UNIVERSITY TEACHING AND FACULTY DEVELOPMENT

HIGHER EDUCATION INSTITUTIONS

PERSPECTIVES, OPPORTUNITIES AND CHALLENGES

University Teaching and Faculty Development

Additional books and e-books in this series can be found on Nova's website under the Series tab.

Education in a Competitive and Globalizing World

Additional books and e-books in this series can be found on Nova's website under the Series tab.

UNIVERSITY TEACHING AND FACULTY DEVELOPMENT

HIGHER EDUCATION INSTITUTIONS

PERSPECTIVES, OPPORTUNITIES AND CHALLENGES

JOE MAXWELL
EDITOR

Copyright © 2019 by Nova Science Publishers, Inc.

All rights reserved. No part of this book may be reproduced, stored in a retrieval system or transmitted in any form or by any means: electronic, electrostatic, magnetic, tape, mechanical photocopying, recording or otherwise without the written permission of the Publisher.

We have partnered with Copyright Clearance Center to make it easy for you to obtain permissions to reuse content from this publication. Simply navigate to this publication's page on Nova's website and locate the "Get Permission" button below the title description. This button is linked directly to the title's permission page on copyright.com. Alternatively, you can visit copyright.com and search by title, ISBN, or ISSN.

For further questions about using the service on copyright.com, please contact:
Copyright Clearance Center
Phone: +1-(978) 750-8400   Fax: +1-(978) 750-4470   E-mail: info@copyright.com.

NOTICE TO THE READER

The Publisher has taken reasonable care in the preparation of this book, but makes no expressed or implied warranty of any kind and assumes no responsibility for any errors or omissions. No liability is assumed for incidental or consequential damages in connection with or arising out of information contained in this book. The Publisher shall not be liable for any special, consequential, or exemplary damages resulting, in whole or in part, from the readers' use of, or reliance upon, this material. Any parts of this book based on government reports are so indicated and copyright is claimed for those parts to the extent applicable to compilations of such works.

Independent verification should be sought for any data, advice or recommendations contained in this book. In addition, no responsibility is assumed by the Publisher for any injury and/or damage to persons or property arising from any methods, products, instructions, ideas or otherwise contained in this publication.

This publication is designed to provide accurate and authoritative information with regard to the subject matter covered herein. It is sold with the clear understanding that the Publisher is not engaged in rendering legal or any other professional services. If legal or any other expert assistance is required, the services of a competent person should be sought. FROM A DECLARATION OF PARTICIPANTS JOINTLY ADOPTED BY A COMMITTEE OF THE AMERICAN BAR ASSOCIATION AND A COMMITTEE OF PUBLISHERS.

Additional color graphics may be available in the e-book version of this book.

Library of Congress Cataloging-in-Publication Data

ISBN: 978-1-53615-717-8

Published by Nova Science Publishers, Inc. † New York

CONTENTS

Preface		**vii**
Chapter 1	Internal Quality Assurance Systems for Higher Education Institutions: Perspectives, Opportunities and Guidelines for a New Maturity Model *Felix Sanchez-Puchol and Joan Antoni Pastor-Collado*	**1**
Chapter 2	We Can Do Better: Building Competencies until Graduation *Rita Payan-Carreira, Gonçalo Cruz and Caroline Dominguez*	**107**
Chapter 3	The Validation of the Total Quality Management Construct Using Confirmatory Factor Analysis *Farooq Miiro and Azam Othman*	**147**
Chapter 4	Measuring and Explaining the Production Efficiency of Higher Education Institutions with an Application to the Public Universities of Spain *Manuel Salas-Velasco*	**169**

Chapter 5	Evolving Entrepreneurial Activities at Post-Soviet Universities *Radzivon Marozau, Maribel Guerrero, David Urbano and Asunción Ibañez*	**201**
Index		**247**
Related Nova Publications		**253**

Preface

In the opening chapter of *Higher Education Institutions: Perspectives, Opportunities and Challenges*, the authors investigate and present the concept of internal quality assurance system implementation maturity, aiming to analyze the existing theoretical underpinnings on how maturity can be understood and approached in terms of an internal quality assurance system.

Some pathways available to the higher education institutions towards the assessment of needs and the improvement of course planning, curriculum design and student guidance systems are discussed.

An empirical study is presented seeking to validate the structure of total quality management construct with an objective of identifying the current total quality management practices employed as perceived by the staff of Islamic University in Uganda.

The penultimate chapter focuses on a deeper understanding of the efficiency measurement and its determinants of the higher education institutions of Spain.

The aim of the closing chapter is to explore the influence of a university environment on entrepreneurial activities of students and alumni in the post-Soviet context.

Chapter 1 - Quality assurance (QA) is currently one of the main concerns for higher education institutions (HEIs) all around the world.

Over the last years, many HEIs have started to institutionalize their QA practices by designing and subsequently implementing a formalized internal quality assurance system (IQAS), aiming to improve the quality of their educational service delivery. The institutionalization process of an IQAS in HEIs is now considered as a risky and challenging task leading, in no few occasions to unsatisfactory implementations. In this vein, available empirical results are still inconclusive on the effectiveness and appropriateness of those systems in HEIs. Against this background, the authors argue that gathering adequate knowledge, tools and frameworks for guiding those actors involved in the design and implementation of IQAS in HEIs would be helpful in order to raise implementation success and satisfaction. Unfortunately, little research has been done on the institutionalization of those critical systems in HEIs. In the authors' view, what many institutions lack today is a real appreciation of where they stand in terms of their current IQAS maturity, understood as the quality of their currently running IQAS "itself". By having more accurate knowledge and better instruments to conveniently self-assess the maturity level of their IQAS would help HEIs to adequately prioritize their IQAS investments and improvement efforts, by focusing on those structural parts of the system that may require these efforts. To cope with these gaps, in this chapter the authors investigate and present the concept of IQAS implementation maturity. The authors aim to analyze the existing theoretical underpinnings on how maturity can be understood and approached in terms of an IQAS and what instruments or frameworks have been suggested for supporting their assessment and measurement. Grounding on the main limitations identified in such tools, the authors will conclude that there is enough room for envisioning improved instruments for assessing and measuring IQAS maturity, and they provide a particular research agenda as well as basic design recommendations for building such artifact. In so doing, the authors contribute to the current existing body of knowledge on QA in HEIs by providing a better understanding on IQAS maturity. The research value relies on the novelty of the study, as, to the best of the authors' knowledge, no similar study of these characteristics has been previously tempted.

Chapter 2 - Today's global economy requests from graduates that they have the competencies at day-1 suiting the workplace, including critical thinking, adaptability, autonomy, teamwork and communication. These competencies go beyond the cognitive achievements or the content knowledge that are often identify as major outcomes in multiple tertiary education providers worldwide. According to published surveys, the hardest positions to fill still require from graduates a combination of technical and transferable soft skills, suggesting that in most cases Higher Education Institutions (HEI) still have difficulties in reaching such a prime goal. It is often claimed that a skills' gap exists between the expectations of employers and HEI regarding the competencies that should be mastered by graduates at the entrance in the labor market. However, even if this opinion is not consensual, and in an attempt to bridge this gap, several initiatives and recommendations have emerged in different countries through the implementation of educational policies and frameworks. In Europe, this has led to the adoption of the philosophy endorsed in the Bologna reform and the Miller pyramid framework for assessment. This skills' gap is evolutive and may present different forms amongst countries or professions. Results from an Erasmus+ project (CRITHINKEDU - Critical Thinking Across the European Higher Education Curricula) have shown that those skills may vary between professional fields, particularly on how they are understood and applied (Dominguez 2018). Moreover, the increased complexity of the professional reality and the tremendous pace at which technology evolves, hinder the efforts taken by the higher education institutions and delay the implementation of adaptative strategies that will foster a constant fitting of the undergraduates to the workplace requirements. The needed adaptation of the HEI is crucial to ensure that their graduates succeed in the current highly competitive professional market. In this sense, and believing that the authors can do better to drive this change, the current chapter discusses some pathways available to HEI towards the assessment of needs and the improvement of course planning, curriculum design and student guidance systems. It will contribute to present/discuss pathways to reduce the existing gaps between day-1 graduates and labor market demands (degree-job match). The complex and multidimensional challenges need to be faced together by higher education and the labor market, as a shared responsibility in establishing educational goals, providing settings and discussing the assessment of outcomes. Such cooperation should also allow to preview for competency-shifts attending to the rapid technological changes, economic and cultural globalization.

Chapter 3 - Purpose: The empirical study sought to validate the structure of total quality management construct with an objective of identifying the current TQM practices employed as perceived by the staff of Islamic University in Uganda. Design/methodology: A cross sectional survey was employed to solicit data from 361 respondents. This was done through randomization and a confirmatory factor analysis of structural equation modelling technique was employed for data analysis. Findings: The results are in congruent with the earlier findings whereby focus on clients, focus on satisfaction of the workers' needs, process improvement, administrative and technological need were found as sound sub-dimensions of TQM. However the research tool merged with on 17 items compared to the earlier tools used. Practical implications: The major implication is that enhancement of a survey tool with 17 items which other universities in future studies at the same level can apply to examine the levels of TQM practices at higher education institutions especially in Uganda. University managers and administrators can employ this tool often to examine how well they can reposition themselves in TQM practices. This kind of approach can lead to creation of a more impressing and interesting environment of teaching and learning and at the same time attract high quality personnel from both students and staff at international levels. The four subcontract tool of TQM is imperative for universities to employ since the current times are more emphatic on customer demands and value for money.

Chapter 4 - Increasing efficiency and productivity in the higher education systems should be at the core of the governments' policy agendas in this time of constrained resources. Expenditure on higher education in the OECD countries accounts for a significant share of public spending. Knowing whether or not public higher education institutions optimize their resources in production is, therefore, an important education policy issue. This chapter begins by exploring the methodology for measuring efficiency in the higher education context. By using several inputs and outputs at the institutional level, the authors can identify the most technically efficient institutions that may work as a benchmark in the sector. Next, the chapter focuses on a deeper understanding of the efficiency measurement and its determinants of the higher education institutions of Spain.

Chapter 5 - Stimulating entrepreneurship inside universities and the consequent development of entrepreneurial universities against the backdrop of global reduction of governmental financial support is one of the current foci of academics, university authorities and policy makers from all around the world. These issues are more critical to post-Soviet economies where the level of the entrepreneurial activity and, as a consequence, of entrepreneurship within universities is lower in comparison with western market economies, while the majority of such countries are still trying to develop an entrepreneurship- and innovation-friendly environment. In this regard, the aim of this chapter is to explore the influence of a university environment on entrepreneurial activities of students and alumni in the post-Soviet context. Methodologically, the authors combined the case study methodology and the regression analysis to embrace two levels of analysis: organizational (a university) and individual (students and alumni). Capitalizing on the nature and uniqueness of the Belarusian context, the authors contribute to the debate on factors shaping an entrepreneurial environment in the context of a post-Soviet university and demonstrate how a university environment influences the entrepreneurial behavior of students and alumni. The general conclusion to be drawn from the study is that underdeveloped entrepreneurial and business competences and the Soviet heritage that is still visible in attitudes and values restrain employing the abundant human and physical resources of the Belarusian State University to contribute to economic development not only by educating job-seekers but by fostering job-creators and transforming research activity into economic value. However, as the regression analysis showed, existing formal business-related education does facilitate the entrepreneurial activity of alumni.

In: Higher Education Institutions
Editor: Joe Maxwell

ISBN: 978-1-53615-717-8
© 2019 Nova Science Publishers, Inc.

Chapter 1

INTERNAL QUALITY ASSURANCE SYSTEMS FOR HIGHER EDUCATION INSTITUTIONS: PERSPECTIVES, OPPORTUNITIES AND GUIDELINES FOR A NEW MATURITY MODEL

Felix Sanchez-Puchol[1,*]
and Joan Antoni Pastor-Collado[2]

[1]Open University of Catalonia (UOC), Barcelona, Spain
[2]Barcelona School of Informatics,
Technical University of Catalonia (UPC), Barcelona, Spain

ABSTRACT

Quality assurance (QA) is currently one of the main concerns for higher education institutions (HEIs) all around the world. Over the last years, many HEIs have started to institutionalize their QA practices by designing and subsequently implementing a formalized internal quality

---

[*] Corresponding Author's E-mail: fsanchezpu@uoc.edu.

assurance system (IQAS), aiming to improve the quality of their educational service delivery. The institutionalization process of an IQAS in HEIs is now considered as a risky and challenging task leading, in no few occasions to unsatisfactory implementations. In this vein, available empirical results are still inconclusive on the effectiveness and appropriateness of those systems in HEIs.

Against this background, we argue that gathering adequate knowledge, tools and frameworks for guiding those actors involved in the design and implementation of IQAS in HEIs would be helpful in order to raise implementation success and satisfaction. Unfortunately, little research has been done on the institutionalization of those critical systems in HEIs. In our view, what many institutions lack today is a real appreciation of where they stand in terms of their current IQAS maturity, understood as the quality of their currently running IQAS "itself". By having more accurate knowledge and better instruments to conveniently self-assess the maturity level of their IQAS would help HEIs to adequately prioritize their IQAS investments and improvement efforts, by focusing on those structural parts of the system that may require these efforts.

To cope with these gaps, in this chapter we investigate and present the concept of IQAS implementation maturity. We aim to analyze the existing theoretical underpinnings on how maturity can be understood and approached in terms of an IQAS and what instruments or frameworks have been suggested for supporting their assessment and measurement. Grounding on the main limitations identified in such tools, we will conclude that there is enough room for envisioning improved instruments for assessing and measuring IQAS maturity, and we provide a particular research agenda as well as basic design recommendations for building such artifact. In so doing, we contribute to the current existing body of knowledge on QA in HEIs by providing a better understanding on IQAS maturity. The research value relies on the novelty of the study, as, to the best of our knowledge, no similar study of these characteristics has been previously tempted.

Keywords: Internal Quality Assurance System, Higher Education Institutions, maturity, information systems

1. INTRODUCTION

Quality assurance (QA) is currently one of the main concerns for modern education institutions all over the world (Steinhardt et al. 2017,

221). Although initially originated in industrial settings, over the last decades QA practices have also made their way into higher education (HE), being progressively adopted by many institutions (Sarrico et al. 2010, 37–43; Seyfried and Pohlenz 2018, 1–2). This fact is especially relevant for western and central European universities under the umbrella of the European Higher Education Area (EHEA), due to the regulatory changes introduced by the Bologna Agreements (Smidt 2015). Among other reforms, the Bologna Agreements forced European Higher Education Institutions (HEIs) to establish a formalized mechanism of internal QA according to a set of standards defined in the Standards and Guidelines for Quality Assurance in the European Higher Education Area (ESG) (ESG 2015). As the standards are non-prescriptive in nature, HEIs are allowed to autonomously implement their own internal quality assurance system (IQAS) according to their strategic goals and operational objectives, whenever compliance with the standards were provided (Kettunen 2012; Manatos, Sarrico, and Rosa 2017b). As a consequence, over the last years many HEIs have started to define, develop and implement their own IQAS in line with the ESG recommendations. As a matter of fact, a recent survey developed by the International Institute for Educational Planning of the United Nations Educational, Scientific and Cultural Organization (IIEP-UNESCO), 92% of 311 HEIs surveyed worldwide rated internal QA as an important or very important component of their respective institutional policy (Martin and Parikh 2017, 28).

Specialized literature reveals that the implementation of an IQAS is a complex and challenging task for HEIs in terms of time, scope, cost and resources invested (Fernández Cruz, Egido Gálvez, and Carballo Santaolalla 2016, 395; Brennan 2018, 255; Leiber, Stensaker, and Harvey 2015, 289). In this sense, O'Mahony and Garavan (2012, 189) argue that HE contexts are particularly challenging as educational institutions face *"a unique set of external drivers for change: they have particular notions of what constitutes quality; complex politics around quality and the conflict between quality for accountability and quality of teaching."* The process of implementing those systems should be viewed more as "a journey" than just a mean for quality improvement (Kamat and Kittur 2017, 516).

Several frameworks, standards, and management philosophies have been proposed as blueprints or reference frameworks to provide assistance to HEI's practitioners in designing and implementing IQAS (Pratasavitskaya and Stensaker 2010; Rosa, Sarrico, and Amaral 2012; Manatos, Sarrico, and Rosa 2017b, 343; Becket and Brookes 2008). Whilst they represent salient and different perspectives for attributes of quality within HEIs (Kamat and Kittur 2017), empirical research results are still inconclusive on the utility of those systems in educational settlements (Fernández Cruz, Egido Gálvez, and Carballo Santaolalla 2016, 395–96; O'Mahony and Garavan 2012, 185; Tavares, Sin, and Amaral 2016, 1294–96). Hence, to be useful for a HEI, the running IQAS should be conveniently deployed according to the requirements and procedures defined and documented in the initial stages (Garza-Reyes, Rocha-Lona, and Kumar 2015, 1299). Nonetheless, this is not always the case: in many HEIs the intended quality effects of the initially designed IQAS are compromised when putting it into practice, leading to unsuccessful implementations. As an IQAS can be defined more or less formally and to a lower or higher degree to fit the HEI's needs, it can also be implemented more or less as an integral part of the whole institution (Živaljević, Bevanda, and Trifunović 2017, 50).

For instance, evaluations of the implemented IQAS must be made to see whether systematic, structured and continuous QA procedures and strategies have been effectively put in place to ensure whether the running IQAS "*produces useful and relevant information for the improvement of its operations and whether it results in effective improvement measures*" (Fernández Cruz, Egido Gálvez, and Carballo Santaolalla 2016, 379; Kettunen 2012, 519). Much has been written on different QA processes and instruments, including self-assessments, peer-reviews, audits, benchmarking, audits, accreditation or certification procedures (Manatos, Sarrico, and Rosa 2017b, 343; Federkeil 2008, 220–23) representing different approaches in terms of why, what, who and how QA is performed, having their own pros and cons (Amaral, Rosa, and Tavares 2007; Leiber, Stensaker, and Harvey 2015, 290–92; Liu 2016, 23; Sarrico et al. 2010, 41–43). However, and from a global perspective, most of them tend to be perceived as being too complicate, subjective, rigid, bureaucratic or even inefficient, especially from the perspective of some HEI's stakeholders, such as the academic staff or institutional managers (Cobham et al. 2014; Leisyte, Zelvys, and Zenkiene 2015, 7–11; Tavares et al. 2017, 1294–97).

In this chapter, we argue that the availability of additional knowledge and tools for guiding and supporting those actors involved in IQAS design and implementation processes would be helpful to better understand and improve the utility of those systems. Drawing on the more generic literature on quality management (QM), more light-weight alternatives to previous approaches can be drawn on the generic concept of "maturity", that is, *"bringing something to a state of full growth or development"* (Cleven et al. 2014, 198–99; Maier, Moultrie, and Clarkson 2012). We believe that what many HEIs really lack today is a real appreciation of where they stand in terms of their current IQAS maturity, understood as the quality of their implemented IQAS, "itself". For instance, having more accurate knowledge and instruments to adequately assess and measure the maturity level of a running IQAS will probably allow educational institutions to prioritise their IQAS improvement initiatives and investments in a better way, focussing on those structural parts of the system that may require priority attention. Such vision is consistent with several recent calls towards developing more holistic and integrative approaches and instruments to QA in HEIs (Kamat and Kittur 2017, 524–25; Manatos, Sarrico, and Rosa 2017a).

There is an important stream of research on maturity of generic (i.e., sector-independent) Quality Management Systems (QMS) (Saraph, Benson, and Schroeder 1989; Flynn, Schroederb, and Sakakibara 1994; Ahire, Golhar, and Waller 1996), but concerns may be arisen on their applicability and suitability for HEIs. Most studies on maturity of QMS focus on profit-oriented business, conceptualizing the effects of those systems in terms of firm's economic performance, effectiveness or competitiveness (Garza-Reyes, Rocha-Lona, and Kumar 2015, 1299; Pereira do Nascimento et al. 2016, 252). However, the focus on IQAS for HEIs should be much more placed on establishing a balance on the dichotomy between regulation/compliance towards society vs. teaching and learning enhancement/improvement (Gamboa and Melão 2012, 385; Liu 2016, 18; O'Mahony and Garavan 2012, 185,187). To date, research conducted on IQAS implementation in HEIs has been primarily focused in studies on critical success factors facilitating the implementation of those systems (Sahu, Shrivastava, and Shrivastava 2013; Malini and Pandi 2018; Bayraktar, Tatoglu, and Zaim 2008) or on exemplary use cases describing in more or less detail the implementation process undertaken in several particular institutional contexts (Mbithi and Moturi 2015; Santos and Dias 2017; O'Sullivan 2017). Unfortunately, and despite recent works providing the first insights on maturity of the institutionalization of QA practices in HEIs (Hrnčiar and Madzík 2017; Vukasovic 2014), research available on such topic is almost inexistent. In addition, the lack of studies on the "*structural/managerial*" elements that configure a "generic" IQAS (Cardoso et al. 2017, 329; O'Mahony and Garavan 2012, 185; Tavares, Sin, and Amaral 2016) further complicates the identification of those factors influencing the maturity of IQAS. Anyway, considering that several authors suggest the suitability of maturity-oriented approaches for addressing QA issues in HE (Bennedsen et al. 2018; Chalaris et al. 2017) we believe that researching in such a field of knowledge seems to be convenient and appropriate.

Given all the previous background, our main aim in this chapter is to investigate the concept of IQAS implementation maturity in HEIs. We do so by adopting a rather explorative and qualitative approach mostly based on an extensive desk research. We basically rely on secondary data information sources published in relevant journals, conference papers, books, research reports as well as the so-called "grey literature", including reports and other complementary documents released by well-known bodies and supranational organizations specialized in QA in HE contexts. In addition, and due to the scarcity of research focused in maturity and QA in HEIs, sources from the more generic literature on QM covering aspects related with "maturity" have been also considered for this study. Next, and on the basis of a careful review of the sources compiled, basic principles of deductive reasoning have been used to synthetize and integrate the results configuring the present work.

Particularly, the remaining parts of the chapter have been structured as follows: first, we provide basic understanding of the concepts of IQAS and maturity in a separate way. Next, we analyze the existing theoretical underpinnings on how maturity can be understood and approached in terms of IQAS in HEIs. We subsequently outline what instruments, frameworks and artifacts have been suggested as plausible for supporting or facilitating IQAS maturity assessment. Finally, and grounding on the main limitations and drawbacks identified in them, we conclude that there is enough room for envisioning new and improved instruments for assessing and measuring IQAS maturity, and therefore, we provide a particular research agenda and basic initial design recommendations for building such an instrument. In so doing, we contribute to current existing body of knowledge on QA in HEIs by elaborating on the lacking foundation's on IQAS implementation maturity, which in turn, would be also valuable for both researchers and practitioners in order to avoid misconceptions and ambiguous understanding on the concept. The research value of our contribution relies on the novelty of the study, as to the best of our knowledge, no similar work of these characteristics on IQAS maturity in HEIs has been previously tempted.

2. THE CONCEPT OF IQAS FOR HEIS

2.1. Terminological Clarification

Before entering in detail, we believe it is worthwhile to briefly comment on the terminological difference between the keywords *Quality Management System (QMS)* and *Internal Quality Assurance System (IQAS)*. We proceed in such way as we concur with Tutko and Naumov (2014, 124) when they state that there generally is *"a use of [ambiguous vocabulary] and imprecise terms concerning internal quality assurance systems."* In this line, and as starting point, an initial simple approach could be considering the term IQAS as just a distinct keyword used particularly in the specialized HE literature to refer to a QMS implemented in an educational settlement. For example, Manatos, Sarrico, and Rosa (2017, 159) state that *"there seems to be an aversion to the word 'management' in much of the literature dealing with higher education. As a consequence (...) it tends to use a different terminology."*

However, certain nuances should be pointed out here. On the one hand, and continuing with the appreciation of previous authors, the HE literature *"habitually refers to QM [quality management] as 'quality assurance' (QA), which is rather odd for QM research, as it reduces the scope of QM to its assurance component"* (Manatos, Sarrico, and Rosa 2017a, 159). Such perspective, considering that QM builds over the concept of QA, seems to be also considered by Asif and Raouf. In their view, QA *"can be described as assurance that requirements for the quality of academic programs offered by the HEI have been (and can be) achieved,"* whilst QM should be understood as rather a *systematic approach [i.e., a model] to achieve quality-related results, [which] purpose is to develop an organisation-wide system to ensure QA of all products/ services"* (Asif and Raouf 2013, 2011). In other words, QM can be viewed as an institutional function including QA tools, that is, the set of mechanisms that make QM possible (Martin and Parikh 2017, 18).

Assuming such vision, it may be argued that the duality between QMS and IQAS can be the consequence of the diversity of meanings and relative semantic overlap among concepts of QA and QM in the particular context of HE. Again, and according to Asif and Raouf (2013, 2011), *"the terms quality assurance, quality management, and total quality management have been used depending upon the scope of the research —whether academic programs or management aspect of the whole HEI."* Hence, the term IQAS is more likely to be found in the educational oriented-literature, where the emphasis preferably tends to be put on the teaching and learning aspects of education. Conversely, the term QMS is much more likely to be found in the management-oriented literature, even when it addresses aspects of these systems within HE contexts. We also interpret that term IQAS can be a form of explicitly emphasizing that traditional QM frameworks do not fit well for the idiosyncrasy of HEIs. Since most of these frameworks have been originally conceived for profit business and organizations, it can be argued that they do not adequately address well domain specific processes, such as teaching, learning or research, which represent the main missions of a modern HEI (Rosa, Sarrico, and Amaral 2012, 129). Finally, the prefix *"internal"* associated to the IQAS term may reinforce the idea of focalizing on the internal tools and mechanisms of QA existing within an educational institution.

Whatever the case, and for the purposes of this work, we assume that an IQAS represents a synonymous term or expression for a QMS in the context of a HEI. In fact, the duality among both terms can be explicitly found in several information sources, showing an interchangeable use of the terms or giving light to a plethora of alternative expressions like *"quality assurance – or management – system"* (Rosa, Sarrico, and Amaral 2012, 129), *"institutional quality assurance schemes"* (O'Sullivan 2017, 191) or *"internal quality assurance management system"* (Aspranawa et al. 2017, 762). In sum, and aiming to respect the original terminology and nomenclature used in the diverse contributions reviewed for this study, in the remaining of the chapter we use both QMS and IQAS keywords indistinctively to refer to the same research entity object.

2.2. Definition of IQAS for HEIs

Whilst several articles can be found in the specialized literature in HE discussing and providing working definitions for concepts like quality, QA or QM (Elassy 2015; Filippakou and Tapper 2008; Harvey and Green 1993; Ryan 2015), no analogous work has been found by this authors devoted to the concept of IQAS. Although several frameworks, models and standards have been posed as blueprints for providing guidance and assistance on how to set up and implement an IQAS in HEIs (Manatos, Sarrico, and Rosa 2017b, 343; Becket and Brookes 2008; Pratasavitskaya and Stensaker 2010; Rosa, Sarrico, and Amaral 2012; Kamat and Kittur 2017; Dahl Jørgensen et al. 2014), in our opinion they fail in providing a consolidated or commonly agreed definition of what is an IQAS. In this sense, and for example, when looking to QA glossaries and catalogues for

HE – for example, the UNESCO glossary of terms and definitions (Vlăsceanu, Grünberg, and Pârlea 2007) or the Analytic Quality Glossary (Harvey, 2004-2018) – we could not identify a formal working definition for the term.

Few documents provide a more or less comprehensible definition of what is an IQAS. As a first approach, it can be argued that several sources refer to an IQAS as a result of the progressive institutionalization of the QA practices, rules and tools undertaken within a HEI; resulting into a *"formal system"* aiming at ensuring the quality of all the institutional activities (Mårtensson, Roxå, and Stensaker 2014, 534; Vukasovic 2014). Tavares et al. (2017, 1294) defend that an IQAS

> "would entail the existence of a quality policy, the creation of formal mechanisms and structures, participation of stakeholders, articulation with information systems, information transparency and continuous quality improvement."

Further, they consider that a formalized IQAS implies:

> "a coherent and structured approach which is meant to ensure quality in every aspect of the institution's activities. This presupposes the existence of a quality policy articulated with the pursuit of the institution's objectives, as well as clearly defined internal procedures, responsibilities and means necessary to attain these objectives" (2017, 1298).

Supplementing the previous view, Kettunen (2008, p. 325) states that an IQAS *"may refer to the environments and quality assurance systems of the international and national levels and the environment and quality assurance system of an individual HEI."* For instance, he stresses the importance on the idea that IQAS may also facilitate HEIs to give answer to external regulations and norms. Nonetheless, and in contrast with previous perspectives that provide a rather static view of what is an IQAS, a more dynamic-oriented vision for these systems can also be identified in other sources. For example, Daromes (2016, p. 89) defines an IQAS "as a plan, implementation, control, and development of the university's quality standards in order to obtain stakeholder satisfaction and ensure that the quality of graduates in accordance with the standard competencies defined."

Whatever the case, and independently of the point of view adopted, according to the Standards and Guidelines for Quality Assurance in the European Higher Education Area (ESG 2.0), the main purpose or goal of an IQAS must be

"to provide information to assure the higher education institution and the public of the quality of the higher education institution's activities (accountability) as well as provide advice and recommendations on how it might improve what it is doing (enhancement)" (ESG 2015).

Earlier definitions of what is an IQAS can be complemented by existing definitions and conceptualizations existing for the more generic term of QMS. For example, the American Society of Quality (ASQ) glossary defines a QMS as a

"formalized system that documents processes, procedures, and responsibilities for achieving quality policies and objectives. A QMS helps coordinate and direct an organization's activities to meet customer and regulatory requirements and improve its effectiveness and efficiency on a continuous basis" (ASQ 2018).

The glossary also refers to the International Organization for Standardization (ISO) 9001 series as the most prominent approach to specify requirements for a general QMS. Particularly, the ISO 9001:2015 version of the standard builds on seven QM principles that represent a *"set of fundamental beliefs, norms, rules and values that are accepted as true and can be used as a basis for quality management"* (ISO 2015): (i) *customer focus*, (ii) *leadership*, (iii) *engagement of people*, (iv) *process approach*, (v) *improvement*, (vi) *evidence-based decision making*, and (vii) *relationship management*. The standard also refers to the *Plan-Do-Check-*

Act (PDCA) cycle of continuous improvement (Deming 1994) as a core approach for defining, building and implementing a QMS. According to the particular application domain of HE in which the present work should be placed, it must be noted here that several extensions of the generic standard tailored to educational institutions have been developed, as the ISO IWA 2:2007 – particular guidelines for applying the ISO 9001 in the education (Abbadi, Bouayad, and Lamrini 2013; Mora et al. 2017, 58–71) – or the new recently released ISO 21001:2018 standard – requirements for a management system for educational organizations (EOMS) (Camilleri 2017; ISO 2018) – . In general, all these frameworks concur in assuming a rather process-oriented approach.

Additional conceptualizations of a QMS can be found in the academic literature. For example, Goetsh and Davies refer to a QMS as

> "all the organization's policies, procedures, plans, resources, processes, and delineation of responsibility and authority, all deliberately aimed at achieving product or service quality levels consistent with customer satisfaction and the organization's objectives. When these policies, procedures, plans, etc., are taken together, they define how the firm works, and how quality is managed" (as cited by Živaljević, Bevanda, & Trifunović, 2017, p. 50).

Hence, a QMS consists of a set of interrelated processes described by the QMS documentation, *"but when applied, [the] quality management system consists of the organizational structure and processes necessary"* (Živaljević, Bevanda, and Trifunović 2017, 50). In similar terms, Garza-Reyes, Rocha-Lona, and Kumar (2015, 1298) argue that QMS are *"an integrated business approach to plan and deploy quality management models, methods and tools across the organisation aligning to their business strategy"* and categorize the elements that compose a QMS in *"human capital, processes, management models-methods-tools, business strategy, and information technology."* Similarly (Mohammad, et al. 2018, 5) define a QMS as a "set of procedures (records, instructions, and guidelines), policies (guidelines, objectives) and manual documentation to provide a framework in the operations of organization; to achieve customer requirements and engaging with continuous improvement of organization and consolidated approach for business in the implementation of quality management (QM) models, methods and tools to achieve the business objective. In HEI, QM is the term used to explain processes involved to ensure properly maintained standards and to optimize quality of education."

Many other examples of definitions for QMS can be found in the literature, but providing a synthesis of them is out of the scope of the present chapter. In any case, previous definitions emerged from academic sources suggest that a QMS could be viewed as rather a set processes, people, structures, tools and physical artifacts working and interacting together, aiming to achieve quality in an organization. In our view, such perspective is consistent with a rather socio-technical approach for a QMS, consisting of both humans and non-humans collaborating in managing the organisation with respect to quality (Øgland 2006; Prida And and Grijalvo 2008).

To sum up, it can be concluded that there is no commonly-agreed definition for the concept of IQAS. Although existing definitions cannot be considered as contradictory as they tend towards certain degree of consensus (i.e., several common structural elements configuring and IQAS/QMS), some of them treat aspects that are disregarded in others, varying therefore in terms of depth and breadth. In this sense, we concur with Tutko and Naumov (2014, 124) that there are opportunities and room for developing a more comprehensible definition of what is an IQAS in HEIs.

2.3. Structural Components of a Typical IQAS for HEIs

The definitions introduced in the previous section seem to stress several elements that configure an IQAS (i.e., human capital, processes, methods and tools, business strategy, information technology, policies, documentation, stakeholders, etc.). Nonetheless, if we turn our attention to the specialized literature in QA for HEIs, studies drawing attention on such structural elements are scarce (Cardoso et al. 2017, 329,339).

Recent disciplinary reviews on quality in HE attest the heterogeneity, complexity, multidisciplinary and scattered situation of the field (Alzafari 2017; Kamat and Kittur 2017; Liu 2016; Manatos, Sarrico, and Rosa 2017a; Prakash 2018; Steinhardt et al. 2017; Tarí and Dick 2016). It is not surprising, hence, that a multiplicity of constructs and frameworks have shed light on in order to characterize and to quantify quality-related constructs in HEIs (Sunder M. 2016; Ryan 2015; Schindler et al. 2015; Kamat and Kittur 2017; Becket and Brookes 2008; Pratasavitskaya and Stensaker 2010; Prakash 2018; Sultan and Wong 2010; Tan, Muskat, and Zehrer 2016; Silva et al. 2017; Farahsa and Tabrizi 2015). In general, and independently of the particular construct addressed by each particular study, it seems that quality practices in HEIs tend to be *"more similar than their label may suggest"* and that *"approaches, concepts and frameworks offered tend to concentrate on many of the same dimensions, although the way in which they discuss and present these may be very different"* (Pratasavitskaya and Stensaker 2010, 47). As a matter of fact, in their recent systematic literature review, Tarí and Dick (2016, 283–84) derive a list of 11 factors, dimensions or facets configuring a multi-dimensional view of QM practices in HEIs: *People management, information and analysis, process management, stakeholder focus, planning, leadership, continuous improvement, programme design* and *supplier management*.

Nonetheless, concerns may arise on the applicability of such factors when addressing the more particular phenomena of IQAS. According to Prakash (2018, 739), if we concentrate on the constructs more related with QA issues, literature is dominated by *"approaches such as audits, accreditation, assessments and continuous improvement."* We concur hence with Abdul Hakeem and Thanikachalam (2014, 430–31) when they argue that such vision does not suit well for the concept of IQAS, since "the purpose of internal quality assurance is distinct from that of accreditation (...) same framework should not be used for both internal quality assurance and accreditation systems. [Considering that] it is evident from the literatures that the ─quality assurance/management system‖ of an institution is an important factor which is assessed for accrediting (...) [the] internal quality assurance system of an institution is a subset of the accreditation process."

For instance, in this section we briefly discuss some studies particularly addressing the structural elements that may characterize a typical implementation of an institutional IQAS, which we have summarized in Table 1. We must acknowledge here the existence of similar studies providing interesting insights but at program level – see for example the works by Mizikaci (2006), Asif and Raouf (2013) or Hakeem and Thanikachalam (2014) to cite a few. Due to space limitations, however, they are not discussed here.

Probably, the most significative empirical study on structural elements of an IQAS is the one conducted by (Cardoso et al. 2017). The authors undertook a content analysis of self-assessment reports of certified IQAS in Portugal, and systematized 7 main structural components, namely *documentation structure, coordination and support structures, processes covered and respective scope, QA mechanisms implemented, support information system, link with the institution's governance*. In another rather conceptual oriented article, Georgiadou and Siakas (2008, 67–68) present a synthesis of the main components and actions involved in implementing an IQAS, namely: *quality culture, expertise, quality policy, central management systems, administrative systems, university-wide data, information knowledge* and *resources*. On the other hand, we also identified studies grounding on stronger theoretical grounds. On the one hand, the work by Hrnčiar and Madzík (2017) presents a theoretical 3D education" model typifying factors (dimensions) that characterize an IQAS.

Table 1. Researched studies addressing structural elements of IQAS for HEIs (institutional-level focus)

Reference	Research/development approach	Scope/generality of the study	Structural components/elements of an IQAS for HEIs
(Georgiadou and Siakas 2008)	Conceptual	Generic	*Quality culture*: assess maturity; identify existing quality practices, best practices and issues. *Expertise*: establish existing in-house expertise, buy-in external expertise, train trainers. *Quality policy*: develop quality policy (taking into account successes/best practices, current social and political needs and specific requirements of internal, national European and International labour market), set up goals & objectives of the QA policy. *Central management Systems*: define quality assurance structures, define and assign roles and responsibilities of the bodies, institutions and committees involved, ensure that QA processes and procedures are understood, identify what data to collect (KPIs), decide where to find information design of targets for comparison (what is the meaning of measures), select research instrument (how to collect data). *Administrative systems*: define and assign the roles and responsibilities of teams and individuals involved, set operational targets, set-up time table and milestones. *University-wide data*: set-up and develop Management Information systems and databases. *Information knowledge*: analyse and interpret data, share knowledge. *Resources*: estimate need, allocate funding.
(Chen 2012)	Theoretical model based on SERVQUAL and PDCA cycle	Generic (applied in a private HEI in Taiwan)	*Plan and do dimensions*: Educational policy and enterprise requirements, educational philosophy, strategy planning and management, resource distribution and management, set up standard of education quality, service process design, establishment of service system, standardize operation process, leadership and management, employee education and training. *Check dimensions*: Quality audit, measurement and monitoring of the service process, customer satisfaction and measurement, employee satisfaction and performance evaluation. *Act dimensions*: Continuous improvement, preventive and corrective action, customer follow-up service.

Reference	Research/development approach	Scope/ generality of the study	Structural components/ elements of an IQAS for HEIs
(Hrnčiar and Madzík 2017)	Theoretical model + surveys and regression analysis	Generic (applied at the Slovak Republic)	*Enabling factors*: Curriculum design, resources, academic's efforts, student's efforts, support services, quality of student experience, standards set for the program and results *Performance results*: Outputs for students (getting and education), outcomes for graduates (employability in certain positions) and employer impacts (demonstrable benefits for organisations)
(Cardoso et al. 2017)	Category content analysis of QA self-assessment reports	Inferred from IQAS of 12 HEIs in Portugal	*IQAs documentation structure*: quality policy, strategic documents, operational plans, etc. *Coordination and support structures*: coordination and strategic decision-making in relation to IQA systems' implementation (QA committees, commissions, boards and councils) and running the system on a daily basis (QA services and offices). *Processes covered and respective scope*: teaching and learning, research, third mission, support processes (services, human resources, documentation, etc.) *QA mechanisms implemented*: procedures to operationalise the teaching and learning process; student surveys; self-assessment and quality monitoring indicators for different processes (special focus on teaching and learning) and appraisal systems for academic and non-academic staff. *Support information system*: institutional mechanisms for the collection, analysis and internal disclosure of information supporting the IQA system. *Link with the institution's governance*: IQA system's interconnection with the institution's governance and management, including the mechanisms facilitating it mechanisms for system's monitoring, evaluation and continuous improvement–information from several external and internal reviews as study programmes' external accreditation, research assessment exercises, self-assessments, or quality audits –often systematised into different types of reports, usually served as the basis for the definition of solutions and actions to overcome weaknesses, and continuously improve the IQAS.

Source: Own elaboration.

The model posed defines both enabling factors (*curriculum design, resources, academic's efforts, student's efforts, support services, quality of student experience, standards set for the program and results*) as well as performance-oriented (*outputs for students –getting and education–, outcomes for graduates –employability in certain positions– and employer impacts – demonstrable benefits for organisations*). In a similar vein, the study by (Chen 2012) also includes a theoretical model for the establishment of a QMS in HEIs, drawing on the SERVQUAL model and PDCA cycle of process improvement. Details for the concrete elements considered in this model are detailed in Table 1.

There are also other studies that can provide further details on the composition of IQAS implemented in different HEIs (see Table 2). In general, these studies are empirical in nature. On the one hand, the recently undertook international project by the IIEP-UNESCO (Martin and Parikh 2017; Martin 2018) offers a macro perspective of the structural configuration of IQAS implemented in several HEIs, including its purpose and scope, organizational structure, policies, documentation, tools, mechanisms, and main drivers and obstacles. When comparing the effective features implemented in practice by participating HEIs in the study with structural elements derived from earlier contributions in Table 1, it can be concluded that institutions analyzed by the IIEP-UNESCO have not yet implemented a notable number of them.

Such fact suggests us that there is still great room for improvement towards more "mature" IQAS. On the other hand, and from a more micro perspective, other works provide valuable information on the specific elements that encompass an IQAS in different particular geographical regions. Hence, the works by Klenk and Seyfried (2016, 236) or Tavares, Sin, and Videira (2017) report on actors involved in the development of IQAS in Germany and Portugal, respectively. The study of Tavares, Sin, and Videira (2017) also provides interesting evidence on the factors that influence the creation and development of IQAS. Finally, the studies by

Klenk and Seyfried (2016, 236) and Leisyte, Zelvys, and Zenkiene (2015) summarize those instruments and mechanisms particularly implemented in IQAS from German and Lithuanian HEIs, respectively.

In sum, existing literature on QA for HE provides evidence on the existence on a certain consensus in that there is a series of structural elements of an IQAS that could be characterized as *typical*, in the sense of their universality as core elements of those systems. In other words, they could be typically identified when reviewing the definition or initial design of an envisioned IQAS. Nonetheless, their effective realization in a particular setting may depend on the level of formalization (i.e., "maturity") of the IQAS implementation achieved by each institution. Analogously, there have also been identified a series of structural elements that could be characterized as rather *discretional*, that is, that may or may not be considered in a generic definition of an IQAS. Such factors are made evident through the different elements considered by each contribution described in Table 1.

According to this rationale, we hypothesize on the feasibility of thinking in some kind of "*reference model/framework*" describing the basic or "typical" form a generic IQAS for HEIs. When we refer to a "*reference model/framework*" we see it as an abstract *blueprint* or *conceptual model* artefact, providing higher levels of detail and specificity on the structural elements (and their main relationships) that configure an IQAS than those provided by other well-known frameworks, as for example, the ESG standards.

We must point out here that assuming the plausibility of a "*reference model/framework*" for an IQAS should not be necessarily interpreted as a claim for a "*one size fits all*" IQAS for HEIs. On the contrary, it should be interpreted as a rather "high level" and ·abstract" model for generalizing and homogenizing commonly-accepted structural elements of an IQAS, but suitable to be conveniently instantiated, adapted and tailored to the specific needs and context of each institution. Disposing of such a kind of artefact may probably facilitate, for example, comparisons and/or benchmarking among existing IQAS implementations in different HEIs.

Table 2. Empirical studies related with structural components of an IQAS

Reference	Scope	Main results
(Martin and Parikh 2017; Martin 2018)	Worldwide survey (311 HEIs from 94 countries)	*Purpose:* Improvement of academic activities, institutional performance assessment, institutional learning, improvement of management (88 per cent), and equitable resource allocation (internally-driven motivations); compliance to requests of external authorities, accountability with government and society (externally driven motivations). *Focus (processes and tools included in the scope of the formalized IQAS):* teaching and learning (enhancement of academic programmes, monitoring of student assessments, monitoring quality of staff performance, staff performance evaluation, availability and use of key information, etc.), graduate employability (curriculum development and review, quality of internships, etc.), governance and management (monitoring of strategic planning objectives, evaluation of administrative units, external certification, service level agreements, etc.), research, community outreach, income generation and community services, international cooperation. *Documentation:* Explicitly written IQA policy and IQA handbook. *People and structures involved:* head of institution, senate, dedicated person/unit/cell, quality committees etc.). *(Contextual) External drivers:* Requirements of the national QA system (i.e., accreditation), requirements of the national qualification framework, government request to develop QM, enhancement of the image of the HEI, international aspiration of the HEI. *(Contextual) Internal drivers:* Leadership support, staff and student participation in the development of the IQAS, clarity on benefits, transparent and well-known procedures, technically qualified staff available, incentives for academic staff to participate, adequate involvement of departments in distributing responsibilities.
(Klenk and Seyfried 2016)	Survey (Germany)	*Actors:* University management, Senate, Deans, Directors, Quality Manager, Commissions, Teams, Students. *Instruments:* Surveys, Controlling/figures, Accreditation, Internal/external evaluations, Benchmarking, Rankings, Monitoring, Personnel development.

Reference	Scope	Main results
(Leisyte, Zelvys, and Zenkiene 2015)	Case study (5 HEIs Lithuania)	*Internal QA mechanisms:* QA unit, Institutional self-assessment, Reviewing study programs, Market/employer survey/ interviews, Assessment of academic staff professional qualification, Student survey, Alumni survey/interviews/ meetings/destination monitoring, Faculty survey.
(Tavares, Sin, and Videira 2017)	Online survey (Portugal)	*Actors:* European Union; National agencies for evaluation and accreditation of higher education; top leadership (rectoral team / presidency); middle managers (faculty Deans, department/ course managers); teaching staff; non-teaching staff; students; external stakeholders. *Factors for the creation and development of IQAS*: Legal requirements and demands from the higher education national agency, promoting continuous improvement of the institution's quality; establishing a system of sanctions and rewards; accountability towards society; promoting the institution's competitiveness; promoting the institution's social recognition; and a favourable environment for innovation.

Source: Own elaboration.

Whatever the case, and aiming to provide an integrated and comprehensive vision of what is an IQAS, we concur with Visscher (2009b) when considering that an IQAS can be seen as an information system (IS) – computer supported or not – designed to support the collection, processing and presentation of data on their functioning relating to institutional quality. Hence, we raise up here the possibility of studying the IQAS implementation phenomena adopting an IS theoretical lens. In this sense, and for example, the feasibility of applying knowledge relative to Enterprise Architecture (EA) and Enterprise Modelling principles (Sandkuhl et al. 2018; Proper and Lankhorst 2014) for improving the quality of IQAS in HEIs has already been suggested by several authors (Haris, Washizaki, and Fukazawa 2017; Olsen and Trelsgård 2016, 807; Riihimaa 2009; Syynimaa 2010). We also deem potential avenues for further research on the phenomena of IQAS implementation in HEIs from the perspective of socio-technical systems theory, that is, involving both social and technical systems working and interacting together to achieve desired outcomes (Bostrom and Heinen 1977a, 1977b; Winter et al. 2014). Such perspective has been also suggested by previous studies on QA for

HEIs (Sahney, Banwet, and Karunes 2008, 505–7; Sahney 2016, 329–31; Mizikaci 2006, 42–48).

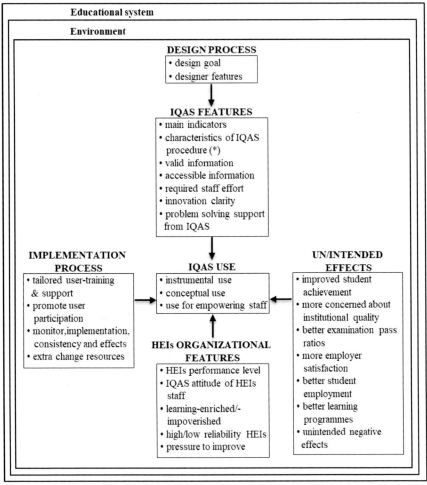

(*) data collection method, respondents, data processing, output, relative-absolute information, data distribution, discussion data, data publication

Source: Slightly adapted from the original proposition by (Visscher 2009a).

Figure 1. An IS-oriented model for IQAS development and implementation success.

Returning to the IS-oriented view of IQAS, Visscher (2009b 7–32) also presents a theoretical framework for the successful implementation of IQAS. The contribution is original in the sense that it grounds on the well-known IS Success Model by DeLone and McLean (2003, 1992). Although we acknowledge that the framework was originally conceived for the particular scope of Vocational Education and Training (VET), we believe that it could also applied in HE contexts. Visscher's characterizes the implementation success of IQAS through 6 main blocks of factors, namely *design process, design features, implementation process, organizational features, use and effects*. The detailed factors emcompassing each block are detailed in Figure 1, which we have slightly adapted from the original contribution, being tailored to more HE-oriented contexts.

We found Visscher's contribution interesting as it can be viewed as an integrated model consolidating, in some way, knowledge from previous studies addressing the structural elements of IQAS for HEIs (see again Table 1). For instance, we see it consistent with both the rather process-oriented approach by Chen (2012) and the more systemic-oriented model of enablers and results by Hrnčiar and Madzík (2017). Moreover, elements considered by Cardoso et al. (2017) or Georgiadou and Siakas (2008, 67–68) could also be relatively easily mapped into the different blocks of factors defined by Visscher's model. Whatever the case, and despite all the above, improved understanding as well as deeper empirical evidence on how HEIs implement IQAS in their own settlements can be better achieved by analysing existing exemplary case studies on this phenomena.

2.4. Exemplary Case Studies on IQAS Implementation in HEIs

There is plenty of literature on how IQAS are being developed and implemented in several real educational contexts, but lots of sources tend to draw on rather informal or anecdotal evidence. In Table 3, we present a non-exhaustive list of case studies reporting on the implementation of an IQAS in different HEIs worldwide, at different stages of the implementation, and grounding on different QA reference frameworks. To guarantee a certain level of rigour in the selected sources, we include only studies published in peer-reviewed journals and conferences. Despite not being exhaustive, collectively, the case studies considered provide rich insights on how context issues may affect the implementation of an IQAS. Further, they can also provide valuable information for establishing or inferring "archetypes" (i.e., standard or typical configurations of best/good practices for those different structural elements encompassing an IQAS) representing the different "stages of maturity" that an IQAS can reach over time. Such conceptualization of "maturity" in terms of IQAS implementation is further explored in the following sections.

Table 3. Case studies reporting on IQAS implementation in HEIs

University name	Country	University type	QA framework/ approach	Reference
Xiamen University	China	Public	'five-in-one' system[1]	(Daguang et al. 2017)
Vienna University of Economics and Business	Austria	Public	European Standards and Guidelines (ESG)	(Vettori et al. 2017)
Daystar University	Kenia	Private	Kenya's National QA Framework	(Kuria and Marwa 2017)
University of Duisburg-Essen	Germany	Public	European Standards and Guidelines (ESG)	(Ganseuer and Pistor 2017)
University of Bahrain	Bahrain	Public	ISO 9001:2000 and Bahrain Excellence Model (BEM)	(AlHamad and Aladwan 2017)
American International University	Bangladesh	Private	ISO 9001:2008 standard	(Lamagna, Villanueva, and Hassan 2017)
University of the Free State	South Africa	Public	Higher Education Qualifications Framework/sub framework (HEQSF /HEQFS)	(Lange and Kriel 2017)
University of Talca	Chile	Public	Chilean's national QA Framework	(Villalobos et al. 2017)
Instituto Politécnico de Setúbal	Portugal	Public	European Standards and Guidelines (ESG)	(Ramos Pires 2010)
University of Oviedo	Spain	Public	European Standards and Guidelines (ESG)	(Álvarez Suárez et al. 2008)
Not specified (IT department)	Republic of Ireland	Public	ISO9001:2000	(O'Mahony and Garavan 2012)

University name	Country	University type	QA framework/ approach	Reference
University do Minho	Portugal	Public	European Standards and Guidelines (ESG)	(Santos and Dias 2017)
King Abdulaziz University (faculty of engineering)	Saudi Arabia	Public	ISO 9001:2008	(El-Morsy et al. 2014)
Universitas Terbuka (Open University)	Indonesia	Public	Asian Association of Open Universities (AAOU) Quality Assurance Framework (QAF)	(Belawati and Zuhairi 2007)
University of Turin (faculty of economics)	Italy	Public	ISO 9001	(Bechis, Biancone, and Tomatis 2008)
Alexander Dubek University of Trenín	Slovak Republic	Public	European Standards and Guidelines (ESG) and ISO 9001:2015	(Jambor, Džubáková, and Habánik 2017)
Eduardo Mondale University	Mozambique	Public	Own adaptation of several references on QA in HEIs derived from literature	(Zavale, Santos, and Da Conceição Dias 2016)

Source: Own elaboration.

[1] Comprising institutional external evaluation (conformance & auditing evaluation), professional accreditation, and evaluation, and international evaluation, as well as the monitoring of teaching quality within institutions.

3. MATURITY AND IQAS FOR HEIS

2.5. Maturity and Maturity Progression

Before entering on the concept of IQAS implementation maturity, we believe that it is worthwhile to provide basic insights on what is mean by maturity in a general sense. Looking at academic contributions addressing topics related with maturity, some of them tend to refer to the definitions proposed by several dictionaries or encyclopedias in order to provide a basic primer understanding. For instance, and in a very broad sense, 'maturity' has been referred as *"the state of being mature"*, *"fullness or perfection of growth or development"*, *"the state of being complete, perfect or ready"* or *"a very advanced or developed form and state"* (Rosemann and De Bruin 2005, 2; Cleven et al. 2014, 198). Similarly, Fraser, Moultrie, and Gregory (2002, 47) state that *"the literal meaning of the word maturity is 'ripeness', conveying the notion of development from some initial state to some more advanced state.* Implicit on the previous definitions is, therefore, the notion of progress or evolution, in the sense that the entity under maturation may pass through a number of intermediate states on the way from an initial to a desired or normally occurring state (Fraser, Moultrie, and Gregory 2002, 47; Mettler 2010, 83).

Nonetheless, and considering that the object or entity under maturity scrutiny could be any type of complex system (Kohlegger, Maier, and Thalmann 2009, 54), the previous notion of a final or normally ending state may be questioned. In this vein, Domingues, Sampaio, and Arezes (2014, 2–3) argue that

> "the system assessment as the notion of equilibrium relates to the chemical reactions. It is a stage favorable to a peculiar characteristic and from where is not advisable to proceed with any further actions. It is not a terminal stage due to the fact that is a dynamic and mobile objective." Therefore, under such perspective, instead of an ending state, maturity should be rather viewed as a mobile objective, "since its main elements change continuously according to the market, business and people. The important thing is not the maturity itself, which is only a state or a point dynamic, but the competence to identify and seek the necessary and sufficient, through the acquisition of knowledge (knowing what), the development of skills (knowing how) and the attitude in aligning it with business objectives (knowing why)" (Tonini, Carvalho, and Spinola 2008, 277).

A couple of corollaries can be derived from the previous rationale. First, maturity can be stated as a *criterion for assessment or measurement* (in one way or another) of the 'goodness' or 'excellence' of the entity under scrutiny (Fitterer and Rohner 2010, 311). Second, it rises up to the notion of maturity factors, that is, those items or capabilities on which the maturity being measured depends on. According to Mettler (2010, 83), the most commonly used basis for assessing maturity in social systems can be generalized into three factors, *people/culture*, *processes/structures*, and *object/technology*. In this sense, increments of (the global) maturity of the assessed entity/domain can be the consequence of either an improvement of just one maturity factor or a combination of several of them (Mettler 2010, 83).

Finally, an important aspect to take into account is the justification on how maturity evolution or progression occurs. Several theories aiming to explain how entities change over time have been posed as plausible justificatory knowledge. For example, Mettler (2010) suggest the use of theories of emergence and diffusion of innovation to explain maturity development. Life cycle theory has also been usually related with maturity, as it describes a typical pathway of change based on a (mostly) unitary sequence of discrete stages of development (Cleven et al. 2014, 194; Lasrado, Vatrapu, and Andersen 2015, 7). In a relatively recent study, Wendler (2012) discusses on how models addressing maturity explain "fullness of growth" of organizational entities and considers two main plausible perspectives. On the one hand, in the (i) lifecycle perspective, an entity evolves automatically over time passing through a series of discrete stages until a perfect or final stage of maturity is inexcusably reached. On the other hand, in the (ii) potential performance perspective, an entity also evolves through a development path of maturity stages, but not following a lifecycle way. Under this latter perspective, the focus is on the potential performance improvements of the entity assessed, which only arise when moving along to higher stages of maturity: "every stage holds an inherent effectiveness and self-evident value, [but] user has to decide by himself which level of maturity (i.e., completeness, perfection) is best for the situation" (Wendler 2012, 1318). Such a performance perspective reinforces the plausibility of thinking in multiple or dynamic paths of maturity evolution since – in line with system's equilibrium vision of maturity – an "entity or system can reach the same outcome from different initial conditions and through many different paths" (Lasrado, Vatrapu, and Andersen 2016, 7). The notion of multiple/dynamic paths of maturity development is in fact implicitly accepted by several researchers (Lasrado, Vatrapu, and Andersen 2015, 7; Cleven et al. 2014; Plattfaut et al. 2011), who typically refer to the work by van de Ven and Poole (1995) on 'idealized types' of organizational change theories (lifecycle, teleology, dialectical and evolutionary theories) as basic theoretical foundations to explain the rationale behind entity maturation.

Finally, and when looking for contributions with a narrower focus on the concept of QMS maturity, Pereira do Nascimento et al. (2016, 2015) conclude that literature on QM allows to synthesize three perspectives on the concept of QSM maturity: (i) maturation time, i.e., the development of an initial state to a more advanced stage in which the temporal notion or aging is implicitly assumed; (ii) capability, assuming the complete development (or perfect condition) of any process/activity under the basis of its inclusion into a cycle of continuous improvement; and (iii) evolution, in which maturity is related to the notion of evolution, in which a balance is supposed between environment adaptation (external point of view) and good practice application (internal point of view) of an entity.

3.2. Unravelling the Theoretical Underpinnings on IQAS Implementation Maturity in HEIs

Earlier rationale provides a basic background to understand how maturity evolves in a general sense. We concentrate now on how maturation can be understood in the scene of IQAS implementation for HEIs. According to Kohlegger, Maier, and Thalmann (2009, 51) the concept of maturity has been used in different ways (analytical, explanatory, normative) in several diverse disciplines. For example, in the IS arena, 'maturity' has been regarded as a *"measure to evaluate the capabilities of an organization"* (Rosemann and De Bruin 2005). Similarly, in the Business Process Management discipline, maturity has been referred as *"the extent to which an organization has explicitly and consistently deployed processes*" (Van Looy, De Backer, and Poels 2011, 1129). In both cases, we perceive that the concept of maturity has rather a performance-oriented connotation, in the sense of moving towards something that is perceived as positive for the whole organization.

Unfortunately, and when collecting and analyzing information available on maturity for the narrower topic of maturity of IQAS in HEIs, we note a general lack of studies trying to address such topic, with the exception, perhaps, of the contribution by Hrnčiar and Madzík (2017) which partially covers it. Paradoxically, we also were able to identify a non-negligible number of sources providing vague references or anecdotal evidence to maturity, or at least, suggesting the need to asses or measure IQAS maturity in some way (Wosik 2009; Bennedsen et al. 2018; Chalaris et al. 2017; Torres Solà et al. 2015, 2015). Whatever the case, and given the scarcity of specialized literature identified, in this section we try to elaborate on this lacking foundation. We do so by drawing on the theoretical foundations on maturity described in the previous section, which we use as reference point to organize, structure, and analyze the little knowledge which we were able to uncover. Again, we deliberately include some contributions with a broader focus of application than just for IQAS within HEIs, with the aim of further strengthening our understanding.

First, when looking for definitions for IQAS maturity, we only were able to detect few contributions with certain degree of significance. In fact, only one of them provides in *stricto senso* a relatively formal definition for the concept of IQAS maturity (see Table 4). Specifically, in his institutional quality assessment handbook, the Commission on Higher Education of the Philippines Government (CHED 2014, 12) states that

> "the maturity of the HEI's internal QA system can be seen in the institutionalization and documentation of systems or processes in the HEI, the extent of implementation of these systems or processes, and the quality outcomes that contribute to program excellence."

In a nutshell, this vision stresses that maturity is related with an institutionalization and systematization process of QA in HEIs. We will return to this idea of institutionalization of QA practices in the following paragraphs.

Other definitions of IQAS maturity identified in other information sources tend to provide, instead, just a partial or blurred vision of what could be understood as IQAS maturity; either highlighting some influential maturity factors or, alternatively, stressing the main intent or goal of an IQAS in HEIs. For example, the key role of documentation as a factor related with IQAS maturity is noted by the Inter-University Council of South Africa (IUCEA 2010, 11): "*The presence of a QA handbook shows the maturity of the institutional IQA system.*" Also, rather process-oriented factors are stressed by the National Agency for Quality Assessment and Accreditation of Spain (ANECA 2014, 13) when noting that maturity of an implemented IQAS "*is reflected in an appropriate review procedure (for example, using appropriate indicators) and putting suitable improvement initiatives into practice.*" Similarly, Massy (2010, 230) states that IQAS implementation maturity is more concerned with QA actors' attitudes, behaviour, and command of quality processes than in the precision of the documentation produced. Finally, Prisăcariu (2014, 138) emphasizes a more performance-oriented perspective on IQAS maturity, putting the focus on "*the responsibility that institutions have [with all its stakeholders] for the quality and continuous development of their education and other operations.*" Such responsibility should be addressed by means of balance between the *QA soft power* (i.e., focus on quality improvement/enhancement, recognition of institutional responsibility and autonomy, stakeholder consensus) and the *QA hard power* (i.e., QA for regulation, outcomes based on institutional performance, consumer information at the heart of QA).

All in all, and despite not considering previous visions as contradictory, we believe that they fail to provide a comprehensive definition of what IQAS implementation maturity is. Such lack of an agreed-upon definition may also be one of the main causes that explain the scarcity of empirical studies addressing it.

Table 4. Researched studies providing underpinning theoretical background for conceptualizing IQAS maturity implementation in HEIs

References	Unit of Analysis	Definition	Influential factors	Maturity progress approach	
				Lifecycle-evolution	Capability-performance
(Pereira do Nascimento et al. 2016)	Generic QMS		✓✓	☑	☐
(Garza-Reyes 2018; Garza-Reyes, Rocha-Lona, and Kumar 2015)	Generic QMS	✓✓	✓✓	☑	☐
(Monkienė and Lamanauskas 2014, 47-48)	QMS for non-university colleges		✓	☑	☐
(Vukasovic 2014)	Institutionalization of an IQAS for HEIs		✓✓	☑	☑
Agencia Nacional de Evaluación de la Calidad y Acreditación (ANECA) 2014)	IQAS for HEIs	✓		☐	☐
Inter-University Council of South Africa (IUCEA 2010, 11)	IQAS for HEIs	✓		☐	☐
Commission on Higher Education of the Philippines Government (CHED 2014, 12)	IQAS for HEIs	✓✓		☐	☐
(Hmčiar and Madzik 2017)	QMS for HEIs	✓	✓✓	☐	☑
(Prisăcariu 2014, 137-38)	IQAS for HEIs		✓	☐	☑
Agência de Avaliação e Acreditação do Ensino Superio (A3ES 2018, 24-30)	Institutional audit of IQAS for HEIs		✓✓	☐	☑
Akkreditierungsagentur für Studiengänge der Ingenieurwissenschaften (ASIIN e.V. 2016)	Institutional accreditation of IQAS for HEIs		✓✓	☐	☑
(Massy 2010)	QA practices (*Educational Quality Work*) in HEIs	✓	✓✓	☐	☑

✓✓ Strong evidence.
✓ Basic evidence.
☑ Addressed.
☐ Non addressed.
Source: Own elaboration.

In this sense, the already referred work by Hrnčiar and Madzík (2017) addresses the relationship among QMS maturity and the HEI's results achieved, but does not provide a formal working definition of IQAS implementation maturity. Instead, the study builds on a theoretical model considering *curriculum design, resources, academic's efforts, student's efforts, support services, quality of student experience, standards set for the program and results* (i.e., outputs, outcomes and impacts) as factors contributing to it. Whilst we do not view such conceptualization as inconsistent with earlier visions (as it implicitly recognises that IQAS implementation maturity depends on multiple influence factors) we neither perceive in it the critical role of documentation (for example) as a factor for maturity. Hence, we clearly see enough room for looking for a wider or more comprehensive definition of IQAS implementation maturity in HEIs.

In order to provide such a working definition, we drawn on the more generic literature on QM, and specifically, on the recent work by Garza-Reyes (2018, 217–18). This study provides a quite holistic definition for QMS maturity, considering that

> "the diagnosis of a QMS (…) must start by defining and understanding the maturity of the organisation's structure, procedures, processes, and resources dedicated to assuring that their products and/or services satisfy their customers' expectations. Here 'maturity' refers to the degree of knowledge, use, effective deployment, and concrete positive results obtained from a company's QMS."

We believe that such generic definition could be relatively easily adapted or instantiated for IQAS implementation maturity in HEIs by replacing the notion of customers with the notion of stakeholders; taking in to account, hence, the different preferences of the several interest groups existing in an education institution. Therefore, we believe that implications for the concept of IQAS implementation maturity in HEIs can be raised here as follows:

i. IQAS maturity should be understood as a rather multidimensional concept on the basis of three interrelated concepts: (i) the (effective) *'deployment'* *of multiple elements*, namely structure, procedures, processes and resources (human and technological), (ii) the *'use'* at both individual (i.e., actors involved) as well as at organizational/institutional level – i.e., dissemination of information across the institution, use for strategic decision making, etc. – and (iii) the *'results'* again at both individual and organizational level – i.e., considering outputs, outcomes and impacts satisficing all HEI's stakeholder expectations – . Note that the underlined concepts on which we rely to define the boundaries of IQAS maturity are not only in line with Garza-Reyes's generic definition but also with the IS-oriented sociotechnical view of IQAS in HEIs mentioned in section 2.2.
ii. IQAS maturity can be established as a criterion for assessment and measurement of the status or level of institutionalization (i.e., formalization) of the QA practices and initiatives implemented in a particular HEI. In other words, it measures the quality degree or "goodness" of the implemented IQAS "itself" or understood as a whole integrated system. Assessment and measurement of IQAS maturity should facilitate to the HEI's quality managers the detection of potential strengths and weaknesses of the QA efforts systematized in the institution.

In a nutshell, and whilst accepting that more research is needed to establish an widely-agreed and comprehensive definition of IQAS maturity, our previous rationale provides a minimum set of consolidated foundations which can be used as a basic theoretical underpinning for future developments. We must also recognize, nonetheless, that the acknowledged multidimensionality and complexity of IQAS maturity as a phenomenon under study certainly complicates the goal of resuming or providing a working definition in the form of a one-sentence or in a few paragraphs.

3.3. Maturation in Terms of IQAS for HEIs

Once portrayed how IQAS implementation maturity can be initially approached, we focus now on further analysing how maturity progress in the particular terms of IQAS implementation in HEIs can be understood. We assume here that the concept can be associated to a criterion for assessing the status level of QA practices' institutionalization undertaken in particular HEIs. Hence, we deem it relevant here to consider the work by Vukasovic (2014), who used institutionalization theory as a lens for describing the formalization of QA practices towards a more systematized and comprehensive IQAS in HEIs.

Institutionalisation can be viewed "as a process through which new, initially ambiguous, unfamiliar and resisted 'ways of doing things' become structured, desirable, appropriate, comprehensible, commonplace and routinise" (Colyvas & Powell, 2006; Scott, 2008, as cited in Vukasovic 2014, 47). In her work, Vukasovic suggests that systematization of HEI's QA practices into a formalized IQAS can be analysed using such a theoretical lens, "which implies the strengthening [and mutual alignment] of the regulative, normative and cultural-cognitive elements of institutions (…) that go in parallel and interact and contribute to each other"[1] (Vukasovic 2014, 47,61). Nonetheless, such process does not necessary occurs in a "linear, uniform and irreversible" manner (Vukasovic 2014, 61). For instance, a distinction can be made between different situations or levels of institutionalization of QA practices, namely (i) low (i.e., QA practices and rules are not systematized but rather developed ad hoc); (ii) medium (i.e., consolidation of QA practices, including the formalization of

---

[1] In terms of IQAS institutionalization, the (i) *regulative dimension* would encompass the development of regulation, structures and procedures, and the assignation of roles and formal relationships between different structures and parts; the (ii) *normative dimension* may include facets as highlighting quality strategic documents and public reports, the use of the IQAS for accountability purposes, work performed to ensure the transparency of QA or the use QA processes' outputs for institutional decision making, and the (iii) *cultural-cognitive* dimension would encompass activities related with the diffusion of improved understanding of what internal QA entails, the elaboration of QA procedures and their expected outcomes/indicators or training activities conducted for those engaged in the IQAS construction (Vukasovic 2014, 49).

rules, procedures, classification of roles and clarification of values); and (iii) high (i.e., QA new introduced norms and values are widely accepted, new practices are clarified and need less explanation and articulation) (Vukasovic 2014, 47–48). Grounding on the previous ideas, it could be concluded that maturity progression of IQAS implementation in HEIs should be better approached through a rather staged-oriented and evolutionary approach.

A more panoramic perspective on maturity progression for IQAS can be achieved reviewing the information collected from a wider number of information sources already summarized in Table 4. On the basis of the interpretation of data shown in it, two main approaches for maturity progression could be inferred:

i. A unidimensional life-cycle oriented approach, in which the unit (i.e., the object) of assessment is the QMS/IQAS as a whole. Maturity evolution is represented here through a rather linear sequence of pre-defined and discrete stages showing the evolution of the QMS/IQAS in terms of certification/accreditation years, which are taken as a reference. Such vision mainly emerges from contributions corresponding to the more generic QM literature. Nonetheless, the work by Monkienė and Lamanauskas (2014, 47–48) suggests a similar pattern for QMS maturity on non-HEI educational colleges in Lithuania.

ii. A multidimensional performance-based approach, in which the IQAS/QMS as a unit of analysis is decomposed (and assessed) into multiple features or structural elements that configure it. Maturity evolution tends to be represented here in rather dynamic or variable way in terms of how well (i.e., level of perfection) each feature is implemented in respect of a determined QA reference standard/best practice. This vision is prone to be found in contributions very focused on QA for HEIs, and more particularly, in documents and reports released by QA agencies/bodies. Hence, different standards/frameworks (ESG standards, CAF Education Model, ASSIN seal, etc.) are taken as a reference depending on each concrete source analysed (A3ES 2018; Hrnčiar and Madzík 2017; ASIIN e.V. 2016).

Finally, and turning back again our attention to Vukasovic's contributions, if we try to place it on one of the previously inferred maturity approaches, results might be somewhat inconclusive. On the one hand, it suggests a three staged-oriented approach based on the global situation of the institutionalization process of the IQAS, which may be viewed as a rather unidimensional life-cycle oriented approach. However this institutionalization process may not progress in a linear, uniform and irreversible form, and can also be described in terms of strengthening *regulative, normative and cultural-cognitive* dimensions. These latter considerations, perhaps, could be more linked to a rather multidimensional performance-based approach. All in all, and from the analysis of the evidences reviewed in this section, it can be concluded that several maturity progress approaches have been considered and seem plausible for assessing IQAS implementation maturity in HEIs. The adoption of either one of the earlier maturity progress approaches has some implications on the concrete instrument or framework used to measure or assess IQAS maturity, as explored in the following sections.

4. INSTRUMENTS FOR ASSESSING AND MEASURING MATURITY OF IQAS IN HEIS

Considering the structural complexity of IQAS, several heterogeneous instruments have been conceived by researchers and practitioners supposed to offer assistance for assessing and measuring IQAS implementation maturity in different ways. Without the aim of being exhaustive, in this section we provide a brief summary of them, with especial emphasis on maturity assessment methods and models.

Both them are generally considered as improvement frameworks providing well-defined support for organizations in order to measure maturity of different organizational entities in an effective way (Paulk 2008).

Differentiating between assessment methods and maturity models may be sometimes difficult, as both terms tend to be used somewhat interchangeably. Adopting a strict Design Science Research perspective, Mettler (2011, 87) refers to them as "maturity assessment models", which tend to be somehow in-between models and methods. For instance, and from an artifact's structural point of view, this instruments can generically be decomposed into a (i) *reference (domain) model;* defining domain areas, capabilities or criteria by which the design domain can be partitioned into more discrete units to be assessed; and an (ii) *assessment method/model*, providing one or more assessment dimensions defining a measurement scale. (Mettler 2011, 85–87; Ofner, Otto, and Österle 2013, 6; Tarhan, Turetken, and Reijers 2016, 129): Hence, *"what is basically assessed is to which extent certain criteria comply with the scale for each assessment dimension"* (Ofner, Otto, and Österle 2013, 6). On the other hand, maturity assessment models may have different utility or purpose, namely (i) *descriptive*, aiming at establishing current (as-is) assessments of the entity under evaluation; (ii) *prescriptive*, enabling the identification and definition of roadmaps for improvement in order to reach future desired (to-be) states; and (iii) *comparative*, providing support for conducting internal or external benchmarking (Pöppelbuß and Röglinger 2011).

In this section, we briefly describe diverse instruments and artifacts that, far away from presenting a more or less formal or accurate measurement for maturity, can provide valuable insights in order to derive criteria for designing and constructing a maturity assessment and measurement instrument for IQAS implementation in HEIs. Collectively, we see all them as an *"ecosystem"* of frameworks representing a multitude of perspectives and viewpoints on how IQAS implementation maturity can be approached.

4.1. Assessment Methods

4.1.1. SWOT Analysis

Several sources refer to the SWOT (strengths-weaknesses-opportunities-threats) analysis as an effective tool in order to achieve a simple understanding of the maturity level of a QMS as well as for the derivation of basic actions for improvement of the QA practices undertaken in an organizational context. For example, Garza-Reyes, Rocha-Lona, and Kumar (2015) propose a conceptual framework for implementing or improving a QMS suitable to be adapted to the needs of specific industries and organizations. In the first stage of their framework, they suggest to determine strengths and opportunities for improvement of the core processes of a QMS (Garza-Reyes, Rocha-Lona, and Kumar 2015, 1300–1302).

Within the application scope of HEIs, the SWOT analysis seems also to be a suitable tool for undertaken an initial maturity evaluation of the QA activities conducted in HEIs, specially where either rudimentary or non-existent formalized IQAS yet exist (Zgodavova, Urbancikova, and Kisela 2015, 9–10; Santos and Dias 2017, 288; RUFORUM 2011). Further, its use is commonly recommended to educational institutions by several national/regional QA agencies and accreditation bodies in their hands-on manuals and supporting guidelines documents (i.e., reports tipically released to facilitate educational institutions the process of developing or assessing their own IQAS).

Obviously, the main advantage of this tool relies on its simplicity and easiness of use, given the fact that it does not require specialised knowledge to be applied in practice. Conversely, it does not provide an accurate measurement index of maturity. As a consequence, calls can be found in the literature recommending the use of this tool in combination with other more sophisticated instruments, as for example, some kind of self-assessment/internal audit method (Garza-Reyes 2018, 217–18).

4.1.2. Business Excellence Model-Oriented Assessment Methods

A more elaborated alternative to SWOT analysis for getting a better understanding of QA practices in HEIs can be the use of self-assessment approaches based on Business Excellence Models (BEMs) (Kamat and Kittur 2017, 520; Rosa, Sarrico, and Amaral 2012). It must be acknowledged at this point that HEIs may consider several alternative quality frameworks as a reference for conducting their assessments, as for example the ISO 9001 standard or Total Quality Management (TQM), to cite only a few (Dahl Jørgensen et al. 2014; Rosa, Sarrico, and Amaral 2012). Nonetheless, there is plenty of literature showing the widespread application of the European Foundation for Quality Management (EFQM) Excellence Model (EFQM 2012) in educational contexts (Calvo-Mora, Alonso-Gonzalez, and Roldán 2006; Tari and Madeleine 2011; Tarí 2006; Rosa and Amaral 2007). Moreover, the use of the Common Assessment Framework (CAF) Education Model (EIPA 2013) – the educational-oriented version of the framework derived from the original model – has been explicitly documented in existing literature as a suitable tool for measuring the maturity of a QMS implemented in HEIs (Hrnčiar and Madzík 2017; Kargytė 2015, 382).

The basic idea here consists in using the dimensions considered by the EFQM framework – namely, *leadership, people, strategy, partnership, process, people results, customer results, society results and key results* – as a proxy to measure the performance or "goodness" of the implemented QMS in an institution. Hence and when compared with the previous SWOT approach, EFQM-oriented assessments allow not only to highlight strengths and weaknesses of institutional QA practices, but also to provide a benchmarking (maturity) measurement by means of a simple scoring system (Garza-Reyes, Rocha-Lona, and Kumar 2015, 1307–8; Kamat and Kittur 2017, 520). Hence, the maturity of the QMS can therefore be regularly or periodically measured and evaluated based on this type of indicator.

Despite that fact that BEMs provide a much more homogeneous and robust framework for self-assessments to HEIs than just a simpler SWOT analysis, criticism may arise due to strong dependence on the pre-defined dimensions. In general, they provide little emphasis regarding the teaching and learning or research and innovation core processes of a modern HEI. Therefore, using an "hybrid" or an own *ad-hoc model* combining the criteria established in different existing frameworks can be also a plausible alternative (Garza-Reyes 2018, 221). In this line, and as previously commented, QA agencies which carry on the responsibility of deploying the external accreditation and/or certification assessment procedures in different countries (Manatos, Sarrico, and Rosa 2017b, 343; Kamat and Kittur 2017, 517) usually develop 'toolkits' containing guidelines, recommendations and text-grids/rubrics providing insights and complementary support for both educational institutions as well as for external auditors on how to proceed on these QA processes. These tools tend to include criteria much more adjusted to the structural components of an IQAS for HEIs and are considered in more detail in the next section.

4.2. Maturity Models

Maturity Models (MMs) probably are the most well-known artifacts used by organizations to achieve maturity measurements for many organizational entities or functional domains. In order to identify potential MMs that could be applied in the scope of QA in HEIs, we extended already conducted reviews targeting MMs for the domain of QA in HEIs from several perspectives (Sanchez-Puchol and Pastor-Collado 2017; Sanchez-Puchol, Pastor-Collado, and Casanovas 2018; Sanchez-Puchol, Pastor-Collado, and Guàrdia 2018). For the purposes of the present chapter, the initial list of existing MMs targeting (in some or another way) our domain of interest was finally reduced to a final set of 12 MMs to be analysed in more detail in this chapter (see Table 5).

Table 5. Uncovered MMs related with applicability for QA issues in HEIs

#	Base references	Model name	Abbrev.	Class of maturity model
MM1	(Garza-Reyes 2018; Garza-Reyes, Rocha-Lona, and Kumar 2015; Rocha-Lona, Garza-Reyes, and Kumar 2013; Dale and Lascelles 1997)	Maturity Diagnostic Instrument	MDI	Sector-independent QMS
MM2	(Pereira do Nascimento et al. 2015, 2016)	Quality Management System Maturity Model	QMS-MM	Sector-independent QMS
MM3	(Książek and Ligarski 2017)	PN-ISO 10014:2008 Self-Assessment	–	Sector-independent QMS
MM4	(Baig, Basharat, and Maqsooud 2006)	Educational Capability Maturity Model	E-CMM	Quality in Higher Education
MM5	(Manjula and Vaideeswaran 2010, 2011, 2012a, 2012b)	Capability Maturity Model for Engineering Education System	E^2-CMM	Quality in Higher Education
MM6	(EIPA 2013; Hrnčiar and Madzík 2017; García Aranda and García Márquez 2015)	CAF-Education Framework	CAF-EFQM	Education-sector QMS
MM7	(Massy 2010)	Education Quality Work	EQW	Higher Education IQAS
MM8	(A3ES 2018)	Criteria for Audits of IQAS	–	Higher Education IQAS
MM9	(Torres Solà et al. 2018)	Criteria for Certification of IQAS	–	Higher Education IQAS
MM10	(ASIIN e.V. 2016)	ASSIN Maturity Model	–	Higher Education IQAS
MM11	(British Columbia 2013)	Quality Assurance Maturity Model	–	Higher Education IQAS
MM12	(Medina García, Méndez Giraldo, and López Quintero 2016; Larrondo Petrie, Medina García, and Méndez Giraldo 2009)	Maturity Model for Learning Ability in Engineering	–	Higher Education IQAS

Source: Own elaboration.

We must acknowledge here that we excluded for final analysis (i) incomplete or under development MMs (Chalaris et al. 2017; Duarte and Ventura Martins 2014) – that is, MMs suggested or proposed for QA issues in HEIs but not providing (yet) enough evidence in terms of their completeness from a MM's structural point of view – , (ii) MMs with a target scope of application limited to one particular institution (Čorejová, Genzorová, and Rostášová 2017; Tovar, Carina, and Castillo 2009), (iii) models considering collaterally aspects related with QA in HEIs –for example, institutional research oriented MMs (Taylor 2015) – or (iv) models related with QA issues in HEIs but rather at program level than at institutional or faculty level (Bennedsen, Georgsson, and Kontio 2014; Rouvrais and Lassudrie 2014; Bennedsen et al. 2015; Bennedsen and Rouvrais 2016; Cocón and Fernández 2011; Bennedsen et al. 2018).

For facilitating the understandability of the final set of reviewed models, we grouped them into generic "classes of MMs", depending on the similarity of their declared maturity object to be addressed. In Annex I, we provide a complete analysis of the main characteristics and properties of each one of the MM analysed. Nonetheless, and due to space constraints, we only briefly comment them just from a very aggregated point of view.

4.2.1. Sector-Independent QMS MMs

These MMs have a focus on assessing maturity of sector-independent QMS, and therefore, and at first sight, they could be a valid option for being applied in HEIs. Nonetheless, IQAS in HEIs require a stronger focus on processes related with teaching, learning and research activities; which are characteristic only of educational organizations. Such processes do not seem to be well-covered by the original reviewed models. A plausible alternative here could be the adaptation or extension of such models providing an adequate support for such lacking elements. The 3 MMs considered in this category present a Likert-like structure and have emerged from rather academic oriented literature. In particular, both the MDI and the QMS-MM have been developed using theoretically-sound scientific procedures, which can be interpreted as a sign of rigour and completeness. Further, they also provide an assessment methodology, which clearly can facilitate their applicability in practical settings.

4.2.2. Quality in Higher Education MMs

These models facilitate maturity measurements for the quality of the educational service delivery in HEIs, in a general sense. They present a strong focus on process-oriented factors and provide a good coverage in terms of the teaching, learning and research activities for these organizations. Unfortunately, this focus on process-oriented factors leads them to underestimate other facets and structural elements that should also be taken into account when measuring the maturity of an IQAS implemented within a HEI. MMs reviewed in this category have their origin in academic sources, and present a CMM-like structure. In addition, the E^2-CMM presents a strong empirical validation and a detailed assessment methodology encompassing a quantitative measurement scale, allowing hence quite accurate maturity measurements.

4.2.3. Education-Sector QMS MMs

Under this typology of MMs we have typified the CAF-Education Framework, which represents a tailored version of the more generic EFQM Excellence Model conveniently adapted for being applied in educational institutions. The use of the EFQM Excellence Models as a foundation for maturity assessments and measurements has been well documented by the literature (García Aranda and García Márquez 2015). It could be applied for maturity assessments either at organizational level or at a narrower perspective being taken as a reference for maturity measurements of the institutional QMS/IQAS. The CAF-Education framework provides a detailed assessment methodology and quantitative maturity measurements. Nonetheless, it must be taken into account that it has been initially conceived for being applied in any type of educational institution, and therefore, it is not particularly tailored for HEIs.

4.2.4. Higher Education IQAs MMs

Under this class of MMs we have categorized a set of instruments that have been conceived for assessing the maturity of IQAS in HEIs from several perspectives. They principally have a practitioner's oriented origin, being conceived and developed by QA-oriented institutions/bodies as support or complementary artifacts for QA accreditation, certification or audit procedures taking a quite a holistic perspective. As a major drawback, it must be argued that they generally have not been developed using a sound scientific procedure, lacking therefore of rigorous empirical validations and accurate assessment procedures.

4.3. Other Alternative Frameworks

4.3.1. Critical Success Factors for QMS/IQAS Implementation in HEIs

A well-established stream of research in the specialized literature of QA for HEIs deals with studies on Critical Success Factors (CSFs). There is a plethora of studies presenting several different instruments/frameworks for measuring the success of QM implementations in HEIs. In general, it can be perceived a great heterogeneity on the constructs used for conceptualizing CSFs, ranging from simple lists of factors to more complex and multidimensional conceptual models. Such variability can also be extended to the underlying theoretical background of the proposed instruments, although a clear predominance on studies relying on Total Quality Management (Owlia and Aspinwall 1997; Bayraktar, Tatoglu, and Zaim 2008) and (perhaps in less measure) on the ISO 9001 standard series (Mohamed, Ghani, and Basir 2016; Thonhauser and Passmore 2006) can be appreciated.

Recent contributions in this research stream seem to confirm general trends and calls towards developing more integrated frameworks to measure QA issues in HEIs (Kamat and Kittur 2017, 524–25; Manatos, Sarrico, and Rosa 2017a). As a matter of fact, Sahu, Shrivastava, and Shrivastava (2013b, 2013a) developed an instrument for measuring QM implementation success grounding on a literature review compiling 64 items into 8 first-order CSFs, namely *roles and responsibilities of senior management, infrastructure in institutions, training development and placement, academic aspects, research and development and consultancy, administration, promoting institution's initiatives, and institution's excellence measures*. Similarly, Pal Pandi and colleagues (Pal Pandi, Paranitharan, and Jeyathilagar 2018; Pal Pandi, Rajendra Sethupathi, and Jeyathilagar 2016b; Pal Pandi et al. 2016; Pal Pandi, Rajendra Sethupathi, and Jeyathilagar 2016a) constructed an Integrated Educational Quality Management System (IEQMS) Model for HEIs as a bundle of several well-known quality frameworks and approaches – including ISO 9001, ISO 14001, Six Sigma, Lean Thinking or Total Quality Management, among others – deriving and grouping 113 items into 10 CSFs first-order variables: *top management commitment, system approach to management, customer (student) satisfaction, employee involvement, training, team work, continuous improvement, corporate social responsibility, academic culture and knowledge audit*. Conducting a formal review on IQAS implementation CSFs for HEIs is out of the scope of the present work, but earlier enumerated CSFs can provide readers with a broad idea of the main factors/criteria considered in the literature.

Although previous CSF-oriented frameworks do not formally provide explicit measurements for the maturity of an IQAS implementation, they can be a very useful resource for constructing maturity measurement instruments, as has been widely recognised by specialized literature in this particular research stream (Lahrmann et al. 2011; Becker, Knackstedt, and Pöppelbuß 2009; van Steenbergen et al. 2010; De Bruin et al. 2005). The earlier referenced studies include empirically-validated instruments based on quantitative indicators and attributes that, together with existing best practices reports (AQU 2011) and existing exemplary use cases of implemented IQAS (see Section 2.4), may be well used or adapted when defining the structural architecture of a maturity measurement instrument for IQAS implemented in HEIs.

4.3.2. Service Quality Models for HEIs

Another important stream of research in the QA-oriented literature for HEIs is based on a set of studies focussed on evaluating the (perceived) educational service quality (or excellence) provided by institutions (Alzafari 2017, 269). Typically, those studies are grounded on generic service quality models like SERVQUAL or SERVPERF, although HE industry-specific variants as HEdPERF or HESQUAL have also been derived (Abdullah 2005; Teeroovengadum, Kamalanabhan, and Seebaluck 2016; Kamat and Kittur 2017, 520). As noted in previous sections of the chapter, service quality models have been recognized as an important "reference frameworks" for defining and conceptualizing QM issues in educational settlements (Becket and Brookes 2008, 44–51; Chen 2012).

From the narrower perspective of measuring the maturity of an IQAS, the importance of such models drawn on the fact that SERVQUAL and derivate service quality models have been related/used for developing capability and process maturity assessments in service-oriented organizations (Radomír 2013). Nonetheless, we were not able to found relevant evidence confirming this point for the particular scope of IQAS implementation in HEIs, far away from mere suggestions considering the potential utility of this models (Đonlagić and Fazlić 2015, 39,55). Further, as they provide a measurement for a very specific construct (service quality), these models tend to be quite inflexible as are based on attributes with strong focus on internal processes and customer satisfaction, but missing factors related with results or outcomes (Kamat and Kittur 2017, 520). For additional details on these education service quality assessment frameworks, readers are referred to the particular reviews conducted on the topic by Sultan and Wong (2010) or Silva et al. (2017).

4.3.3. Reference Models and Enterprise Reference Architectures for HEIs

An alternative perspective for approaching maturity of IQAS in HEIs can be funded on the potential synergies that can emerge from QMS and IS lifecycle's integration; and more particularly, on the development, implementation and deployment of EAs (Rupino da Cunha and Dias de

Figueiredo 2005, 2245). According to Barata and Cunha (2017, 290) *"new approaches should be developed, which include practical artifacts to assist the users. Examples of artifacts can be architectural documentation of both systems and patterns of action that IS and QMS practitioners can adopt."* In this sense, several authors have suggested the potential of EA artifacts for QA purposes in HEIs (Oderinde 2010; Olsen and Trelsgård 2016; Svensson and Hvolby 2012; Riihimaa 2009). EA artifacts are documents describing and representing the structure of a system at high level of abstraction (Kotusev 2019; Greefhorst, Koning, and Vliet 2006). In the following, we focus on Reference Models (RMs) and Enterprise Reference Architectures (ERAs) as concrete types of EA's abstract artifacts (Niemi and Pekkola 2017; Cloutier et al. 2010; Fettke and Loos 2007) for which we envision a great potential as facilitators for building and improving IQAS and related practices in HEIs.

RMs can be viewed as a frame of reference for a concrete *"class of objects."* They are generic (abstract) conceptual models providing a universal (i.e., idealized) or standardized representation for an application domain, entity or field of interest (Thomas 2006). Hence, they formalize and encapsulate a set of generally accepted well practices, reusable designs and domain knowledge which must be next conveniently adjusted and adapted to the specific requirements of the concrete object or entity to be modelled (Pajk, Indihar-Štemberger, and Kovaþiþ 2012; Fettke and Loos 2007).

There are several types of RMs representing the content of various different domains. For the scope of HEIs, most of the existing proposals have been targeted to represent the standard processes that should be deployed in an idealized educational institution – i.e., the so-called *Business Process Reference Models*. There also exists some contributions more directed to represent the landscape of applications and data objects/entities that should cover the overall informational needs of HEIs (Sanchez-Puchol, Pastor-Collado, and Borrell 2018). When such abstract RMs provide an integrated description of the business, IS (applications, data) and technological domains (layers) of a concrete type or class of enterprises, they are known as ERAs[2] (ten Harmsen van der Beek, Trienekens, and Grefen 2012, 99–100). In other words, an ERA can be considered as anything else than a reference representation (i.e., a RM) of the EA of a concrete type of business (Timm 2018, 209). In Table 5, we provide a comprehensive list enumerating several of the most outstanding RMs and ERAs developed specifically for HEIs. Due to readability purposes, complementary information for each one of them can be found in Annex II.

Table 6. Enterprise Reference Architectures and Models for Higher Education Institutions[*]

Enterprise reference architectures (ERAs)	Business-oriented reference models (RMs)	Information systems & technology oriented reference models (RMs)
Hoger Onderwijs Referentie Architectuur (Dutch's Higher Education Reference Architecture (SURF 2018)	UCISA UK Higher Education Capability Model (UCISA 2018)	Higher Education Information Systems in Croatia (Frackmann 2007)
ITANA Reference Architecture for Teaching and Learning (ITANA Working Group 2012; Abel, Brown, and Suess 2013)	Colombian Higher Education Enterprise Architecture (Llamosa-Villalba et al. 2015, 2014)	Unified Information Systems Reference Model for Higher Education Institutions (Sanchez-Puchol, Pastor-Collado, and Borrell 2017)
CAUDIT Enterprise Architecture Commons for Higher Education (CAUDIT 2016, 2017)	Charles Sturt University Higher Education Business Process Reference Model (Charles Sturt University 2010)	e-education Application Framework (Fagan 2003)
Trust and Identity (TIER) Reference Architecture (TIER-Data Structures and APIs Working Group 2016)	Business Process Reference Model for Higher Education (Svensson and Hvolby 2012)	Reference Model of University Information Technology Architecture (Chen, Tang, and Li 2016)

[*] Classification of artifacts based on authors' own appreciation.
Font: Own elaboration.

---

[2] It must be acknowledged that many contributions labelled as "*Reference Architectures*" do not provide such a complete view. Hence, in many times they tend to just provide the integrated view of the business and part of the IS layers (especially, the data object layer).

RMs and ERAs are much appreciated artifacts in several scientific disciplines as they are susceptible to be taken as a *"reference framework"* for defining the dimensions or focus areas under which to anchor and configurate a maturity assessment instrument/framework. Relatively similar RMs or ERAs have been used, for example, for building maturity instruments in domains like EA management (Meyer, Helfert, and O'Brien 2011) or Software Engineering (Bekkers et al. 2010). Moreover, RMs and ERAs are also useful artifacts to develop improvement plans (roadmaps) for a particular object or domain of analysis, describing how to migrate from a starting or baseline "as-is" state towards a future desired "to-be" state (Cloutier et al. 2010, 18–19; Niemi and Pekkola 2017; Kotusev 2019). In this sense, they have been also used in combination with other already existing MMs to perform maturity assessments and measurements (Barn, Clark, and Hearne 2013). Considering this background, we believe that a similar approach can be adopted grounding on RMs and ERAs for HEIs in order to facilitate the definition, construction and improvement of their IQAS. Hence, they can be very valuable resources for several activities conducted during the formalization and systematization of IQAS in HEIs, including among others, the description and documentation of how processes are carried out, how responsibilities are assigned inside the institution, the identification of information flows between involved entities, the identification of critical data records for certification/auditing purposes or the definition of technological infrastructure to adequately collect and store performance indicators of the running IQAS (Riihimaa 2009; Rupino da Cunha and Dias de Figueiredo 2005, 2250–51; Kahveci et al. 2012; Svensson and Hvolby 2012; Haris, Washizaki, and Fukazawa 2017).

Despite the previous advantages, it must be noted however, that RMs and ERAs are very focused on business-, IS- and technology-oriented aspects. Therefore, other important dimensions or factors contributing to IQAS implementation maturity may be neglected or underestimated by these artifacts (see Section 2.3). In addition, there is still a lack of systematic methods and procedures on how to apply/instantiate the existing RMs and ERAs in order to derive context-oriented architectural solution designs, which, in turn, may complicate the realization of the practical utility of these artifacts (ten Harmsen van der Beek, Trienekens, and Grefen 2012; Timm 2018).

5. Towards a New Instrument for Assesing and Measuring IQAS Maturity in HEIs

5.1. Opportunity and Need for a New MM Instrument for Measuring IQAS Implementation in HEIs

Given all the background considered during this chapter, and despite accepting the existence of basic foundational knowledge and some instruments for addressing in some or another way IQAS implementation maturity in HEIs, we believe that there still is room for improvement and further research on the topic. In general, we argue that the research stream devoted to IQAS maturity assessments in HEIs is still its infancy stage, as only scattered and limited research on the topic already exists. Hence, several unresolved problems can be identified, which can be arguably summarized into two major gaps: (i) the lack of an agreed-upon definition and conceptualization of what is an IQAS for HEIs, (ii) the lack of an holistic, integrated, and theoretically-sound instrument providing an accurate and effective measurement of IQAS implementation maturity in HEIs.

The opportunity for envisioning such a new MM instrument can be framed in line with current research calls from further studying QA in HEIs adopting a "maturity oriented" perspective. Moreover, and in terms of justifying the practical relevance of the envisioned artifact, the authors of the present work have had the opportunity to confirm its relevance by means of several informal interviews undertaken over the last months with quality managers and HEIs' stakeholders in different international conferences related with QM and HE issues. In all cases, all people interviewed welcomed the initiative and expressed their enthusiasm on the possibility of having such a practical-oriented MM.

Grounding on the information sources reviewed this chapter, and specially, on major drawbacks and deficiencies identified in the existing artifacts conceived for measuring IQAS maturity in HEIs, in the following lines we provide a synthetized set of functional and non-functional "meta-requirements" [MR] representing (in a consolidated way) the main design objectives to be accomplished by our envisioned MM for IQAS implementation in HEIs. Inevitably, some level of subjectivity at this point must be acknowledged.

5.1.1. [MR1] Robustness

The envisioned MM should be developed by using theoretically-sound scientific methodologies, providing an adequate justification of its theoretical foundation, the underlying maturity concept and how the artifact has been validated and verified.

5.1.2. [MR2] Comprehensiveness

As IQAS implementation maturity can be not captured by a single dimension or facet of analysis. For instance, the envisioned model should cover the IQAS domain as a whole, providing multiple dimensions or focus areas of analysis, representing all the aspects encompassing the structural elements as well as its main impacts at institutional level (i.e., maturity factors).

5.1.3. [MR3] Granularity

The envisioned MM should provide an adequate support for allowing maturity measurements at different levels of granularity, that is, both at an aggregate level and at a more particular or fine-trained factor level.

5.1.4. [MR4] Prescriptiveness

The envisioned MM should provide adequate support for practitioners in terms of best practices, recommendations and detailed improvement measures on how to make progress or step up to further levels of IQAS implementation maturity.

5.1.5. [MR5] Accuracy

The MM should provide an effective assessment methodology for making reliable and accurate assessments of IQAS implementation maturity. The assessment methodology should allow for self-assessments as well as assessments by external parties.

5.1.6. [MR6] Flexibility

Considering that there is no one-size-fits-all reference model for IQAS in HEIs, the envisioned MM should provide context-specific configuration mechanisms specifying how the MM should be adapted to the particular requirements of IQAS implemented in different HEIs.

5.2. A Particular Research Agenda for Building a MM for IQAS Implementation in HEIs

Once the need of a new instrument has been conveniently justified and its basic design objectives appropriately inferred from existing basic foundational knowledge, the question arises now on how to construct such a new envisioned MM.

In Figure 2 we portray a research agenda based on a rather constructive-oriented Design Science Research (DSR) approach, reflecting a plausible pathway to build and evaluate a MM instrument for IQAS implementation in HEIs based in four major stages or phases. According to the potentially important role that mixed/multimethod research can play in DSR (Ågerfalk 2013, 253), we also depict suitable research methods and data collection techniques that could be used or applied in each of the particular considered stages (Venable, Pries-Heje, and Baskerville 2016, 2012; Peffers et al. 2012). In addition, the main expected outputs for each stage are also summarized at the bottom part of the image.

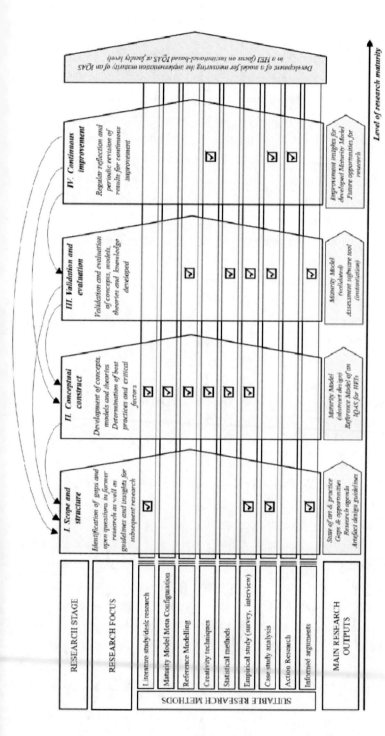

Figure 2. Elements of the proposed research agenda based on a Design Science Research approach for building a MM for IQAS implementation maturity. Font Own elaboration inspired on previous examples by Krüger and Teuteberg (2015) and Oesterreich and Teuteberg (2016).

First, existing theoretical and practical knowledge on the research topic should be collected, analyzed and organized to identify possible existing research gaps and/or potential lines and opportunities for research. Such task can be undertaken basically by means of science review approaches, which may also incorporate and integrate expert knowledge emerged from practitioners and experts in the field. This could be achieved, for example, by means of exploratory empirical analysis or representative case studies. In this vein, contents and considerations presented in this chapter could be assimilated to be a representative initial attempt of this first stage. Next and grounding on this knowledge gained in the first stage; constructs, models and assessment criteria should be derived in order to design the structural architecture (including maturity dimensions, maturity level stages, assessment variables, etc.) of the envisioned instrument. This can be achieved by using different research methods, as MM meta-configuration, creativity techniques, reference modelling or statistical methods, among others (Lahrmann et al. 2011; Patas, Pöppelbuß, and Goeken 2013; Lahrmann and Marx 2010).

Thirdly, the constructed MM should be rigorously evaluated and validated by means of empirical studies, expert focus groups, in-depth case studies or even by means of an action research approach. The main goal of this stage should be the demonstration of the MM's feasibility and applicability in many different HE contexts. Hence, the more studies conducted testing in some or another way in as many as possible heterogeneous and diverse particular HE contexts, the more generalizability for the new MM may be claimed. Finally, and after being applied in multiple natural real contexts, during the last stage of the research process the initially constructed MM should be continuously improved in a regular basis with the aim to incorporate new trends, regulatory changes, emerged best practices or technological innovations that may gradually arise in the field of QA in HEIs. At this point of time, several research methods could be susceptible of being applied to enhance the initial version of the artefact by means of an iterative and cyclical approach.

5.3. Design Guidelines and Recommendations for Developing a MM for IQAS Implementation in HEIs

The previous research agenda provides a high-level roadmap for developing a MM measurement instrument for IQAS implementation in HEIs. However, it still represents a too abstract course of action. For instance, having of more fine-grained and detailed recommendations would be advisable, as essential design decisions to be adopted across the pathway for building the envisioned MM are not properly detailed in the proposed research agenda. For instance, we further extend it now by providing more explicit design recommendations and guidelines for building the MM drawing on the well-known framework of design parameters for MMs proposed by Mettler (2011, 2010). Reasons for using such framework are three-fold:

- First, it is a generic framework for domain-independent MMs. For instance, it can be applied for building any kind of MM, whether it is a generic MM or a more specific one, suitable for being applied only to a particular entity or concrete scenario.
- Secondly, it has already been successfully applied in several research domain areas, either as a simple reference guide for constructing new MMs (Mettler and Blondiau 2012) or as a template for comparing (similar) existing ones in a chosen domain or field (Vezzetti, Violante, and Marcolin 2014; Carvalho et al. 2018).
- Finally, this framework is a widely-accepted and well-known decision framework grounding on the DSR paradigm. For instance, it suits perfectly well with our suggested four-stage-based research agenda. Therefore, it will allow us to derive additional in-depth design recommendations complementing the research outputs suggested for each one of the stages proposed in the research agenda.

Table 7. Design recommendations and guidelines for the developing a well-grounded MM for IQAS implementation in HEIs

Research Agenda	Design Activity	Design parameter	Design characteristic/options	Design guidelines recommendations	Justificatory knowledge
Stage 1	1. Identify need or new opportunity	*Novelty*	☑ Emerging ☐ Pacing ☐ Disruptive ☐ Mature	• The envisioned MM addresses the implementation of IQAS in HEIS, which still is a relatively new phenomenon for many educational institutions over the world, which is especially relevant for in Western and Central European countries belonging to the EHEA area.	[Sect. 1 & 2.4]
		Innovation	☐ New ☑ Variant ☐ Version	• Existing knowledge and MMs devoted to assessing similar QA issues may provide valuable knowledge for not having to create a new MM from scratch.	[Sect 2.2-2.4 & 4.2]
		Breadth/focus	☐ General issue ☑ Specific issue	• IQAS represent a specific type of artefact deployed in HEIs, which should be adequately addressed by means of a specific issue-oriented MM. As no one-size-fits-all approach is acknowledged for such kind of artifacts, the envisioned MM should include adaptation mechanism for being particularized to different HE contexts.	[Sect 2.2, 2.3 & 4.2]
	2. Define scope	*Depth/level of analysis*	☐ Individual/group ☑ Organization ☐ Inter-organizational ☑ Global-Society	• The envisioned MM is expected to be applied at institutional/faculty level, and therefore, it must basically encompass intra-organizational aspects. • Global-society issues related to third-mission function of educational institutions should also be taken into account.	[Sect. 2.2, 2.3]
		Target Audience	☑ Management-oriented ☑ Quality assurance-oriented ☐ Technology-oriented ☐ Education-oriented	• The main target audience is deemed to be quality- and management-oriented staff with decision authority within HEIs. • External professionals belonging to QA bodies and entities also may potentially be interested in using the MM	[Sect. 2.3, 2.4] & subjective consideration
		Dissemination	☑ Open ☐ Exclusive	• Free or open dissemination of the MM will probably foster its acceptance and widespread among institutions.	Subjective consideration
		Stakeholders	☑ Academic researchers ☑ Industry practitioners ☐ Government bodies ☐ Combination	• Academic researchers and HEIs practitioners can be viewed as main interested parties in the development of the envisioned MM.	Subjective consideration

Research Agenda	Design Activity	Design parameter	Design characteristic/options	Design guidelines recommendations	Justificatory knowledge
Stage 2	3. Design model	*Maturity definition*	☐ Process-oriented ☐ Object-oriented ☐ People-oriented ☑ Combination	• Complex socio-technical systems like the implementation of IQAS HEIs require a multi-dimensional definition of maturity combining several factors of maturity. • Multi-dimensional definitions of maturity facilitate both aggregate and particular dimension-level measurements.	[Sect 3.2, 3.3]
		Goal function	☐ One-dimensional ☑ Multi-dimensional		[Sect 3.2, 3.3 & 4.2]
		Design process	☑ Theory-driven (top-down) ☐ Practitioner-based (bottom-up) ☐ Combination	• Adoption of a rather theory-driven & top-down development approach grounding in existing knowledge and similar MMs, according to recommendations for building MMs to be applied in rather immature domains.	[Sect 2.4 & 4.2]
		Design product	☐ Textual description of form ☑ Textual description of form and function ☑ Instantiation (software assessment tool)	• Clear description of principles of form (i.e., structure) and function (i.e., effects) of the MM should be provided. • MM could be instantiated in the form of a prototype fostering its applicability in real HE contexts.	[Sect 2.3] & Subjective consideration
		Application method	☑ Self-assessment ☑ Third-party assisted ☐ Certified professionals	• Primary utility of the MM directed for self-assessment of the maturity of the IQAS implementation in HEIs. • Potential utility for external QA-professionals in terms of comparative/benchmarking purposes.	[Sect 4.2]
		Respondents	☑ Management (internal) ☑ Staff (internal) ☐ QA bodies (external) ☐ Partners (external)	• Most suitable respondents for collecting data may well be the internal actors engaged with the institutionalization of the IQAS.	Subjective consideration

Table 7. (Continued)

Research Agenda	Design Activity	Design parameter	Design characteristic/options	• Design guidelines recommendations	Justificatory knowledge
Stage 3	4. Evaluate design	*Subject of evaluation*	☐ Design process ☐ Design product ☑ Both	• Evaluation of both design process and product in order to achieve a good balance among (scientific) rigor and (practical) relevance.	Subjective consideration
		Point of time	☐ Ex-ante ☐ Ex-post ☑ Both	• Ideally, multiple evaluation episodes should be conducted considering multiple scenarios. • Ex-post naturalistic evaluation in terms of MM's utility in a particular real HE strongly recommended • At worst, ex-ante naturalistic evaluations must be conducted.	Subjective consideration
		Evaluation method	☐ Artificial ☐ Naturalistic ☑ Combination		Subjective consideration
Stage 4	5. Reflect evolution	*Subject of change*	☐ None ☐ Form ☐ Functioning ☑ Form and functioning	• Dynamics of the MM should consider both structural as well as functional adaptability-mechanisms to suit well the particular HE context of application.	Subjective consideration
		Frequency of change	☐ Non-recurring ☑ Continuous	• A clear release management policy could provide traceability on changes applied to the MM over time.	Subjective consideration
		Structure of change	☑ External/open ☐ Internal/exclusive	• No a priory perceived reason for limiting the origin and source of changes suggested to the initial MM	Subjective consideration

Font: Own elaboration, based on minor extensions/modification of the original model proposed by Mettler.

In Table 7, we synthetize our suggested design guidelines and recommendations for developing our envisioned MM in terms of the decision parameters considered in original Mettler's framework. We do so by indicating, for each design parameter defined in the original model, the most suitable option (in our view), according to the uncovered knowledge presented in earlier sections of this chapter. Collectively, and combined with the previous research agenda, we believe that they provide a clear and valuable pathway containing interesting foundations for those readers especially interested in the construction of the poised artefact. In the following paragraphs, we provide brief additional justification for the specific suggested options.

5.3.1. Identify Need or New Opportunity Activity

Two main parameters have to be considered in this first design activity: novelty and innovation. According to Mettler "considerations about the novelty of the topic covered by the MM play a key role, since it determines whether there is a need for explanation in practice (…) as well as some use cases to underpin the theoretical assumptions on the maturity levels" (2010, 81–82). Our envisioned MM can be generally framed into the QA in HE disciplinary field, which we consider as a rather mature and developed research area. As a matter of fact, in a recent scientometric study Alzafari (2017, 264) refers to it as a complex and multidisciplinary field due to the overlapping and interlinking of the topics covered in the enormous amount of studies devoted to it. Further, the field's maturity can be also perceived by the great number of recently released disciplinary reviews synthetizing the already existing body of knowledge (Manatos, Sarrico, and Rosa 2017a; Tarí and Dick 2016; Prakash 2018; Kamat and Kittur 2017; Steinhardt et al. 2017).

However, if we circumscribe to the narrower topic of systematization of IQAS in HEIs, we believe this one to be a relatively new (*emerging*) phenomena for many HEIs, especially in Western-central European universities (Kwiatkowska-Sujka and Socha 2017; Harutyunyan and Ohanyan 2016, 5; Sá, Sampaio, and Rosa 2012). Assuming that many HEIs started to formalize their IQAS at the end of the first decade of the

2000s as a consequence of the legal requirements derived from the Bologna Process agreements (Seyfried and Pohlenz 2018, 1), it could be considered as rather immature subject in practice. As shown in Section 2.4, whilst accepting the existence of an increasingly larger database of rigorous use cases available, we believe that they do not yet provide appropriate evidence on well-accepted QA practices, especially for higher levels of IQAS implementation maturity.

On the other hand, the second parameter to be considered before starting the explicit development of a MM is innovation. Hence, a decision should be made in terms of deciding on building a completely new model, a version, or a variant of an already existing model. We believe that several alternatives and recommendations are plausible here. On the one hand, assuming than no fully-focused MM on IQAS maturity implementation has been found (see Section 4.2), a first recommendation could be building a completely (*new*) maturity model. Nonetheless, we believe that a better plausible alternative could be to either adapt or improve (*variant*) the content of an already existing MM. Existing knowledge and contributions highlighted in the initial sections of this chapter could provide quite valuable knowledge for being used to such purposes.

5.3.2. Define Scope

The define scope stage is devoted to defining the main boundaries of the MM to be constructed. The first decision involves considering the breadth/focus (i.e., magnitude) of the phenomena to be addressed by the MM. In this sense, generic MMs are those that can be applied across different domains, whilst domain-specific MMs are coupled to rather more particular scenarios or entities. We assume here that sector-independent MMs for QMS (as for example, those analyzed in section 4.2) do not provide an adequate support for assessing particularities of IQAS in HEIs – i.e., consider the idiosyncrasies of educational institutions and their need to specifically monitor and control the quality of teaching and learning service delivery –. Hence, a *specific-issue* oriented MMs seems to be a more adequate approach. Further, we deem that the envisioned MM should be applied at institutional/centre level, and therefore, its main focus should be set to the *intra-organizational* dimensions of the IQAS (processes, actors, structure, information and documentation needs, etc.). Nonetheless, *global-society* aspects and impacts characteristics of the third-mission function of educational institutions should be considered, too.

The implementation of an IQAS mostly involves *quality-oriented* and *management-oriented* actors, which we see as the target potential audience of the envisioned artefact. Nonetheless, we also hypothesize that external QA-oriented professionals associated to accreditation/certification bodies and agencies may also use the resulting artifact. Whatever the case, the target audience of the MM should not be confused with MM's stakeholders, that is, all those who may have an interest in the creation of the MM. A priori, we consider that both *academic researchers* and *practitioners* in HEIs could be the most interested stakeholders, as the constructed MM would provide them valuable insights and data for illustrating QA best-practices associated to different levels of IQAS implementation maturity. Finally, and regarding the dissemination of the MM, we propose an *open and free* approach, aiming to foster as much as possible the widespread and use of the MM anywhere.

5.3.3. Design Model

The design model activity represents the starting point for constructing the MM itself. Hence, the first decision to be adopted is the definition of a proper conceptualization of the "maturity" to be assessed. According to the sociotechnical approach considered for those systems over the chapter, we believe that a rather multi-faceted (i.e., *combination* of process-oriented, object-oriented and people-oriented) definition and a multi-dimensional goal function conceptualization of maturity could be the most adequate approach. In other words, IQAS implementation maturity should be view as a "optimization indicator" of the formalization of the technical system (infrastructure, information, documentation, etc.), the social system (people capabilities, etc.) and a managerial system (processes, structure, etc.) that encompass the whole IQAS. In addition, the MM to be constructed should operate at different levels of granularity, being able to measure not only the maturity of the IQAS implemented at aggregated level, but also at a narrower level, in terms of each sub-area (dimension) or maturity factors being considered.

Next, the nature of the design process for building the MM should be considered. In this sense, we recommend a rather *top-down* approach drawing on knowledge presented in this chapter, and in line with similar existing examples of other MM's developed for addressing relatively immature phenomena (Mettler 2010). There is also a need to decide on both the method of application (i.e., whether data collection for assessment is based upon self/third-party assessments) and the expected respondents (i.e., actors who collect real data for assessment) for the MM. In our view, the constructed model should be primarily devoted for *self-assessment* purposes by quality managers within HEIs. Nonetheless, and as noted earlier, we also perceive certain potential utility of the MM for external professionals embarked in accreditation/certification QA procedures or even in benchmarking/comparative exercises (a consistent and reliable assessment instrument should be provided, in this case). To conclude, the most suitable respondents for collecting data may be the *internal staff* (teaching or administrative) of the HEI, or alternatively, those HEI's internal actors engaged in tasks related with the design, implementation and improvement the IQAS.

5.3.4. Evaluate Design

Once properly constructed, the MM should be evaluated in terms of three main decision parameters: subject of evaluation (what), point of evaluation (when) and paradigm of evaluation (how).

Regarding the subject of evaluation, we believe that both the *design product* (i.e., the MM itself, both in terms of principles of form and function) as well as the *design process* (i.e., the way the MM has been built) must be evaluated. Adopting such approach will foster not only the transparency and the traceability of the conceived MM, but also will allow to achieve a good balance in terms of scientific rigor and practical relevance. On the other hand, decisions regarding the temporal frame and the paradigm of evaluation can be adopted together in an integrated way. The temporal frame refers to whether evaluations are undertaken during (*ex-ante*) or after (*ex-post*) artefact construction. The paradigm of evaluation refers to whether evaluation is made on a contrived and non-realistic way (*artificial*) or alternatively in its real environmental context (*naturalistic*) (Venable, Pries-Heje, and Baskerville 2012).

As a starting point, we recommend undertaking multiple evaluation episodes in order to encompass as much as possible casuistry. Also, involving in the evaluation episodes potential real users who were expected to use the artifact in practice could be an interesting possibility. If this scenario were not possible, an ex-post naturalistic evaluation of the MM's utility within a real particular HE context would be highly recommended. In the worst case, an ex-ante artificial evaluation must be conducted. Multiple evaluation episodes considering different types of HEIs – i.e., private vs. public institutions, virtual vs. traditional universities, polytechnics vs. specialized institutes, etc. – would also boost generalizability of the constructed model.

5.3.5. Reflect Evolution

Finally, decisions related with the dynamics of the MM constructed should be addressed, that is, issues related with its maintenance and improvement in order to sustain its practical utility over time. For instance, in the following, we suggest generic recommendations for decisions regarding the subject, frequency and structure of the change dynamics. Nonetheless, they should be adequately nuanced (or even reconsidered) based on real and true feedback obtained once the earlier described activities were effectively executed.

First, we assume that there could be room for improvements and adaptations of the initial version realized of the MM in terms of both *form* (i.e., adapting the structure of the MM to either new QA regulations and standards or new emerged QA best practices) and *function* (i.e., adapting the MM instrument for collecting data on the basis of the feedback received from previous users of the artifact). In terms of frequency of change of the MM, we consider that such mutability issues would be better managed by means of the establishment of an adequate release management policy. In other words, new versions (i.e., releases) of the

MM could be *recurrently* drafted after certain predefined periods of time, integrating in the new version of the model all the improvements or adaptations collected over such temporal frame. Last but not least, regarding the structure of change of the MM we do not see a priori any reason for establishing restrictions neither in terms of the source nor the origin of the improvement recommendations and suggestions to be considered.

CONCLUSION

This study has elaborated on the topic of IQAS implementation maturity in HEIs. It provides new insights into the underlying assumptions of current IQAS maturity by grounding them on an IS-oriented perspective, which was not previously available in the literature. Given the former insights, this work highlights deficiencies found in existing instruments available for its assessment and measurement, which in turn, have seldom been examined. Finally, both a high-level research agenda and more specific practical guidelines and recommendations for developing a new MM for IQAS implementation in HEIs have been provided in the last section of the chapter, aiming to cope with previously identified lackings.

As any other piece of research, the present study comes with its own limitations. First, and despite the broad number of information sources considered, we cannot guarantee to have covered all relevant publications regarding the phenomena under study. Hence, results and conclusions achieved in the present chapter are limited to the selected information sources reviewed. For instance, these results and conclusions should be appropriately validated and corroborated by means of additional studies. Further, caution should be taken regarding the interpretations and findings achieved during the chapter due to the inherent subjectivity derived from the authors' subjectivity as well as the fact that several non-peer reviewed sources have been considered for analysis, containing therefore information which could not have been properly corroborated.

Notwithstanding these limitations, we believe that the present chapter adds value for both scholars and practitioners. On the one hand, by providing improved understanding on the concept of IQAS implementation maturity, the present study would help scholars to avoid confusions and inappropiate assumptions derived from currently scattered and varied existing literature on the discussed phenomena. On the other hand, practitioners are also supported by providing a catalogue describing the main features and limitations of currently existing artifacts for conducting IQAS maturity assesments and measuraments in HEIs, which in turn, shed light on the need and opportunity for developing a new MM instruments coping with existing deficiencies of the reviewed existing artifacts.

ACKNOWLEDGMENTS

We acknowledge the support of the Industrial Doctorates Plan of the Generalitat de Catalunya (DI77 2014) for partly financing this work.

REFERENCES

Abbadi, Laila El, Aboubakr Bouayad, and Mohamed Lamrini. 2013. "ISO 9001 and the Field of Higher Education: Proposal for an Update of the IWA 2 Guidelines." *Quality Approaches in Higher Education*, 2013.

Abdul Hakeem, M.A., and V. Thanikachalam. 2014. "A Multi-Dimensional Approach in Developing a Framework for Internal Quality Assurance of Second Cycle Engineering Programmes." *European Scientific Journal*, 10 (12): 414–41.

Abdullah, Firdaus. 2005. "HEdPERF versus SERVPERF: The Quest for Ideal Measuring Instrument of Service Quality in Higher Education Sector." *Quality Assurance in Education* 13 (4): 305–28. https://doi.org/10.1108/09684880510626584.

Abel, Rob, Malcolm Brown, and Jack Suess. 2013. "A New Architecture for Learning." *EDUCAUSE Review*, 2013.

Agência de Avaliação e Acreditação do Ensino Superior (A3ES). 2018. *"Activity Plan 2018."* Agência de Avaliação e Acreditação do Ensino Superior (A3ES). https://www.a3es.pt/sites/default/files/ActivityPlan 202018_1.pdf.

Agència per a la Qualitat del Sistema Universitari de Catalunya (AQU). 2011. *"Support Programme. Final Report."* January 2012. Barcelona: © Agència per a la Qualitat del Sistema Universitari de Catalunya. http://.aqu.cat/doc /doc_37106735_1.pdf.

Ågerfalk, Pär J. 2013. "Embracing Diversity through Mixed Methods Research." *European Journal of Information Systems* 22 (3): 251–56. https://doi.org/10.1057/ejis.2013.6.

Ahire, Sanjay L., Damodar Y. Golhar, and Matthew A. Waller. 1996. "Development and Validation of TQM Implementation Constructs." *Decision Sciences* 27 (1): 23–56. https://doi.org/10.1111/j.1540-5915.1996.tb00842.x.

Akkreditierungsagentur für Studiengänge der Ingenieurwissenschaften, der Informatik, der Naturwissenschaften und der Mathematik e. V. (ASIIN e.V.). 2016. [*Institutional Accreditation/Evaluation Criteria for the ASIIN System Seal. Requirements for Good Teaching and Successful Learning*]. Düsseldorf, Germany: ASIIN. https://www.asiin.de/en/quality-management/accreditation-of-systems-and-institutions/quality-criteria.html?file=files/content/kriterien/0.4_Institutional_Accreditation_Evaluation_Criteria_for_the_ASIIN_System_Seal_2016-06-20.pdf.

AlHamad, Bassam, and Rama Aladwan. 2017. *From Externally to Internally Driven Quality Assurance*. Paris, France: International Institute for Educational Planning, UNESCO.

Álvarez Suárez, Alberto, Javier Alonso Álvarez, Ramiro Martís Florez, and Miguel A. López Cabana. 2008. "Internal Quality Assurance Systems of University Education at the University of Oviedo." In *Proceedings of the 11th Toulon-Verona International Conference on Quality in Services. Higher Education, Health Care, Local Government, Tourism, Banking*, edited by Rocco Molinterni and

Jacques Martin, 1000–1012. University of Florence, 4-5 September 2008: Firenze University Press.

Alzafari, Khaled. 2017. "Mapping the Literature Structure of 'Quality in Higher Education' Using Co-Word Analysis." *Quality in Higher Education* 23 (3): 264–82. https://doi.org/10.1080/13538322.2017.1418607.

Amaral, Alberto, Maria João Rosa, and Diana Tavares. 2007. "Assessment as a Tool for Different Kinds of Action: From Quality Management to Compliance and Control." In *Quality Assessment for Higher Education in Europe. Symposium on Quality Assessment for Higher Education in Europe*, edited by A. Cavalli, 43–53. Portland Press. http://www.portlandpresspublishing.com/sites/default/files/Editorial/Wenner/QAHEE/0010043.pdf.

American Association for Quality (ASQ). 2018. *ASQ Quality Glossary. ASQ. The Global Voice of Quality.* 2018. https://asq.org/quality-resources/quality-glossary/q.

Anderson, Ian. n.d. "UK HE Capability Model." Web Portal. *UCISA* (blog). Accessed October 14, 2018. https://www.ucisa.ac.uk/representation/activities/cap_model.

Asif, Muhammad, and Abdul Raouf. 2013. "Setting the Course for Quality Assurance in Higher Education." *Quality & Quantity* 47 (4): 2009–2024. https://doi.org/10.1007/s11135-011-9639-2.

Aspranawa, Anang Dwi Putransu, Bambang Budi Wiyono, Imron, and Muhamad Huda AY. 2017. "Management System Internal Quality Assurance Higher Education." *Journal of Social Sciences* 6 (4): 762–74. https://doi.org/ 10.25255/jss.2017.6.4.762.774.

Baig, Moazzam, Sidra Basharat, and Manzil-e Maqsooud. 2006. "A Maturity Model for Quality Improvement in Higher Education." In *International Conference on Assessing Quality in Higher Education (ICAQHE) 2006*, 1–15. 11–13 December 2006, Lahore, Pakistan. https://pdfs.semanticscholar.org/123b/e17a89011487bb9ad6d1fcfc28391c9b133a.pdf.

Barata, João, and Paulo Rupino Cunha. 2017. "Synergies between Quality Management and Information Systems: A Literature Review and Map for Further Research." *Total Quality Management & Business Excellence* 28 (3–4): 282–95. https://doi.org/10.1080/147833 63.2015.1080117.

Barn, Balbir S., Tony Clark, and Gary Hearne. 2013. "Business and ICT Alignment in Higher Education: A Case Study in Measuring Maturity." In *Building Sustainable Information Systems: Proceedings of the 2012 International Conference on Information Systems Development*, edited by Henry Linger, Julie Fisher, Andrew Barnden, Chris Barry, Michael Lang, and Christoph Schneider, 51–62. Springer Science + Business Media New York. https://doi.org/10.1007/978-1-4614-7540-8_4.

Bayraktar, E., E. Tatoglu, and S. Zaim. 2008. "An Instrument for Measuring the Critical Factors of TQM in Turkish Higher Education." *Total Quality Management and Business Excellence* 19 (6): 551–74. https://doi.org/ 10.1080/14783360802023921.

Bechis, Marco, Paolo Pietro Biancone, and Laura Tomatis. 2008. "The Quality Certification and Accreditation Experience in the Faculty of Economics of the University of Turin (Note 2)." In *Proceedings of the 11th Toulon-Verona International Conference on Quality in Services. Higher Education, Health Care, Local Government, Tourism, Banking*, edited by Rocco Molinterni and Jacques Martin, 41–46. University of Florence, 4-5 September 2008: Firenze University Press.

Becker, Jörg, Ralf Knackstedt, and Jens Pöppelbuß. 2009. "Developing Maturity Models for IT Management: A Procedure Model and Its Application." *Business & Information Systems Engineering* 1 (3): 213–22. https://doi.org/ 10.1007/s12599-009-0044-5.

Becket, Nina, and Maureen Brookes. 2008. "Quality Management Practice in Higher Education - What Quality Are We Actually Enhancing?" *Journal of Hospitality, Leisure, Sport and Tourism Education* 7 (1): 40–54. https://doi.org/10.3794/johlste.71.174.

Bekkers, Willem, Inge van de Weerd, Marco Spruit, and Sjaak Brinkkemper. 2010. "A Framework for Process Improvement in Software Product Management." In *Systems, Software and Services Process Improvement*, edited by Andreas Riel, Rory O'Connor, Serge Tichkiewitch, and Richard Messnarz, 1–12. Berlin, Heidelberg: Springer Berlin Heidelberg.

Belawati, T., and A. Zuhairi. 2007. "The Practice of a Quality Assurance System in Open and Distance Learning: A Case Study at Universitas Terbuka Indonesia (The Indonesia Open University)." *International Review of Research in Open and Distance Learning* 8 (1). https://www.scopus.com/inward/record.uri?eid=2s2.033947376860&partnerID=40&md5=a552a915391f76a7cf05376a91985635.

Bennedsen, J., S. Rouvrais, J. Roslöf, J. Kontio, F. Georgsson, and C. D. McCartan. 2018. "Collaborative Quality Enhancement in Engineering Education: An Overview of Operational Models at a Programme Level." *European Journal of Engineering Education*, 1–16. https://doi.org/10.1080/03043797.2018.1443058.

Bennedsen, Jens, Fredrik Georgsson, and Juha Kontio. 2014. "Evaluating the CDIO Self-Evaluation." In *Proceedings of the 10th International CDIO Conference*, 19:1–11. Barcelona, Spain, June 15-19 2014. http://www.cdio.org/files/document/cdio2014/69/69_Paper.pdf.

Bennedsen, Jens, and Siegfried Rouvrais. 2016. "Finding Good Friends to Learn from and to Inspire." In *Frontiers in Education Conference (FIE), 2016*, 1–8. IEEE.

Bennedsen, Jens, Siegfried Rouvrais, Robin Clark, and Katriina Schrey-Niemenmaa. 2015. "Using Accreditation Criteria for Collaborative Quality Enhancement." In *Interactive Collaborative Learning (ICL), 2015 International Conference On*, 334–341. IEEE.

Bostrom, Robert P., and J. Stephen Heinen. 1977a. "MIS Problems and Failures: A Socio-Technical Perspective. Part I: The Causes." *MIS Quarterly* 1 (3): 17–32. https://doi.org/10.2307/248710.

———. 1977b. "MIS Problems and Failures a Socio-Technical Perspective Part II: The Application of Socio-Technical Theory." *MIS Quarterly* 1 (4): 11–28. https://doi.org/10.2307/249019.

Brennan, John. 2018. "Success Factors of Quality Management in Higher Education: Intended and Unintended Impacts." *European Journal of Higher Education*, May, 1–9. https://doi.org/10.1080/21568235. 2018.1474776.

British Columbia. 2013. *"Quality Assurance Framework British Columbia."* Green Paper. March 2013. https://www.ufv.ca/media/assets/senate/academic-planning--priorities-committee/agenda-packages-and-minutes/Green-Paper-on-Quality-Assurance.pdf.

Calvo-Mora, Arturo, Antonio Alonso-Gonzalez, and José L. Roldán. 2006. "Using Enablers of the EFQM Model to Manage Institutions of Higher Education." *Quality Assurance in Education* 14 (2): 99–122. https://doi.org/10.1108/ 09684880610662006.

Camilleri, Anthony F. 2017. "Standardizing Management Systems for Educational Organizations: Implications for European Higher Education." In *12th European Quality Assurance Forum*. 23-25 November 2017, Riga, Latvia.

Cardoso, Sónia, Maria João Rosa, Pedro Videira, and Alberto Amaral. 2017. "Internal Quality Assurance Systems: 'Tailor Made' or 'One Size Fits All' Implementation?" *Quality Assurance in Education* 25 (3). https://doi.org/10.1108/QAE-03-2017-0007.

Carvalho, João Vidal, Álvaro Rocha, José Vasconcelos, and António Abreu. 2018. "A Health Data Analytics Maturity Model for Hospitals Information Systems." *International Journal of Information Management*, July. https://doi.org/ 10.1016/j.ijinfomgt.2018.07.001.

Chalaris, Manolis, Ioannis Chalaris, Stefanos Gritzalis, and Cleo Sgouropoulou. 2017. "Maturity Level of the Quality Assurance Evaluation Procedures in Higher Education: A Qualitative Research." In *Proceedings of the 21st Pan-Hellenic Conference on Informatics*, 63:1–63:2. PCI 2017. New York, NY, USA: ACM. https://doi.org/ 10.1145/3139367.3139438.

Charles Sturt University. 2010. "Higher Education Process Reference Model." *Charles Sturt University - Work Process Improvement* (blog). 2010. http://www.csu.edu.au/special/wpp/resources/reference-model.

Chen, Shaoyong, Yirong Tang, and Zhefu Li. 2016. "UNITA: A Reference Model of University IT Architecture." In *Proceedings of the 2016 International Conference on Communication and Information Systems*, 73–77. Bangkok, Thailand, December 16 - 18, 2016: ACM Press. https://doi.org/10.1145/ 3023924.3023949.

Chen, Shun-Hsing. 2012. "The Establishment of a Quality Management System for the Higher Education Industry." *Quality & Quantity* 46 (4): 1279–96. https://doi.org/10.1007/s11135-011-9441-1.

Cleven, Anne Katharina, Robert Winter, Felix Wortmann, and Tobias Mettler. 2014. "Process Management in Hospitals: An Empirically Grounded Maturity Model." *Business Research* 7 (2): 191–216. https://doi.org/10.1007/s40685-014-0012-x.

Cloutier, Robert, Gerrit Muller, Dinesh Verma, Roshanak Nilchiani, Eirik Hole, and Mary Bone. 2010. "The Concept of Reference Architectures." *Systems Engineering* 13 (1): 14–27. https://doi.org/ 10.1002/sys.v13:1.

Cobham, David, Bruce Hargrave, Kevin Jacques, and John Lewak. 2014. "Promoting Paperless Approaches to Quality Assurance and Enhancement Procedures: A University Departmental Case Study." In *8th International Technology, Education and Development Conference (INTED 2014)*. 10-12 March 2014, Valencia, Spain. http://iated.org/inted2014/.

Cocón, Felipe, and Eugenio Fernández. 2011. "MMCbEEES: Maturity Model in the e-Learning Teaching Environment Adapted to the EHEA." In *6th Iberian Conference on Information Systems and Technologies*, 1–7. 15-18, June 2011. Chaves, Portugal. http://ieeexplore.ieee.org/document/5974198.

Commission on Higher Education (CHED). 2014. "*Handbook on Typology, Outcomes-Based Education, and Institutional Sustainability Assessment.*" Quezon City, Philippines: Commission on Higher Education, Office of Institutional Quality Assurance and Governance. http://downloads. chedcaraga.com/typology.

Čorejová, Tatiana, Tatiana Genzorová, and Mária Rostášová. 2017. "On the University Strategy in the Education Quality Assurance: Case Study." In *16th International Conference on Information Technology Based Higher Education and Training (ITHET), 2017*, 1–4. Ohrid; Macedonia; 10-12 June, 2017: Institute of Electrical and Electronics Engineers Inc (IEEE). https://doi.org/10.1109/ITHET.2017.8067795.

Council of Australian University Directors of Information Technology (CAUDIT). 2016. "Enterprise Architecture Commons for Higher Education." *CAUDIT. Council of Australian University Directors of Information Technology* (blog). 2016. https://www.caudit.edu.au/EA-Framework.

———. 2017. "CAUDIT Higher Education EA Reference Models Roll out to 147 Universities - and Counting!" *CAUDIT. Council of Australian University Directors of Information Technology* (blog). 2017. https://www.caudit.edu.au/news/caudit-higher-education-ea-reference-models-roll-out-147-universities-and-counting.

Daguang, Wu, Xie Zuoxu, Wu Fan, and Qi Yanjie. 2017. *Enhancing Teaching and Learning through Internal Quality Assurance*. Paris, France: International Institute for Educational Planning, UNESCO.

Dahl Jørgensen, Malene, Regitze Sparre Kristensen, Alexandre Wipf, and Stefan Delplace. 2014. *Quality Tools for Professional Higher Education Review and Improvement*. © 2014, PHExcel Consortium. https://www.eurashe.eu /phexcel-report-tools/.

Dale, B.G., and D.M Lascelles. 1997. "Total Quality Management Adoption: Revisiting the Levels." *The TQM Magazine* 9 (6): 418–28. https://doi.org/10.1108/09544789710186957.

Daromes, Fransiskus E. 2016. "Strengthening Beliefs Systems on the Development and Implementation Internal Quality Assurance Systems on Higher Education." In *Quality Assurance: Analysis, Methods and Outcomes*, edited by Craig Coleman, UK ed., 69–80. Nova Science Publishers, Incorporated.

De Bruin, Tonia, Ronald Freeze, Uday Kaulkarni, and Michael Rosemann. 2005. "Understanding the Main Phases of Developing a Maturity Assessment Model." In *Australasian Conference on Information Systems (ACIS)*, edited by B. Campbell, J. Underwood, and D. Bunker, 8–19. November 30 - December 2 2005, Sydney, New South Wales, Australia. https://eprints.qut.edu.au/25152/.

DeLone, William H., and Ephraim R. McLean. 1992. "Information Systems Success: The Quest for the Dependent Variable." *Information Systems Research* 3 (1): 60–95. https://doi.org/dx.doi.org/10.1287/isre.3.1.60.

———. 2003. "The DeLone and McLean Model of Information Systems Success: A Ten-Year Update." *Journal of Management Information Systems* 19 (4): 9–30. https://doi.org/dx.doi.org/10.1080/07421222.2003.11045748.

Deming, William E. 1994. *The New Economics for Industry, Government, Education*. 2nd Edition. Cambridge, MA: MIT Press.

Domingues, Pedro, Paulo Sampaio, and P. Arezes. 2014. "A Model Proposal for Integrated Management Systems Maturity Assessment." In *58th European Organization for Quality Congress*, 1–12. Gothenburg, Sweden, June 11-12, 2014. http://hdl.handle.net/1822/36207.

Đonlagić, Sabina, and Samira Fazlić. 2015. "Quality Assessment in Higher Education Using the SERVQUAL Model." *Management* 20: 39–57.

Duarte, Duarte, and Paula Ventura Martins. 2014. "Higher Education Business Process Improvement: Achieving BPMM Level 3." In *9th International Conference on the Quality of Information and Communications Technology 2014*, 18–27. IEEE. https://doi.org/10.1109/QUATIC.2014.10.

Elassy, Noha. 2015. "The Concepts of Quality, Quality Assurance and Quality Enhancement." *Quality Assurance in Education* 23 (3): 250–61. https://doi.org/10.1108/QAE-11-2012-0046.

El-Morsy, A.-W., H. Shafeek, A. Alshehri, and S.A. Gutub. 2014. "Implementation of Quality Management System by Utilizing ISO 9001:2008 Model in the Emerging Faculties." In *4th International Arab Conference on Quality Assurance in Higher Education*, 11:119–25. April 1-3, 2014, Zarqa, Jordan. https://www.scopus.com/inward/record.uri?eid=2-s2.0-84899833187&partnerID=40&md5=d10626cb8ecddc30006813479ca774b4.

European Foundation for Quality Management (EFQM). 2012. *EFQM Excellence Model*. Brussels, Belgium: ©European Foundation for Quality Management.

European Institute of Public Administration (EIPA). 2013. *CAF 2013. Improving Public Organisations through Self-Assessment*. Research Report Part 1: Content of the model. Maastricht, The Netherlands: European Institute of Public Administration (EIPA). http://ec.europa.eu/eurostat/ramon/ statmanuals/files/CAF_2013.pdf.

Fagan, Mary Helen. 2003. "Exploring E-Education Applications: A Framework for Analisys." *Campus-Wide Information Systems* 20 (4): 129–36. http://dx.doi.org/10.1108/10650740310491298.

Farahsa, Sahar, and Jafar Sadegh Tabrizi. 2015. "How Evaluation and Audit Is Implemented in Educational Organizations? A Systematic Review." *Research and Development in Medical Education* 4 (1): 3–16. https://doi.org/10.15171/rdme.2015.002.

Federkeil, Gero. 2008. "Rankings and Quality Assurance in Higher Education." *Higher Education in Europe* 33 (2–3): 219–231. https://doi.org/10.1080/03797720802254023.

Fernández Cruz, Francisco José, Inmaculada Egido Gálvez, and Rafael Carballo Santaolalla. 2016. "Impact of Quality Management Systems on Teaching-Learning Processes." *Quality Assurance in Education* 24 (3): 394–415. https://doi.org/10.1108/QAE-09-2013-0037.

Fettke, Peter, and Peter Loos, eds. 2007. *Reference Modeling for Business Systems Analysis*. IGI Global. DOI: 10.4018/978-1-59904-054-7.

Filippakou, Ourania, and Ted Tapper. 2008. "Quality Assurance and Quality Enhancement in Higher Education: Contested Territories?" *Higher Education Quarterly* 62 (1–2): 84–100.

Fitterer, René, and Peter Rohner. 2010. "Towards Assessing the Networkability of Health Care Providers: A Maturity Model Approach." *Information Systems and E-Business Management* 8 (3): 309–333. https://doi.org/10.1007/s10257-009-0121-9.

Flynn, Barbara B., Roger G. Schroederb, and Sadao Sakakibara. 1994. "A Framework for Quality Management Research and an Associated Measurement Instrument." *Journal of Operations Management*, 339–66.

Frackmann, Edgar. 2007. *"Higher Education Information Systems. Proposal for an Overall Concept for Higher Education Information Systems in Croatia.*" Furtherance of the Agency of Science and Higher Education in Its Quality Assurance Role and the Development of a Supporting Information System. Croatia: Agency of Science and Higher Education. http://forum.azvo.hr/cd/LinkedDocuments/Higher_Education_Information_Systems.pdf.

Fraser, P., J. Moultrie, and M. Gregory. 2002. "The Use of Maturity Models/Grids as a Tool in Assessing Product Development Capability." In *IEEE International Engineering Management Conference*, 244–249. 18-20 August 2002, Cambridge, UK. https://doi.org/10.1109/ IEMC.2002.1038431.

Gamboa, António Jorge, and Nuno Filipe Melão. 2012. "The Impacts and Success Factors of ISO 9001 in Education: Experiences from Portuguese Vocational Schools." *International Journal of Quality & Reliability Management* 29 (4): 384–401. https://doi.org/10.1108/ 02656711211224848.

Ganseuer, Christian, and Petra Pistor. 2017. *"From Tools to an Internal Quality Assurance System.*" Paris, France: International Institute for Educational Planning, UNESCO.

García Aranda, Jose Ramón, and Fausto Pedro García Márquez. 2015. "Use of Excellence Models as a Management Maturity Model (3M)." In *Advanced Business Analytics*, edited by Fausto Pedro García Márquez and Benjamin Lev, 165–79. Cham: Springer International Publishing. https://doi.org/10.1007/978-3-319-11415-6_8.

Garza-Reyes, Jose Arturo. 2018. "A Systematic Approach to Diagnose the Current Status of Quality Management Systems and Business Processes." *Business Process Management Journal* 24 (1): 216–33. https://doi.org/10.1108/BPMJ-12-2016-0248.

Garza-Reyes, Jose Arturo, Luis Rocha-Lona, and Vikas Kumar. 2015. "A Conceptual Framework for the Implementation of Quality Management Systems." *Total Quality Management & Business Excellence* 26 (11–12): 1298–1310. https://doi.org/10.1080/14783363.2014.929254.

Georgiadou, Eli, and Kerstin Siakas. 2008. "Towards a Workable Framework for Internal Quality Assurance in Higher Education." In *Proceedings of the Dissemination Workshop Internal Quality Assurance: Experience, Problems, Trends*, 60–67. 23-24 September, Yerevan, Armenia.

Greefhorst, Danny, Henk Koning, and Hans van Vliet. 2006. "The Many Faces of Architectural Descriptions." *Information Systems Frontiers* 8 (2): 103–13. https://doi.org/10.1007/s10796-006-7975-x.

Hakeem, M A Abdul, and V Thanikachalam. 2014. "A Multi-Dimensional Approach in Developing a Framework for Internal Quality Assurance of Second Cycle Engineering Programmes." *European Scientific Journal* 10 (12): 414–41. https://doi.org/10.19044/esj.2014.v10n12p%25p.

Haris, Ali Sajjad, Hironori Washizaki, and Yoshiaki Fukazawa. 2017. "Utilization of ICTs in Quality Assurance and Accreditation of Higher Education: Systematic Literature Review." In *Proceedings of 2017 Ieee 6th International Conference on Teaching, Assessment, and Learning for Engineering (Tale)*, 354–59.

Harmsen van der Beek, Wijke ten, Jos Trienekens, and Paul Grefen. 2012. "The Application of Enterprise Reference Architecture in the Financial Industry." In *TEAR 2012 and PRET 2012, LNBIP 131*, edited by Stephan Aier, Mathias Ekstedt, Florian Matthes, Erik Proper, and Jorge L. Sanz, 93–110. Springer Berlin Heidelberg. http://dx.doi.org/10.1007/978-3-642-34163-2_6.

Harutyunyan, Hovhannes, and A. Ohanyan. 2016. "The Role of Internal Audit in Continuous Improvement of Quality Management Systems at Private HE Institutions: A Case Study of Eurasia International University (Armenia)." *Journal of Business & Financial Affairs* 5 (1): 1–10. https://doi.org/10.4172/ 2167-0234.1000170.

Harvey, Lee. 2004. *Analytic Quality Glossary, Quality Research International.* [Lee Harvey's Homepage]. 2004. www.qualityresearch international.com/glossary/.

Harvey, Lee, and D. Green. 1993. "Defining Quality." *Assessment & Evaluation in Higher Education* 18 (1): 9–34. https://doi.org/10.1080/0260293930180102.

Hrnčiar, Miroslav, and Peter Madzík. 2017. "A 3D View of Issues of Quality in Higher Education." *Total Quality Management & Business Excellence* 28 (5–6): 633–62. https://doi.org/10.1080/14783363.2015.1105100.

International Organization for Standardization (ISO). 2015. "ISO 9001:2015 (En): Quality Management Systems — Requirements." [Web portal]. *ISO Online Browsing Platform (OBP)* (blog). 2015. https://www.iso.org/obp/ui/#iso:std:66266:en.

———. 2018. "ISO 21001:2018 (En): Educational Organizations — Management Systems for Educational Organizations — Requirements with Guidance for Use." [Web portal]. *ISO Online Browsing Platform (OBP)* (blog). 2018. https://www.iso.org/obp/ui/#iso:std:66266:en.

Inter-University Council for East Africa (IUCEA). 2010. "*A Road Map to Quality. Handbook for Quality Assurance in Higher Education.*" Vol 4 - Implementation of a Quality Assurance System. The Inter-University Council for East Africa/Deutscher Akademischer Austausch Dienst (DAAD). https://www.iucea.org/index.php?option=com_phocadown load& view=category&id=22:qa-hand&Itemid=613#.

ITANA Working Group. 2012. "Reference Architecture for Teaching and Learning." Web Page. *ITANA Wiki* (blog). 2012. https://spaces.internet2.edu/display/itana/Reference+Architecture+for+Teaching+and+Learning.

Jambor, Jaroslav, Martina Džubáková, and Josef Habánik. 2017. "Integration of ESG 2015 and ISO 9001:2015 Standards in the Higher Education Organization (Case Study)." *AD ALTA: Journal Of Interdisciplinary Research (07/02)* 07 (02): 87–91.

Kahveci, Tuba Canvar, Özer Uygun, Ulaş Yurtsever, and Sinan İlyas. 2012. "Quality Assurance in Higher Education Institutions Using Strategic Information Systems." *Procedia - Social and Behavioral Sciences* 55 (October): 161–67. https://doi.org/10.1016/j.sbspro.2012.09.490.

Kamat, Vivek B., and Jayant K. Kittur. 2017. "Quantifying the Quality of Higher and Technical Education: Salient Perspectives." *International Journal of System Assurance Engineering and Management* 8 (2): 515–527. https://doi.org/ 10.1007/s13198-016-0428-0.

Kargytė, Virginija. 2015. "Application of Generic Quality Management Models in European Universities." *Management Theory and Studies for Rural Business and Infrastructure Development* 37 (3): 381–98. https://doi.org/10.15544/ mts.2015.33.

Kettunen, Juha. 2008. "A Conceptual Framework to Help Evaluate the Quality of Institutional Performance." *Quality Assurance in Education* 16 (4): 322–32. https://doi.org/10.1108/09684880810906472.

———. 2012. "External and Internal Quality Audits in Higher Education." *The TQM Journal* 24 (6): 518–528. https://doi.org/10.1108/17542731211270089.

Klenk, Tanja, and Markus Seyfried. 2016. "Institutional Isomorphism and Quality Management: Comparing Hospitals and Universities." In *Towards a Comparative Institutionalism: Forms, Dynamics And Logics Across The Organizational Fields Of Health Care And Higher Education*, 217–42. https://doi.org/10.1108/S0733-558X20150000045020.

Kohlegger, Michael, Ronald Maier, and Stefan Thalmann. 2009. "Understanding Maturity Models Results of a Structured Content Analysis." In *Proceedings of I-KNOW '09 and I-SEMANTICS '09*, 11. 2-4 September 2009, Graz, Austria. http://iwi.uibk.ac.at/download/downloads/Publikationen/KMM.pdf.

Kotusev, Svyatoslav. 2019. "Enterprise Architecture and Enterprise Architecture Artifacts: Questioning the Old Concept in Light of New Findings." *Journal of Information Technology*, February, 026839621881627. https://doi.org/ 10.1177/0268396218816273.

Krüger, Nicolai, and Frank Teuteberg. 2015. "From Smart Meters to Smart Products: Reviewing Big Data Driven Product Innovation in the European Electricity Retail Market." In *INFORMATIK 2015. Lecture Notes in Informatics (LNI)*, edited by Douglas Cunningham, Petra Hofstedt, Klaus Meer, and Ingo Schmitt, Gesellschaft für Informatik e.V., 1171–82. Bonn. https://dl.gi.de/handle/20.500.12116/2271.

Książek, D., and M. Ligarski. 2017. "Assessment of the Level of Maturity of the Quality Management System–applied Models and Sample Test Results." *Systemy Wspomagania w Inżynierii Produkcji, 6.* 6 (4): 118–24.

Kuria, Mike, and Simmy M Marwa. 2017. "Shaping Internal Quality Assurance from a Triple Heritage." Paris, France: International Institute for Educational Planning, UNESCO.

Kwiatkowska-Sujka, Izabela, and Mieczyslaw W. Socha. 2017. "Embedding of ESG Part 1 into IQA Systems– EIQAS Project Survey's Results on ESG Part 1 and IQA: State of Arts and Challenges." *Quality Assurance Review for Higher Education* 7 (1): 36–55.

Lahrmann, Gerrit, and Frederik Marx. 2010. "Systematization of Maturity Model Extensions." In *Global Perspectives on Design Science Research: 5th International Conference, DESRIST 2010, St. Gallen, Switzerland, June 4-5, 2010. Proceedings.*, edited by Robert Winter, J. Leon Zhao, and Stephan Aier, 522–525. Springer Berlin Heidelberg. https://doi.org/10.1007/978-3-642-13335-0_36.

Lahrmann, Gerrit, Frederik Marx, Tobias Mettler, Robert Winter, and Felix Wortmann. 2011. "Inductive Design of Maturity Models: Applying the Rasch Algorithm for Design Science Research." In *Service-Oriented Perspectives in Design Science Research*, edited by Hemant Jain, Atish P. Sinha, and Padmal Vitharana, 176–191. Springer Berlin Heidelberg.

Lamagna, Carmen, Charles C Villanueva, and Farheen Hassan. 2017. "*The Effects of Internal Quality Assurance on Quality and Employability.*" Paris, France: International Institute for Educational Planning, UNESCO.

Lange, Lis, and Lise Kriel. 2017. *Integrating Internal Quality Assurance at a Time of Transformation.* Paris, France: International Institute for Educational Planning, UNESCO.

Larrondo Petrie, María Mercedes, Víctor Hugo Medina García, and Germán Méndez Giraldo. 2009. "Modelo de Registro y Acreditación de Instituciones de Educación Superior Basado En El Modelo CMMI [In Spanish]." In *Seventh LACCEI Latin American and Caribbean Conference for Engineering and Technology (LACCEI'2009)*, 1–8. San Cristóbal, Venezuela, June 2-5, 2009. http://www.laccei.org/LACCEI2009-Venezuela/p116.pdf.

Lasrado, Lester Allan, Ravi Vatrapu, and Kim Normann Andersen. 2015. "Maturity Models Development in IS Research." In *IRIS: Selected Papers of the Information Systems Research Seminar in Scandinavia.* Vol. 6. Oulu, Finland. https://doi.org/10.13140/RG.2.1.3046.3209.

———. 2016. "A Set Theoretical Approach to Maturity Models: Guidelines and Demonstration." In *Proceedings of the 37th International Conference on Information Systems (ICIS 2016)*, 1–20. 11-14 December 2016, Dublin, Ireland. https://aisel.aisnet.org/icis2016/Methodological/Presentations/12/.

Leiber, Theodor, Bjørn Stensaker, and Lee Harvey. 2015. "Impact Evaluation of Quality Assurance in Higher Education: Methodology and Causal Designs." *Quality in Higher Education* 21 (3): 288–311. https://doi.org/10.1080/ 13538322.2015.1111007.

Leisyte, Liudvika, Rimantas Zelvys, and Lina Zenkiene. 2015. "Re-Contextualization of the Bologna Process in Lithuania." *European Journal of Higher Education* 5 (1): 49–67. https://doi.org/10.1080/21568235.2014.951669.

Liu, Shuiyun. 2016. "Higher Education Quality Assessment and University Change: A Theoretical Approach." In *Quality Assurance and Institutional Transformation: The Chinese Experience*, edited by

Shuiyun Liu, 15–46. Singapore: Springer Singapore. https://doi.org/10.1007/978-981-10-0789-7_2.

Llamosa-Villalba, Ricardo, Luz Torres Carreño, Q. Ana M. Paez, Q. Dario J. Delgado, Andres Bueno Barajas, and Edgar Garcia Sneyder. 2015. "Enterprise Architecture of Colombian Higher Education." In *2015 IEEE Frontiers in Education Conference (FIE)*, 1–9. 21-24 October 2015, El Paso, TX, USA: IEEE.

Llamosa-Villalba, Ricardo, Dario J. Delgado, Heidi P. Camacho, Ana M. Paéz, and Raúl F. Valdivieso. 2014. "Organizational Leadership Process for University Education." In *International Conference on Cognition and Exploratory Learning in Digital Age* (CELDA 2014), 119–26. Porto, Portugal, 25 - 27 October 2014: International Association for the Development of the Information Society (IADIS).

Maier, A. M., J. Moultrie, and P. J. Clarkson. 2012. "Assessing Organizational Capabilities: Reviewing and Guiding the Development of Maturity Grids." *IEEE Transactions on Engineering Management* 59 (1): 138–59. https://doi.org/10.1109/TEM.2010.2077289.

Malini, Siva, and A. Pal Pandi. 2018. *Suitability of IEQMS Model Practice in Business Education-An Empirical Study* 8 (6): 92. https://doi.org/10.5958/2249-7307.2018.00056.7.

Manatos, Maria J., Cláudia S. Sarrico, and Maria J. Rosa. 2017a. "The Integration of Quality Management in Higher Education Institutions: A Systematic Literature Review." *Total Quality Management & Business Excellence* 28 (1–2): 159–75. https://doi.org/10.1080/14783363.2015.1050180.

———. 2017b. "The European Standards and Guidelines for Internal Quality Assurance: An Integrative Approach to Quality Management in Higher Education?" *The TQM Journal* 29 (2): 342–56. https://doi.org/10.1108/ TQM-01-2016-0009.

Manjula, R., and J. Vaideeswaran. 2010. "A New CMM-EDU Process Improvement and Assessment Model Using SEI-CMM Approach-Engineering Education Capability Maturity Model: (E2-CMM)." *International Journal of Software Engineering & Applications* 1 (4): 39–52. https://doi.org/10.5121/ijsea.2010. 1403.

———. 2011. "A New Framework for Measuring the Quality of Engineering Education System Using SEI-CMM Approach - (E2-CMM)." *International Journal of Software Engineering & Applications* 2 (1): 28–43. https://doi.org/10.5121/ijsea.2011.2103.

———. 2012a. "A New CMM-Quality Education (CMM-QE) Framework Using SEI-CMM Approach and Calibrating for Its Process Quality and Maturity Using Structural Equation Modeling–PLS Approach." *International Journal of Software Engineering and Its Applications* 6 (4): 117–130.

———. 2012b. "A Bootstrap Approach of Benchmarking Organizational Maturity Model of Software Product With Educational Maturity Model." *International Journal of Modern Education and Computer Science* 4 (6): 50–58. https://doi.org/10.5815/ijmecs.2012.06.07.

Mårtensson, Katarina, Torgny Roxå, and Bjørn Stensaker. 2014. "From Quality Assurance to Quality Practices: An Investigation of Strong Microcultures in Teaching and Learning." *Studies in Higher Education* 39 (4): 534–45. https://doi.org/10.1080/03075079.2012.709493.

Martin, Michaela. 2018. "Development, Drivers, and Obstacles in IQA: Findings on an International Survey." In *Internal Quality Assurance: Enhancing Higher Education Quality and Graduate Employability*, edited by Michaela Martin, 39–59. Paris, France: International Institute for Educational Planning (IIEP-UNESCO). http://unesdoc.unesco.org/images/0026/002613/261356e.pdf.

Martin, Michaela, and Shreya Parikh. 2017. "*Quality Management in Higher Education: Developments and Drivers. Results from an International Survey.*" Paris, France: International Institute for Educational Planning (IIEP-UNESCO). http://unesdoc.unesco.org/images/0026/002602/260226E.pdf.

Massy, William F. 2010. "Education Quality Audit as Applied in Hong Kong." In *Public Policy for Academic Quality*, edited by David D. Dill and Maarja Beerkens, 30:203–25. Dordrecht: Springer Netherlands. https://doi.org/ 10.1007/978-90-481-3754-1_11.

Mbithi, Peter M. F., and Christopher Moturi. 2015. "ISO 9001: 2008 Implementation and Impact on the University of Nairobi: A Case Study." *The TQM Journal* 27 (6): 752–60. https://doi.org/10.1108/ TQM-04-2015-0053.

Medina García, Víctor Hugo, Germán Andrés Méndez Giraldo, and José Fernando López Quintero. 2016. "Model Accreditation for Learning in Engineering Based on Knowledge Management and Software Engineering." In *New Advances in Information Systems and Technologies*, edited by Álvaro Rocha, Ana Maria Correia, Hojjat Adeli, Luis Paulo Reis, and Marcelo Mendonça Teixeira, 79–88. Cham: Springer International Publishing. https://doi.org/ 10.1007/978-3-319-31232-3_8.

Mettler, Tobias. 2010. "Thinking in Terms of Design Decisions When Developing Maturity Models:" *International Journal of Strategic Decision Sciences* 1 (4): 76–87. https://doi.org/10.4018/jsds.2010 100105.

———. 2011. "Maturity Assessment Models: A Design Science Research Approach." *International Journal of Society Systems Science* 3 (1/2): 81–98. https://doi.org/10.1504/IJSSS.2011.038934.

Mettler, Tobias, and André Blondiau. 2012. "HCMM - a Maturity Model for Measuring and Assessing the Quality of Cooperation between and within Hospitals." In *25th IEEE International Symposium on Computer-Based Medical Systems (CBMS2012)*, 1–6. 20-22 June 2012, Rome, Italy. https://doi.org/10.1109/CBMS.2012.6266397.

Meyer, Martin, Markus Helfert, and Conor O'Brien. 2011. "An Analysis of Enterprise Architecture Maturity Frameworks." In *Perspectives in Business Informatics Research*, edited by Janis Grabis and Marite Kirikova, 167–177. Berlin, Heidelberg: Springer Berlin Heidelberg.

Mircea, Marinela, and Anca Ioana Andreescu. 2011. "Using Cloud Computing in Higher Education: A Strategy to Improve Agility in the Current Financial Crisis." *Communications of the IBIMA*, June, 1–15. https://doi.org/ 10.5171/2011.875547.

Mizikaci, Fatma. 2006. "A Systems Approach to Program Evaluation Model for Quality in Higher Education." *Quality Assurance in Education* 14 (1): 37–53. https://doi.org/10.1108/09684880610643601.

Mohamed, Hasan Al-Banna, Ab. Mumin Ab. Ghani, and Siti Arni Basir. 2016. "Factors Influencing the Implementation of Islamic QMS in a Malaysian Public Higher Education Institution." *Total Quality Management & Business Excellence* 27 (9–10): 1140–57. https://doi.org/10.1080/14783363.2015.1064765.

Mohammad, Mohammad Fakhrulnizam, Rusli Abdullah, Marzanah A. Jabar, Rozi Nor Haizan, and Nor Aida Abdul Rahman. 2018. "Towards the Integration of Quality Management System And Knowledge Management System In Higher Education Institution: Development of Q-Edge Kms Model." *Acta Informatica Malaysia* 2 (2): 04–09. https://doi.org/10.26480/aim.02.2018.04.09.

Monkienė, Aistė, and Vincentas Lamanauskas. 2014. "Quality Management Systems in Lithuanian Colleges: Websites Information Analysis." *Quality Issues and Insights in the 21st Century* 3 (1): 41–49.

Mora, Manuel, Fen Wang, Jorge Marx Gómez, Mahesh S. Rainsinghani, and Valentyna Savkova. 2017. "Decision-Making Support Systems in Quality Management of Higher Education Institutions: A Selective Review." *International Journal of Decision Support System Technology* 9 (2): 56–79. https://doi.org/10.4018/IJDSST.2017040104.

National Agency for Quality Assessment and Accreditation (ANECA). 2014. *Report on the State of External Quality Assessment at Spanish Universities.* Madrid, Spain. http://deva.aac.es/include/files/deva/ informes/evaluacion_ externa/Informe_Calidad_2014_en.pdf.

Niemi, Eetu, and Samuli Pekkola. 2017. "Using Enterprise Architecture Artifacts in an Organisation." *Enterprise Information Systems* 11 (3): 313–38. https://doi.org/10.1080/17517575.2015.1048831.

Oderinde, Dumebi. 2010. "Using Enterprise Architecture (EA) as a Business-IT Strategy Alignment for Higher Educational Institutions (HEIs)." In *Proceedings of UK Academy for Information Systems* (UKAIS) Conference, 1–10. 23 March 2010, Oriel College, Oxford,

UK. https://pdfs.semanticscholar.org/ba69/4577c87388fa4d604c51f87c763dba5f46b5.pdf.

Oesterreich, Thuy Duong, and Frank Teuteberg. 2016. "Understanding the Implications of Digitisation and Automation in the Context of Industry 4.0: A Triangulation Approach and Elements of a Research Agenda for the Construction Industry." *Computers in Industry* 83: 121–39. https://doi.org/10.1016/j.compind.2016.09.006.

Ofner, Martin, Boris Otto, and Hubert Österle. 2013. "A Maturity Model for Enterprise Data Quality Management." *Enterprise Modelling and Information Systems Architectures* 8 (2): 4–24. https://doi.org/10.1007/s40786-013-0002-z.

Øgland, Petter. 2006. "Designing Quality Management Systems with Minimal Management Commitment." *Systemist* 28 (2): 2–13.

Olsen, D.H., and K. Trelsgård. 2016. "Enterprise Architecture Adoption Challenges: An Exploratory Case Study of the Norwegian Higher Education Sector." *Procedia Computer Science* 100: 804–11. https://doi.org/10.1016/j.procs.2016.09.228.

O'Mahony, Kim, and Thomas N. Garavan. 2012. "Implementing a Quality Management Framework in a Higher Education Organisation: A Case Study." *Quality Assurance in Education* 20 (2): 184–200. https://doi.org/10.1108/09684881211219767.

O'Sullivan, David. 2017. "Evolution of Internal Quality Assurance at One University – a Case Study." *Quality Assurance in Education* 25 (2): 189–205. https://doi.org/10.1108/QAE-03-2016-0011.

Owlia, Mohammad S., and Elaine M. Aspinwall. 1997. "TQM in Higher Education - a Review." *International Journal of Quality & Reliability Management* 14 (5): 527–43. https://doi.org/10.1108/02656719710170747.

Pajk, Dejan, Mojca Indihar-Štemberger, and Andrej Kovaþiþ. 2012. "Reference Model Design: An Approach and Its Application." In *Proceedings of the 34th International Conference on Information Technology Interfaces (ITI 2012)*, 1–6. June 25-28, 2012, Cavtat, Croatia.

Pal Pandi, A., K.P. Paranitharan, and D. Jeyathilagar. 2018. "Implementation of IEQMS Model in Engineering Educational Institutions – a Structural Equation Modelling Approach." *Total Quality Management & Business Excellence* 29 (1–2): 29–57. https://doi.org/10.1080/14783363.2016. 1154431.

Pal Pandi, A., P.V. Rajendra Sethupathi, and D. Jeyathilagar. 2016a. "Quality Sustainability in Engineering Educational Institutions - A Theoretical Model." *International Journal of Productivity and Quality Management* 18 (2–3): 364–84. https://doi.org/10.1504/IJPQM.2016. 076715.

———. 2016b. "The IEQMS Model for Augmenting Quality in Engineering Institutions – an Interpretive Structural Modelling Approach." *Total Quality Management & Business Excellence* 27 (3–4): 292–308. https://doi.org/10.1080/14783363.2014.978647.

Pal Pandi, A., P.V. Rajendra Sethupathi, D. Jeyathilagar, and R. Rajesh. 2016. "Structural Equation Modelling for Analysing Relationship between IEQMS Criteria and Performance of Engineering Institutions." *International Journal of Enterprise Network Management* 7 (2): 87–97. https://doi.org/10.1504/ IJENM.2016. 077525.

Pardeshi, Vaishali H. 2014. "Cloud Computing for Higher Education Institutes: Architecture, Strategy and Recommendations for Effective Adaptation." *Procedia Economics and Finance* 11: 589–99. https://doi.org/10.1016/ S2212-5671(14)00224-X.

Patas, Janusch, Jens Pöppelbu\s s, and Matthias Goeken. 2013. "Cherry Picking with Meta-Models: A Systematic Approach for the Organization-Specific Configuration of Maturity Models." In *Design Science at the Intersection of Physical and Virtual Design*, edited by Jan vom Brocke, Riitta Hekkala, Sudha Ram, and Matti Rossi, 353–368. Springer Berlin Heidelberg.

Paulk, Mark C. 2008. "A Taxonomy for Improvement Frameworks." In *4th World Congress for Software Quality*, 1–16. September 15-18, 2008, Bethesda, Maryland, US. http://citeseerx.ist.psu.edu/viewdoc/ summary?doi=10.1.1.141. 6438.

Peffers, Ken, Marcus Rothenberger, Tuure Tuunanen, and Reza Vaezi. 2012. "Design Science Research Evaluation." In *Design Science Research in Information Systems. Advances in Theory and Practice: 7th International Conference, DESRIST 2012, Las Vegas, NV, USA, May 14-15, 2012. Proceedings*, edited by Ken Peffers, Marcus Rothenberger, and Bill Kuechler, 398–410. Springer Berlin Heidelberg. https://doi.org/10.1007/978-3-642-29863-9_29.

Pereira do Nascimento, Adelson, Marcos Paulo Valadares de Oliveira, Marcelo Bronzo Ladeira, and Hélio Zanquetto Filho. 2016. "Key Transition Points: The Climbing to Quality Management System Maturity." *Gestão & Produção* 23 (2): 250–66. https://doi.org/10.1590/0104-530x2222-15.

Pereira do Nascimento, Adelson, Marcos Paulo Valadares de Oliveira, Hélio Zanquetto Filho, and Marcelo Bronzo Ladeira. 2015. "Idade Versus Maturidade: Uma Pesquisa Empírica sobre Sistemas de Gestão da Qualidade [In Portuguese]." *Sistemas & Gestão* 10 (1): 108–23. https://doi.org/10.7177/ sg.2015.v10.n1.a9. [Age Versus Maturity: An Empirical Survey on Quality Management Systems. *Systems & Management*]

Plattfaut, Ralf, Björn Niehaves, Jens Pöppelbuß, and Jörg Becker. 2011. "Development of BPM Capabilities – Is Maturity the Rigth Path?" In *Proceedings of the 19th European Conference on Information Systems (ECIS 2011)*, 1–13. Helsinki, Finland, June 9-11. https://aisel.aisnet.org/ecis2011/ 27.

Pöppelbuß, Jens, and Maximilian Röglinger. 2011. "What Makes a Useful Maturity Model? A Framework of General Design Principles for Maturity Models and Its Demonstration in Business Process Management." In *Proceedings of the 19th European Conference on Information Systems (ECIS 2011)*, 1–12. Helsinki, Finland, June 9-11. https://eref.uni-bayreuth.de/id/eprint/8260.

Prakash, Gyan. 2018. "Quality in Higher Education Institutions: Insights from the Literature." *The TQM Journal* 30 (6): 732–48. https://doi.org/10.1108/TQM-04-2017-0043.

Pratasavitskaya, Halina, and Bjørn Stensaker. 2010. "Quality Management in Higher Education: Towards a Better Understanding of an Emerging Field." *Quality in Higher Education* 16 (1): 37–50. https://doi.org/10.1080/1353832 1003679465.

Prida And, Bernardo, and Mercedes Grijalvo. 2008. "The Socio-Technical Approach to Work Organisation. An Essential Element in Quality Management Systems." *Total Quality Management & Business Excellence* 19 (4): 343–52. https://doi.org/10.1080/147833607 01594568.

Prisăcariu, Anca. 2014. "Approaches of Quality Assurance Models on Adult Education Provisions." *Procedia - Social and Behavioral Sciences* 142 (August): 133–39. https://doi.org/10.1016/j.sbspro.2014.07.623.

Proper, Henderik A., and Marc M. Lankhorst. 2014. "Enterprise Architecture Towards Essential Sensemaking." *Enterprise Modelling and Information Systems Architectures* 9 (1): 5–21. http://doi.org/10.18417/emisa.9.1.1.

Radomír, Šerek. 2013. "Service Quality and Process Maturity Assessment." *Journal of Competitiveness* 5 (4): 43–56. https://doi.org/10.7441/joc.2013.04.03.

Ramos Pires, António. 2010. "Quality Management System in a Portuguese Higher Polytechnic Institute: Difficulties and Potentialities." In *Proceedings of the 13th Toulon-Verona International Conference on Quality in Services*. 2–4 September 2010, Coimbra, Portugal.

Regional Universities Forum for Capacity Building Agriculture (RUFORUM). 2011. *Quality Assurance Mechanism and Credit Accumulation and Transfer System - QAM/CATS. Handbook for Strengthening Postgraduate Training and Research Programmes in Eastern, Central and Southern Africa*. Kampala, Uganda. https://repository.ruforum.org/system/tdf/RUFORUM%20QAM-CATS%20Handbook_2011_0.pdf?file=1&type=node&id=33594&force=.

Riihimaa, Jaakko. 2009. "Combining Enterprise Architecture and Quality Assurance System from Data Administration Viewpoint." In *Proceedings of the International Conference EUNIS 2009*, 1–7. June 23rd to 26th, 2009, Santiago de Compostela, Spain.

Rocha-Lona, Luis, Jose Arturo Garza-Reyes, and Vikas Kumar. 2013. *Building Quality Management Systems: Selecting the Right Methods and Tools*. Boca Raton, FL: CRC Press, Taylor & Francis Group.

Rosa, Maria João, and Alberto Amaral. 2007. "A Self-Assessment of Higher Education Institutions from the Perspective of the EFQM Excellence Model." In *Quality Assurance in Higher Education: Trends in Regulation, Translation and Transformation*, edited by Don F. Westerheijden, Bjørn Stensaker, and Maria João Rosa, 181–207. Dordrecht: Springer Netherlands. http://dx.doi.org/10.1007/978-1-4020-6012-0_7.

Rosa, Maria João, Claudia S. Sarrico, and Alberto Amaral. 2012. "Implementing Quality Management Systems in Higher Education Institutions." In *Quality Assurance and Management*, edited by M. Savsar, 129–146. JanezaTrdine, Rijeka: InTech. http://cdn.intechopen.com/pdfs/33265/InTechImplementing_quality_management_systems_in_higher_education_institutions.pdf.

Rosemann, Michael, and Tonia De Bruin. 2005. "Towards a Business Process Management Maturity Model." In *Proceedings of the 13th European Conference on Information Systems (ECIS 2005)*. 26-28 May 2005, Germany, Regensburg. https://eprints.qut.edu.au/25194/.

Rouvrais, Siegfried, and Claire Lassudrie. 2014. "An Assessment Framework for Engineering Education Systems." In *Software Process Improvement and Capability Determination*, edited by Antanas Mitasiunas, Terry Rout, Rory V. O'Connor, and Alec Dorling, 250–255. Cham: Springer International Publishing.

Rupino da Cunha, Paulo, and António Dias de Figueiredo. 2005. "Quality Management Systems and Information Systems: Getting More than the Sum of the Parts." In *Proceedings of the 11th Americas Conference on Information Systems*, Paper 236:2245–53. Omaha, NE, USA August 11-14th 2005. http://aisel.aisnet.org/amcis2005/236.

Ryan, Tricia. 2015. "Quality Assurance in Higher Education: A Review of Literature." *Higher Learning Research Communications* 5 (4). https://doi.org/10.18870/hlrc.v5i4.257.

Sá, Paula S., Paulo Sampaio, and Maria J. Rosa. 2012. "Quality in Higher Education: Internal Quality Assurance Systems and the Quality Management Models." In *XVIII International Conference on Industrial Engineering and Operations Management (ICIEOM 2012)*, 171.1-171.9. Guimarães, Portugal, July 9-11, 2012. http://repositorium.sdum.uminho.pt/handle/1822/36139.

Sahney, Sangeeta. 2016. "Use of Multiple Methodologies for Developing a Customer-Oriented Model of Total Quality Management in Higher Education." *International Journal of Educational Management* 30 (3): 326–53. https://doi.org/10.1108/IJEM-09-2014-0126.

Sahney, Sangeeta, D.K. Banwet, and S. Karunes. 2008. "An Integrated Framework of Indices for Quality Management in Education: A Faculty Perspective." *The TQM Journal* 20 (5): 502–19. https://doi.org/10.1108/17542730810898467.

Sahu, Anil R., Rashmi R. Shrivastava, and R. L. Shrivastava. 2013a. "Development and Validation of an Instrument for Measuring Critical Success Factors (CSFs) of Technical Education–a TQM Approach." *International Journal of Productivity and Quality Management* 11 (1): 29–56.

Sahu, Anil R., Rashmi R. Shrivastava, and R.L. Shrivastava. 2013b. "Critical Success Factors for Sustainable Improvement in Technical Education Excellence: A Literature Review." *The TQM Journal* 25 (1): 62–74. https://doi.org/10.1108/17542731311286432.

Sanchez-Puchol, Felix, and Joan A. Pastor-Collado. 2017. "Focus Area Maturity Models: A Comparative Review." In *Information Systems: 14th European, Mediterranean, and Middle Eastern Conference, EMCIS 2017, Coimbra, Portugal, September 7-8, 2017, Proceedings*, edited by Marinos Themistocleous and Vincenzo Morabito, 531–44. Cham: Springer International Publishing. https://doi.org/10.1007/978-3-319-65930-5_42.

Sanchez-Puchol, Felix, Joan A. Pastor-Collado, and Baptista Borrell. 2017. "Towards a Unified Information Systems Reference Model for Higher Education Institutions." *Procedia Computer Science (Special Issue CENTERIS 2017 - International Conference on ENTERprise Information Systems)* 121: 542–53. https://doi.org/10.1016/j.procs.2017.11.072.

———. 2018. "A Critical Review on Reference Architectures and Models for Higher Education Institutions." In *Proceedings of the International Conferences Big Data Analytics, Data Mining and Computational Intelligence 2018; Theory and Practice in Modern Computing 2018; and Connected Smart Cities 2018 - Part of the Multi Conference on Computer Science and Information Systems (MCCSIS 2018)*, edited by Ajith P. Abraham, Jörg Roth, and Guo Chao Peng, 113–20. Madrid, Spain, 17-20 July 2018. http://www.iadisportal.org/digital-library/a-critical-review-on-reference-architectures-and-models-for-higher-education-institutions.

Sanchez-Puchol, Felix, Joan A. Pastor-Collado, and Josep Casanovas. 2018. "Theoretical Comparison of Universitary Quality Assurance Maturity Models." In *Proceedings Book of the 3rd International Conference on Quality Engineering and Management, 2018*, edited by Jasmina Berbegal-Mirabent, Frederic Marimon, Martí Casadesús, and Paulo Sampaio, 401–19. July 11-13, Universitat Internacional de Catalunya, Barcelona (Spain). http://icqem.dps.uminho.pt/icqem18_proceedingsbook.pdf.

Sanchez-Puchol, Felix, Joan A. Pastor-Collado, and Lourdes Guàrdia. 2018. "Maturity Models for Improving the Quality of Digital Teaching." In *10th EDEN Research Workshop. Conference Proceedings (Towards Personalized Guidance and Support for Learning)*, edited by Josep M. Duart and András Szűcs, 238–53. Barcelona, Spain 24-26 October 2018. http://www.eden-online.org/wp-content/uploads/2018/11/RW10_2018_Barcelona_Proceedings.pdf.

Sandkuhl, Kurt, Hans-Georg Fill, Stijn Hoppenbrouwers, John Krogstie, Florian Matthes, Andreas Opdahl, Gerhard Schwabe, Ömer Uludag, and Robert Winter. 2018. "From Expert Discipline to Common

Practice: A Vision and Research Agenda for Extending the Reach of Enterprise Modeling." *Business & Information Systems Engineering* 60 (1): 69–80. https://doi.org/10.1007/ s12599-017-0516-y.

Santos, Isabel M., and Graciete Dias. 2017. "A Comprehensive Internal Quality Assurance System at University of Minho." *International Journal of Quality & Reliability Management* 34 (2): 278–94. https://doi.org/10.1108/IJQRM-04-2015-0063.

Saraph, Jayant V., P. George Benson, and Roger G. Schroeder. 1989. "An instrument for measuring the critical factors of quality management." *Decision Sciences* 20 (4): 810–29.

Sarrico, Claudia, Maria João Rosa, Pedro Teixeira, and Margarita Cardoso. 2010. "Assessing Quality and Evaluating Performance in Higher Education: Worlds Apart or Complementary." *Minerva* 48 (1): 35–54. https://doi.org/ 10.1007/s11024-010-9142-2.

Schindler, Laura, Sarah Puls-Elvidge, Heather Welzant, and Linda Crawford. 2015. "Definitions of Quality in Higher Education: A Synthesis of the Literature." *Higher Learning Research Communications* 5 (3): 3. https://doi.org/ 10.18870/hlrc.v5i3.244.

Seyfried, Markus, and Philipp Pohlenz. 2018. "Assessing Quality Assurance in Higher Education: Quality Managers' Perceptions of Effectiveness." *European Journal of Higher Education*, May, 1–14. https://doi.org/10.1080/ 21568235.2018.1474777.

Silva, Danilo Soares, Gustavo Herminio Salati Marcondes de Moraes, Ieda Kanashiro Makiya, and Francisco Igncio Giocondo Cesar. 2017. "Measurement of Perceived Service Quality in Higher Education Institutions A Review of HEdPERF Scale Use." *Quality Assurance in Education* 25 (4): 415–39. https://doi.org/10.1108/QAE-10-2016-0058.

Smidt, Hanne. 2015. "European Quality Assurance—A European Higher Education Area Success Story [Overview Paper]." In *The European Higher Education Area: Between Critical Reflections and Future Policies*, edited by Adrian Curaj, Liviu Matei, Remus Pricopie, Jamil Salmi, and Peter Scott, 625–37. London, UK: Springer, Cham. doi: 10.1007/978-3-319-20877-0_40.

Standards and Guidelines for Quality Assurance in the European Higher Education Area (ESG). 2015. Approved by the Ministerial Conference, European, Association for Quality Assurance in Higher Education. Yerevan, 14-15 May: Brussels, Belgium. http://www.eua.be/Libraries/quality-assurance/esg_2015.pdf?sfvrsn=0.

Steenbergen, Marlies van, Rik Bos, Sjaak Brinkkemper, Inge van de Weerd, and Willem Bekkers. 2010. "The Design of Focus Area Maturity Models." In *DESRIST 2010, LNCS 6105*, edited by Robert Winter, J. Leon Zhao, and Stephan Aier, 317–332. Springer Berlin Heidelberg. https://doi.org/10.1007/978-3-642-13335-0_22.

Steinhardt, Isabel, Christian Schneijderberg, Nicolai Götze, Janosch Baumann, and Georg Krücken. 2017. "**Mapping the Quality Assurance of Teaching and Learning in Higher Education: The Emergence of a Specialty?**" *Higher Education* 74 (2): 221–37. https://doi.org/10.1007/s10734-016-0045-5.

Sultan, Parves, and Ho Yin Wong. 2010. "Service Quality in Higher Education – a Review and Research Agenda." *International Journal of Quality and Service Sciences* 2 (2): 259–72. https://doi.org/10.1108/17566691011057393.

Sunder M., Vijaya. 2016. "Constructs of Quality in Higher Education Services." *International Journal of Productivity and Performance Management* 65 (8): 1091–1111. https://doi.org/10.1108/IJPPM-05-2015-0079.

SURF. 2018. "Hoger Onderwijs Referentie Architectuur [In Dutch]." Web Page. *Hoger Onderwijs Referentie Architectuur* (blog). 2018. https://hora.surf.nl/index.php/Hoger_Onderwijs_Referentie_Architectuur.

Svensson, Carsten, and Hans-Henrik Hvolby. 2012. "Establishing a Business Process Reference Model for Universities." *Procedia Technology* 5 (2012): 635–42. https://doi.org/10.1016/j.protcy.2012.09.070.

Syynimaa, Nestori. 2010. "HMEF: Framework to Evaluate Merging of Higher Education Institutions – Application of Enterprise Architecture." In *3rd Conference of the Nordic Section of the Regional*

Studies Association (NORSA 2010), 1–5. June 21–23, 2010 Seinäjoki, Finland.

Tan, Adrian Heng Tsai, Birgit Muskat, and Anita Zehrer. 2016. "A Systematic Review of Quality of Student Experience in Higher Education." *International Journal of Quality and Service Sciences* 8 (2): 209–28. https://doi.org/10.1108/IJQSS-08-2015-0058.

Tarhan, Ayca, Oktay Turetken, and Hajo A. Reijers. 2016. "Business Process Maturity Models: A Systematic Literature Review." *Information and Software Technology* 75 (July): 122–34. https://doi.org/10.1016/j.infsof.2016.01.010.

Tarí, Juan José. 2006. "An EFQM Model Self-Assessment Exercise at a Spanish University." *Journal of Educational Administration* 44 (2): 170–88. https://doi.org/10.1108/09578230610652051.

Tarí, Juan José, and Gavin P.M. Dick. 2016. "Trends in Quality Management Research in Higher Education Institutions." *Journal of Service Theory and Practice* 26 (3): 273–96. https://doi.org/10.1108/JSTP-10-2014-0230.

Tari, Juan José, and Carolina Madeleine. 2011. "Preparing Jordanian University Services to Implement a Quality Self-Assessment Methodology." *International Review of Administrative Sciences* 77 (1): 138–58. https://doi.org/10.1177/0020852310390540.

Tavares, Orlanda, C. Sin, and P. Videira. 2017. "Actors and Factors behind the Development of Internal Quality Assurance Systems." In *EDULEARN17 Proceedings*, 8402–9. 9th International Conference on Education and New Learning Technologies. Barcelona, Spain: IATED. https://doi.org/10.21125/edulearn.2017.0559.

Tavares, Orlanda, Cristina Sin, and Alberto Amaral. 2016. "Internal Quality Assurance Systems in Portugal: What Their Strengths and Weaknesses Reveal." *Assessment & Evaluation in Higher Education* 41 (7): 1049–1064.

Tavares, Orlanda, Cristina Sin, Pedro Videira, and Alberto Amaral. 2017. "Academics' Perceptions of the Impact of Internal Quality Assurance on Teaching and Learning." *Assessment & Evaluation in Higher*

Education 42 (8): 1293–1305. https://doi.org/10.1080/02602938. 2016.1262326.

Taylor, John. 2015. "The Evolution of Institutional Research: Maturity Models of Institutional Research and Decision Support and Possible Directions for the Future." In *Institutional Research and Planning Higher Education: Global Contexts and Themes*, edited by Karen Webber and Angel Calderon, 213–28. New York: Routledge.

Teeroovengadum, V., T.J. Kamalanabhan, and A.K. Seebaluck. 2016. "Measuring Service Quality in Higher Education: Development of a Hierarchical Model (HESQUAL)." *Quality Assurance in Education* 24 (2): 244–58. https://doi.org/10.1108/QAE-06-2014-0028.

Thomas, Oliver. 2006. "Understanding the Term Reference Model in Information Systems Research: History, Literature Analysis and Explanation." In *Business Process Management Workshops*, edited by Christoph J. Bussler and Armin Haller, 484–496. Berlin, Heidelberg: Springer Berlin Heidelberg.

Thonhauser, Theresa, and David L. Passmore. 2006. "ISO 9000 in Education: A Comparison between the United States and England." *Research in Comparative and International Education* 1 (2): 156–73. https://doi.org/10.2304/rcie.2006.1.2.156.

TIER-Data Structures and APIs Working Group. 2016. "The TIER Reference Architecture (RA)." 2016. https://spaces.internet2.edu/pages/viewpage. action?pageId=98306902.

Timm, Felix. 2018. "An Application Design for Reference Enterprise Architecture Models." In *Advanced Information Systems Engineering Workshops*, edited by Raimundas Matulevičius and Remco Dijkman, 209–221. Springer International Publishing.

Tonini, Antonio Carlos, Marly Monteiro de Carvalho, and Mauro de Mesquita Spinola. 2008. "Contribuição dos modelos de qualidade e maturidade na melhoria dos processos de software [In Portuguese]." *Production* 18 (2): 275–86. https://doi.org/10.1590/S0103-651320080 00200006.

Torres Sol, Josep Manel, Miquel Vidal Espinar, Caterina Cazalla Lorite, and Esther Huertas Hidalgo. 2018. "*Guide to the Certification of*

Internal Quality Assurance Systems (IQAS) Implementation." Barcelona, January 2018: © Agència per a la Qualitat del Sistema Universitari de Catalunya. http://www.aqu.cat/doc/doc_47139484_1.pdf.

Torres Solà, Josep Manel, Manel Vidal Espinar, Caterina Cazalla Lorite, and Esther Huertas Hidalgo. 2015. "Certification of IQAS Implementation." *El Butlletí - A Quarterly Publication of AQU Catalunya*, no. 77 (April). http://www.aqu.cat/elButlleti/butlleti77/articles1_en.html#.XBkQbvZFwic.

Tovar, Edmundo, Paola Carina, and Karen Castillo. 2009. "Critical Success Factors for Implementing Quality Systems in European Higher Education." In *Proceedings of the 2009 American Society for Engineering Education (ASEE) Annual Conference & Exposition*, 14:1093.1-1093.12. June 14 - 17, 2009 - Austin, Texas. https://peer.asee.org/5767.

Tutko, Marta, and Vìtalìj Naumov. 2014. "Quality assurance systems in Polish and Ukrainian higher education. A comparative analysis." *Studia Humanistyczne AGH* 13 (1): 117. https://doi.org/10.7494/human.2014.13.1.117.

Universities and Colleges Information Systems Association (UCISA). 2018. "Launch of the UK HE Capability Model." Web Portal. *UCISA* (blog). 2018. https://www.ucisa.ac.uk/news/2018-03_15_capmodel.

Van Looy, Amy, Manu De Backer, and Geert Poels. 2011. "Defining Business Process Maturity. A Journey towards Excellence." *Total Quality Management* 22 (11): 1119–1137. https://doi.org/10.1080/14783363.2011.624779.

Ven, Andrew H. van de, and Marshall Scott Poole. 1995. "Explaining Development and Change in Organizations." *The Academy of Management Review* 20 (3): 510. https://doi.org/10.2307/258786.

Venable, John, Jan Pries-Heje, and Richard Baskerville. 2012. "A Comprehensive Framework for Evaluation in Design Science Research." In *Design Science Research in Information Systems. Advances in Theory and Practice. DESRIST 2012.*, edited by Ken Peffers, Marcus Rothenberger, and Bill Kuechler, 423–438. Lecture

Notes in Computer Science 7286. Berlin, Heidelberg: Springer Berlin Heidelberg. https://doi.org/10.1007/978-3-642-29863-9_31.

———. 2016. "FEDS: A Framework for Evaluation in Design Science Research." *European Journal of Information Systems* 25 (1): 77–89. https://doi.org/10.1057/ejis.2014.36;

Vettori, Oliver, Karl Ledermüller, Christoph Schwarzl, Julia Höcher, and Julia Zeeh. 2017. *"Developing a Quality Culture through Internal Quality Assurance."* Paris, France: International Institute for Educational Planning, UNESCO.

Vezzetti, Enrico, Maria Grazia Violante, and Federica Marcolin. 2014. "A Benchmarking Framework for Product Lifecycle Management (PLM) Maturity Models." *The International Journal of Advanced Manufacturing Technology* 71 (5): 899–918. https://doi.org/10.1007/s00170-013-5529-1.

Villalobos, Pablo, Álvaro Rojas, Francisco Honorato, and Sebastián Donoso. 2017. *"Mainstreaming Internal Quality Assurance with Management."* Paris, France: International Institute for Educational Planning, UNESCO.

Visscher, Adrie J. 2009a. "A Theoretical Framework for Analysing the Implementation and Effects of Quality Assurance Systems in European VET. In: Visscher A.J. (Eds) Improving Quality Assurance in European Vocational Education and Training. Springer, Dordrecht." In *Improving Quality Assurance in European Vocational Education and Training*, edited by Adrie J. Visscher. Dordrecht: Springer Netherlands. https://doi.org/10.1007/978-1-4020-9527-6_2.

———. , ed. 2009b. *Improving Quality Assurance in European Vocational Education and Training. Factors Influencing the Use of Quality Assurance Findings*. Dordrecht: Springer Netherlands. https://doi.org/10.1007/978-1-4020-9527-6.

Vlăsceanu, Lazăr, Laura Grünberg, and Dan Pârlea. 2007. *Quality Assurance and Accreditation a Glossary of Basic Terms and Definitions*. Edited by Melanie Seto and Peter J. Wells. Bucharest: Unesco-CEPES. http://www.bibl.ulaval.ca/doelec/lc/L/Qualityassuranceaccreditation_Unesco.pdf.

Vukasovic, Martina. 2014. "Institutionalisation of Internal Quality Assurance: Focusing on Institutional Work and the Significance of Disciplinary Differences." *Quality in Higher Education* 20 (1): 44–63. https://doi.org/10.1080/13538322.2014.889430.

Wendler, Roy. 2012. "The Maturity of Maturity Model Research: A Systematic Mapping Study." *Information and Software Technology* 54 (12): 1317–39. https://doi.org/10.1016/j.infsof.2012.07.007.

Winter, Susan, Nicholas Berente, James Howison, and Brian Butler. 2014. "Beyond the Organizational 'Container': Conceptualizing 21st Century Sociotechnical Work." *Information and Organization* 24 (4): 250–69. https://doi.org/10.1016/j.infoandorg.2014.10.003.

Wosik, Dawid. 2009. "Towards Excellence in Higher Education Through Quality Awareness." In *INQAAHE 2009 Biennial Conference*. 30 March - 2 April. Abu Dhabi, United Arab Emirates. http://www.inqaahe.org/sites/default/files/pictures/26_Wosik_Towards%20excellence%20in%20HE%20trough%20quality%20awareness.pdf.

Zavale, Nelson Casimiro, Luisa Alcantra Santos, and Maria Da Conceição Dias. 2016. "Main Features and Challenges of Implementing Internal Quality Assurance within African Higher Education Institutions: The Case of Eduardo Mondlane University." *International Journal of African Higher Education* 2 (1). https://doi.org/10.6017/ijahe.v2i1.9262.

Zgodavova, Kristina, Natasa Urbancikova, and Matus Kisela. 2015. "Enhancement of the Quality Assurance Model at the Slovak University: Case Study." *Quality Innovation Prosperity* 19 (2): 01. https://doi.org/10.12776/qip.v19i2.610.

Živaljević, Aleksandra, Vuk Bevanda, and Dragana Trifunović. 2017. "Life Cycle of Quality Management System in Organizations." *Management:Journal of Sustainable Business and Management Solutions in Emerging Economies*, October. https://doi.org/10.7595/management.fon.2017.0012.

ANNEX I. MATURITY MODELS RESEARCHED IN THE CHAPTER

	[#MM1] MDI	[#MM2] QMS-MM	[#MM3]
Name of the model	Maturity Diagnostic Instrument	Quality Management System Maturity Model	PN-ISO 10014:2008 Self-Assessment
Unit of analysis	Business organizations	Business organizations	Business organizations
Declared maturing object	QMS business process	QMS	QMS
Target audience	Quality Managers (implicit)	Experts, consultants and managers (implicit)	Not declared
Dimensions explored	No primary dimensions or areas 84 sub-factors directly detailed	1. Leadership and Communication 2. Agility and Integration by IT 3. Efficient Management Processes 4. Valuing employees 5. Information Availability 6. Cost Valuing management	1. Customer-oriented approach 2. Leadership 3. Commitment of people 4. Process approach 5. Systems approach to management 6. Continuous improvement 7. Fact-based decisions 8. Mutually beneficial relationships with suppliers
Number of dimensions	0 Primary 84 Secondary	6 Primary 27 Secondary	8 Primary 24 Secondary
Maturity stages/levels	1. Uncommitted 2. Drifters 3. Tool pushers 4. Improvers 5. Award winners 6. World-class	1. Level 1 2. Level 2 3. Level 3 4. Level 4 5. Level 5	1. No or false 2. Little true 3. Partly true 4. Mostly true 5. Yes, always true
# of maturity levels	6 Levels	5 Levels	5 Levels
Composition	Likert-Like	Likert-like	Likert-like
Assessment Method	Yes, detailed	No evidence found	No evidence found
Empirically tested?	Yes, but results are not provided	Yes, exploratory factor analysis	No evidence found
Measurement tool disclosed	No evidence found	No evidence found	No evidence found
Guidelines for implementation	Yes, generic recommendations	No evidence found	No evidence found
Documentation	Book chapter, journal articles	Journal article	Journal article

Annex I. (Continued)

	[#MM4] E-CMM	[#MM5] E²-CMM
Name of the model	Educational Capability Maturity Model	Capability Maturity Model for Engineering Education System
Unit of analysis	Higher Education Institutions	Engineering Education Institutions
Declared maturing object	Quality (of processes)	Quality (of processes)
Target audience	(Higher) Education providers (Explicit)	Not declared
Dimensions explored	No primary dimensions or areas 20 sub factors directly detailed	Adhoc process, Resource Management, Financial resource, allocation and utilization, Physical facilities, Learning Resources, Course Curriculum, Administrative Support, Leadership, Staff and Students relationship, Management and organization skills, Communication and social skills, Teamwork, Resources(faculty and staff), Human Resources(students), Management Responsibility, Product realization, Measurement, analysis and improvement, Educational Change Management, Teaching-Learning and assessment practices, Educational subcontract management, Educational organization process focus, Student support and progression, Supplementary practices, Healthy practices, Strategy planning, Opportunities for knowledge up-gradation, Learning outcomes, Technical Competencies Technology driven teaching aids, Generic Competencies, Teaching – Learning and Evaluation, Research, Consultancy and Extension, Redefining educational quality in terms of outcomes, Internal Quality Assurance Cell (IQAC),Process management, Personality development Academics, Industry Institute Interface, Responsiveness, Organizational performance results, Quantitative and qualitative focus on teaching and learning, Measurement Analysis and knowledge mgt., Maturity and stability of the institution, Educational Quality Assurance, Continuous Evaluation System
Number of dimensions	0 Primary 20 Secondary	44 Primary 234 Secondary
Maturity stages/levels	1. Initial 2. Repeatable 3. Defined 4. Management 5. Optimized	1. Initial 2. Repeated 3. Defined 4. Refined 5. Quantifiable matured
# of maturity levels	5 Levels	5 Levels
Composition	CMMI-like	CMM-like
Assessment Method	No evidence found	Yes, detailed
Empirically tested?	No evidence found	Yes, structural equation modelling with PLS support

	[#MM4] E-CMM	[#MM5] E²-CMM
Measurement tool disclosed	No evidence found	Yes, but not accessible
Guidelines for implementation	Yes, basic (limited) recommendations	Yes, clear recommendations
Documentation	Book chapter	Conference papers

	[#MM6] CAF-EFQM	[#MM7] EQW	[#MM8]
Name of the model	Common Assessment Framework	Education Quality Work	Criteria for Audits of IQAS
Unit of analysis	Education institutions	Higher education institutions (Asia-Pacific)	Higher education institutions (Portugal)
Declared maturing object	Organization/QMS	QA practices (quality work)	IQAS Audit (ESG standard-oriented)
Target audience	Quality practitioners	QA bodies and accreditation agency experts / HEI's QA staff	QA bodies and accreditation agency experts / HEI's QA staff

Dimensions explored	1. Leadership
	2. Strategy and Planning
	3. People
	4. Partnerships and Resources
	5. Processes
	6. Citizen/Customer-oriented Results
	7. People Results
	8. Social Responsibility Results
	9. Key Performance Results
		1. Learning objectives
		2. Curriculum and cu-curriculum
		3. Teaching and learning processes
		4. Assessment of student learning
		5. Assuring educational quality
			1. Institutional policy for QA
			2. Scope and effectiveness of the procedures and structures of QA
			  2.1. Teaching and learning
			  2.2. Research and development /targeted research and high level professional development
			  2.3. Interaction with society
			  2.4. Policies for staff management
			  2.5. Support services
			  2.6. Internationalisation
			3. Relationship between the IQAS and the strategic management of the institution
			4. Participation of internal and external stakeholders in the processes for QA
			5. Information Management– mechanisms for the collection, analysis and internal dissemination of information
			6. Publication of relevant information to external stakeholders
			7. Monitoring, evaluation and continuous improvement of the IQAS

Annex I. (Continued)

	[#MM6] CAF-EFQM	[#MM7] EQW	[#MM8]
Number of dimensions	9 Primary 28 Secondary	9 Primary Variable number Secondary	7 Primary | 5 Secondary (related with dimension 2)
Maturity stages/levels	1. Unable to demonstrate 2. Limited ability to demonstrate 3. Able to demonstrate 4. Fully able to demonstrate 5. Recognized as a global role model	1. No effort at all 2. Firefighting 3. Informal effort 4. Organized effort 5. Mature effort	1. Insufficient development 2. Partial development 3. Substantial development 4. Very advanced development
# of maturity levels	5 Levels	5 Levels	4 Levels
Composition	Likert-Like	CMM-like	Text-Grid
Assessment Method	Yes, detailed	Yes, but items for assessment can be variable	No (implicit use of the rubric)
Empirically tested?	Refers academic studies and practical use cases as evidence	No evidence found	No evidence found
Measurement tool disclosed	Evidence found on an eTool	No evidence found	No evidence found
Guidelines for implementation	Yes, clear recommendations	Yes, basic recommendation	Yes, basic recommendations
Documentation	Specific and detailed hands-on manual, journal articles, books	Book chapter	Practical hands-on manual

	[#MM9]	[#MM10]
Name of the model	Criteria for Certification of IQAS	ASIIN Maturity Model
Unit of analysis	Higher education institutions (Catalonia)	Higher education institutions
Declared maturing object	IQAS certification (ESG standard-oriented)	IQAS Accreditation (ASIIN seal)
Target audience	QA bodies and accreditation agency experts | HEI's QA staff	QA bodies and accreditation agency experts

Dimensions explored	1. IQAS review and improvement.
	  1.1. IQAS process have been implemented.
	  1.2. IQAS process map consistent with processes implemented.
	  1.3. Evidence of people responsible for IQAS review & improvement.
	  1.4. The unit has a system for the management of IQAS documentation.
	  1.5. The unit has an easily accessible information management system.
	  1.6. Evidence that IQAS is periodically reviewed/improved/enhanced.
		1. Definition of quality.
		  1.1. Objectives.
		  1.2. (Quality-) management systems/ governance.
		2. Educational programmes/courses/training Creation & development of programmes/courses/training.
		  2.2. Implementation of programmes/courses/training.
		  2.3. Cooperation.
		  2.4. Examination systems and organization of exams.

[#MM9]	[#MM10]

2. Design, review and improvement of study programmes.
  2.1. Evidence of people responsible for study programmes.
  2.2. Assessment in accordance with processes implemented in the IQAS.
  2.3. Information is compiled for review of study programmes.
  2.4. Evidence that study programmes are periodically reviewed/improved/enhanced.
3. Learning support and guidance systems for students.
  3.1. Evidence of the people responsible for learning support and guidance systems.
  3.2. Actions related to learning support & guidance systems carried out in accordance with IQAS processes.
  3.3. Information compiled for review/improvement of learning support & guidance systems.
  3.4. Evidence that learning support & guidance systems are periodically reviewed /improved.
4. Academic staff.
  4.1. Evidence of people responsible for processes related to academic staff.
  4.2. IQAS processes for academic staff are coherent with QA recommendations.
  4.3. Information is compiled for the review of learning resources management.
  4.4. Learning resources management is periodically reviewed/improved/enhanced.
5. Physical resources and services.
  5.1. Evidence of the people responsible for physical resources and services.
  5.2. Information is compiled for review of physical resources and service management.
  5.3. Physical resources and service management reviewed/ improved /enhanced.
6. Public information.
  6.1. Evidence of people responsible for processes related to public information.
  6.2. Information compiled for review, improvement and enhancement.
Public information is periodically reviewed, improved and enhanced.
	2.5. Recognition of achievements.
	  2.6. Assistance and support.
	3. Management of resources Material and human resources.
	  3.2. Human resources development.
	  3.3. Interaction with research.
	  3.4. Interaction with administration.
	4. Transparency and documentation Rules & regulations for programmes/courses/training.
	  4.2. Documentation

Annex I. (Continued)

Number of dimensions	6 Primary | 24 Secondary	4 Primary | 14 Secondary
Maturity stages/levels	1. Good 2. Satisfactory 3. Unsatisfactory	1. Not existent 2. Defined 3. Implemented 4. Established & controlled 5. Predictive & proactive
# of maturity levels	3 Levels	5 Levels
Composition	Text-Grid	Text-Grid
Assessment Method	No (implicit use of the rubric)	No (implicit use of the rubric)
Empirically tested?	No evidence found	No evidence found
Measurement tool disclosed	No evidence found	No evidence found
Guidelines for Implementation	Yes, basic recommendations	Yes, basic recommendations
Documentation	Practical hands-on manual	Practical hands-on manual

	[#MM11]	[#MM12]
Name of the model	Quality Assurance Maturity Model	Maturity Model for Learning Ability in Engineering
Unit of analysis	Post-secondary institutions (Canada)	Engineering higher education institutions LACCEI (Latin American & Caribbean)
Declared maturing object	QA processes' autonomy & independence from external QA governing bodies	QA capabilities for Accreditation
Target audience	Not declared	Not declared
Dimensions explored	1. Program Quality 2. Faculty and staff 3. Governance 4. Students 5. Innovation and change management 6. Sustainability 7. External stakeholders	1. Potentiality (capacity) 2. Processes
Number of dimensions	7 Primary	2 Primary | 3 Secondary
Maturity stages/levels	1. Lack or minimal awareness 2. Basic awareness	1. Initial 2. Managed

# of maturity levels	5 Levels	5 Levels
Composition	CMM-like	CMM-like
Assessment Method	No evidence found	No evidence found
Empirically tested?	No evidence found	No evidence found
Measurement tool disclosed	No evidence found	Yes, but not accessible
Guidelines for implementation	Yes, basic recommendations	Yes, specific recommendations
Documentation	Practical hands-on manual	Conference papers

(levels: 3. Maturing / 4. Good practice / 5. Best practice; and 3. Defined / 4. Quantitative managed / 5. Optimization)

Source: Own elaboration.

ANNEX II. REFERENCE MODELS AND ENTERPRISE REFERENCE ARCHITECTURES FOR HEIS

Artifact Name (including base references)	Type[1]	Origin	Detail	Accesibil.	Scope of application						
					Width				Depth	
					Teaching	Research	Support Services	Third mission	Business	Data	Applications	Technology
Hoger Onderwijs Referentie Architectuur (SURF 2018)	ERA	Both	High	Free	✓	✓	✓		✓	✓	✓	✓
ITANA Reference Architecture for Teaching and Learning (ITANA Working Group 2012; Abel, Brown, and Suess 2013)	ERA	Practice	High	Free	✓	✓	✓	✓	✓	✓		
CAUDIT Enterprise Architecture Commons for Higher Education (Council of Australian University Directors of Information Technology (CAUDIT) 2016, 2017)	ERA	Both	High	Restricted	✓	✓	✓	✓	✓	✓		

Annex II. (Continued)

Artifact Name (including base references)	Type[1]	Origin	Detail	Accesibil.	Width: Teaching	Research	Support Services	Third mission	Business	Depth: Data	Applications	Technology
Trust and Identity (TIER) Reference Architecture (TIER-Data Structures and APIs Working Group 2016)	ERA	Practice	Medium	Free			✓				✓	✓
Cloud Computing Architecture for Higher Education (Pardeshi, 2014; Mircea and Andreescu, 2011)	ERA	Academia	Low	Free	✓	✓	✓	✓			✓	✓
UCISA UK Higher Education Capability Model (Anderson n.d.; UCISA 2018)	BU-RM	Practice	High	Free	✓	✓	✓		✓			
Colombian Higher Education Enterprise Architecture (Llamosa-Villalba et al. 2015, 2014)	BU-RM	Both	Medium	Restricted	✓	✓	✓		✓			
Charles Sturt Univ. HE Business Process Reference Model (Charles Sturt University 2010)	BU-RM	Practice	High	Free	✓	✓	✓		✓			
Business Process Reference Model for Higher Education (Svensson and Hvolby 2012)	BU-RM	Academia	Low	Free	✓		✓					
Higher Education Information Systems in Croatia (Frackmann 2007)	IS/IT-RM	Practice	Low	Free	✓	✓	✓		✓		✓	
Unified Information Systems Reference Model for Higher Education Institutions (Sanchez-Puchol, Pastor-Collado, and Borrell 2017)	IS/IT-RM	Academia	Medium	Free	✓		✓		✓		✓	
e-education Application Framework (Fagan 2003)	IS/IT-RM	Academia	Low	Free	✓		✓				✓	
Reference Model of University IT Architecture (S. Chen, Tang, and Li 2016)	IS/IT-RM	Academia	Low	Free	✓		✓					✓

[1] Based on own authors appreciation.

ERA → Enterprise Reference Architecture | BU-RM → Reference Model | IS/IT-RM → Reference Model.

✓ → Covered | — → Not evaluated due to ongoing development, lack of evidence or translation problems to the original source.

Font: Own elaboration.

In: Higher Education Institutions
Editor: Joe Maxwell

ISBN: 978-1-53615-717-8
© 2019 Nova Science Publishers, Inc.

Chapter 2

WE CAN DO BETTER: BUILDING COMPETENCIES UNTIL GRADUATION

Rita Payan-Carreira[1,*], *Gonçalo Cruz*[2]
and Caroline Dominguez[2,3]

[1]Department of Veterinary Medicine, Universidade de Évora, Pole at Mitra, Évora, Portugal
[2]Department of Engineering, University of Trás-os-Montes e Alto Douro, Vila Real, Portugal
[3]LabDCT-CIDTFF, University of Trás-os-Montes e Alto Douro, Vila Real, Portugal

ABSTRACT

Today's global economy requests from graduates that they have the competencies at day-1 suiting the workplace, including critical thinking,

---

[*] Corresponding Author's E-mail: rtpayan@gmail.com.

adaptability, autonomy, teamwork and communication. These competencies go beyond the cognitive achievements or the content knowledge that are often identify as major outcomes in multiple tertiary education providers worldwide. According to published surveys, the hardest positions to fill still require from graduates a combination of technical and transferable soft skills, suggesting that in most cases Higher Education Institutions (HEI) still have difficulties in reaching such a prime goal.

It is often claimed that a skills' gap exists between the expectations of employers and HEI regarding the competencies that should be mastered by graduates at the entrance in the labor market. However, even if this opinion is not consensual, and in an attempt to bridge this gap, several initiatives and recommendations have emerged in different countries through the implementation of educational policies and frameworks. In Europe, this has led to the adoption of the philosophy endorsed in the Bologna reform and the Miller pyramid framework for assessment.

This skills' gap is evolutive and may present different forms amongst countries or professions. Results from an Erasmus+ project (CRITHINKEDU - Critical Thinking Across the European Higher Education Curricula) have shown that those skills may vary between professional fields, particularly on how they are understood and applied (Dominguez 2018). Moreover, the increased complexity of the professional reality and the tremendous pace at which technology evolves, hinder the efforts taken by the higher education institutions and delay the implementation of adaptative strategies that will foster a constant fitting of the undergraduates to the workplace requirements. The needed adaptation of the HEI is crucial to ensure that their graduates succeed in the current highly competitive professional market.

In this sense, and believing that we can do better to drive this change, the current chapter discusses some pathways available to HEI towards the assessment of needs and the improvement of course planning, curriculum design and student guidance systems. It will contribute to present/discuss pathways to reduce the existing gaps between day-1 graduates and labor market demands (degree-job match). The complex and multidimensional challenges need to be faced together by higher education and the labor market, as a shared responsibility in establishing educational goals, providing settings and discussing the assessment of outcomes. Such cooperation should also allow to preview for competency-shifts attending to the rapid technological changes, economic and cultural globalization.

Keywords: higher education, competency-based education, workplace-based competencies, labor market integration, educational policy, quality frameworks, soft-skills

1. New Paradigms Shaping Competencies: From Professional and Societal Needs to Effective Acquisition

Labor market agents in different fields have been claiming for some decades that there is a gap between the expectations of the labor market and the skills new graduates present, regarding the competencies that should be mastered by graduates at the entrance in the labor market.

In an attempt to bridge this gap, several initiatives and recommendations towards the implementation of educational policies and frameworks have emerged. Yet, the gap tends to persist, albeit assuming different forms cross-countries. In 2015, Cedefop published a report about the skill shortages and gaps in European enterprises. This report refers that EU firms struggle not with a generalized lack of skills, but with difficulties in finding staff with the right skills (Cedefop 2015). This report also reveals that this skill mismatch varies markedly across Member States (Figure 1).

Besides, the reported mismatches seem to vary between professional fields as results from an Erasmus+ project (CRITHINKEDU - Critical Thinking Across the European Higher Education Curricula) have shown. These skills seem to be understood and applied differently within each professional context (Dominguez 2018). The differences among sectors is also acknowledged in the Cedefop 2018 report (Cedefop 2018). They are driven by the increased complexity of the professional reality and the tremendous pace at which technology evolves.

The ever-growing pace of the market complexity and competitivity has represented a great challenge for higher education institutions to implement adaptative strategies to foster a constant fitting of the undergraduates to the workplace requirements. Projections of the Mckinsey Society reported that in 2030, the global labor force will reach 3.5 billion persons, but a shortage of competent, highly-skilled workers who are needed to raise productivity and drive the growth of businesses and national economies is expected, which may reach the number of 38 to

40 million (ca. 13% of the demand) (Dobbs et al. 2012). In parallel, a surplus of low-skill workers will occur.

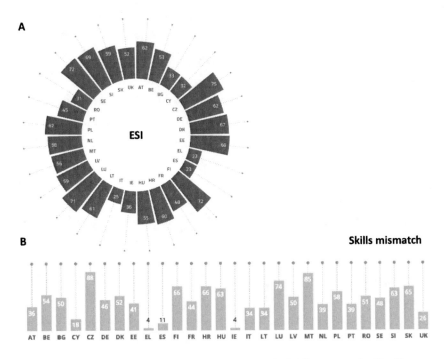

Figure 1. A - European Skills Index measuring countries' "distance to the ideal" performance over a period of 7 years and covering three pillars: skills development (representing the training and education activities of the country and the immediate outputs of that system in terms of the skills developed and attained), activation (that includes indicators of the transition from education to work) and matching (representing the degree of successful utilisation of skills, i.e., the extent to which skills are effectively matched in the labor market.). B - Detail of skills mismatching across EU countries [https://skillspanorama.cedefop.europa.eu/en/indicators/european-skills-index].

The mismatch gap may escalate following the evergrowing digital transformation of the economy and the development of the artificial intelligence era. The way people work and do business keeps changing, reshaping the landscape of skills needed, namely in terms of technological and digital skills (European Commission 2016). Some defend that skills gaps will always persist, as they arise from seniority and in answer to the dynamic changes and the uncertainty in job markets. Therefore, they will never be completely abrogated. However, they can be mitigated. To reduce the impact of such forces, the active engagement of workers in flexible thinking and lifelong learning is of utmost importance. Such a paradigm/shift requires a different mindset, raising important challenges to Higher Education Institutions (Table 1).

Table 1. Different levels of responsibility in the roadmap supporting the skills gaps and general approaches for mitigation. Policy-makers have a role to play in the skills offered by recent graduates, while lifelong learning is a joint responsibility of the individuals and the employers

Claims	Graduates	Policy-makers	Employers
Difficulties	Are ill-prepared to modern workplaces; Might be over-skilled in some cases	Struggle to match the pace at which the workplace demands evolve	The growing complexity of the workplaces increased the mutation in the demanded skills
Consequences	Often experience feelings of insecurity and frustration; More prone to career stagnation and inequities	The offered one-shot policies tend to fail; Have difficulties in matching the skills supply with skills demands	Risk of lower productivity; Increases the risk of delaying or failing proposed outcomes
To foster the change	Need to invest in lifelong learning; Need to cope with skills adaptation and transferability	To draw policies orientating the competency-based education; Foster the education for transferability of critical thinking and other soft skills	Offer tailored skills formation through time; Offer deployment scenarios for training; Foster skills transition into new settings

How can the HE Institutions contribute to minimize the mismatch between the skills offered and demanded?

Preparing students for yet non-existent jobs demands calls for an educational approach that teaches them how to learn and think more than merely absorb content or develop technical skills. Critical thinking, entrepreneurship, problem solving or digital competencies are some of the qualifications listed in the EU New Skills Agenda or identified by the Manpower Group (2013) or the Mckinsey Society (2013), together with adaptability, autonomy, teamwork and communication, essential to develop good-quality jobs and to fulfil the potential of future professionals and confident active citizens. Albeit it is widely desirable to strengthen key-competencies (understood as the results of the interaction of knowledge with skills) and soft skills within the Higher education curricula, it is also crucial to provide better career guidance and training for skills' transference, enabling the efficient and timely reallocation of skills that emerge from labor market complexity and unforeseen changes.

This evolving landscape has gradually called on HEI worldwide to start reforming their curricula, going beyond knowledge and gearing them towards a competency-based education. To empower future professionals and citizens, education must focus on developing competencies. A competency-based approach to education requires the identification and definition of key-competencies and higher, more complex skills to drive change. It should offer the tools to anticipate market evolution and transformations while fostering students' thinking about the consequences of choices in terms of economic, social and environmental sustainability. Therefore, education should be flexible, allow the development of transferable competencies and foster continuous self-improvement/ empowerment.

Since competence is a complex term with different interpretations and since efforts have been made by different international and national bodies to guide high education institution towards the implementation of competency-based education, in the next section we will present some educational frameworks designed to meet the challenge of reducing the skills' gaps/mismatches.

2. Shaping Concepts towards Competency-Based Higher Education: A Perspective Based on Some Educational Frameworks

Worldwide, the concept of competence and competency-based education in higher education has gained particular attention due to the increased demands and emphasis in terms of quality, costs, assessment and accountability (Burnette 2016). On the one hand, educational policy-makers and the public, in general, strengthened the pressure over the universities to innovate towards the offer of high-quality educational experiences, and to improve the match between the learning and the demands of the labor market and society. On the other hand, governments and funding partners (e.g., workforce) need substantive evidence to ensure their investments' results. Even considering the lack of clarity and the plurality of competence definitions or perspective of competency-based education prevailing between the different higher education stakeholders (i.e., agencies, universities, teachers, students and business companies), they are usually stated as learning outcomes and assumed as a combination of cognitive, affective, motivational, volitional, and social dispositions that form the basis for performance (Shavelson 2013).

Thus, this section intends 1) to present an overview of some competency-based frameworks relevant to higher education and lifelong learning, attending to the educational, social and professional perspectives; 2) to compare frameworks and report the challenges, difficulties, and barriers in their use and implementation. The frameworks reviewed herein were selected within those used in higher education and lifelong learning (population criteria), which are used transversally and across disciplines (scope criteria), and which provide operational definitions of competencies, knowledge, skills, abilities, attitudes, or values (specificity criteria). It was intended to provide a global overview of some of the most known frameworks proposed worldwide for higher education (e.g., Europe, North America, Latin America, Australia), from earliest initiatives (e.g., Tuning) and derived efforts (e.g., QF-EHEA, DEP) to recent works grounded and sustainably aligned with the 21st century labor market and societal needs (e.g., KSAVE, ERF-LLL). Other frameworks were also included, namely those widely adopted by higher education institutions and promoted by governmental entities or recognized higher education bodies and associations (e.g., AQF, LEAP, CAS). Given these criteria, we identified ten frameworks for revision (see Table 2).

All the frameworks were reviewed upon six main categories of analysis (see Table 2 and Table 3): scope, purpose orientation, learning orientation, targeted competencies and learning outcomes, implementation, and impact. In terms of the scope, a framework can reach a wide or a limited range of educational settings and outcomes (e.g., cross- disciplinary vs. subject-specific), or both. Concerning the second and third categories, i.e., purpose orientation and learning orientation, respectively, we adopted Prøitz's conceptual model (Prøitz 2010) for analysis. This two-axis continuum model proposes two opposite poles for *purpose orientation* - accountability *vs.* educational, instructional planning and curriculum development -, and two opposite poles for *learning orientation* - process-oriented, open-ended and limited measurability *vs.* result-oriented, full-ended and measurable (Prøitz 2010; Havnes and Prøitz 2016). Learning outcomes can either be perceived as tools for educational, instructional planning and curriculum development, or as tools for measuring effectiveness and accountability (e.g., political, legal, bureaucratic, professional, educational, market accountability), on one hand, but they can also be understood as "what one ends up with, intended or not, after some form of engagement" (Eisner, 1979, 101), or as "refined understanding of the learning process and thus permits a drawing of relatively precise implications for the design of instruction" (Gagné, 1974, 51). Eisner was concerned with the role of curriculum in the learning process and the complexity of learning outcomes, which depended on different variables such as the student, subject, teacher, making impossible to sort all of the variables into pre-defined terms (Eisner, 1979). Contrastingly, Gagné was concerned with the instructional design and interested in determining the kind of learning needed to achieve specific tasks requiring planning and sequencing (Gagné, 1974).

Thus, the learning outcomes may be either described as process-oriented, open-ended and with limited measurability, or result-oriented, full-ended and measurable

The fourth category, *targeted competencies* and *learning outcomes*, intend to spot the main competencies each framework targets as essential for being developed by higher education students and beyond. The *implementation* category aims to identify the main guidelines, recommendations, and methodologies provided by the frameworks to support the implementation and assessment of the competencies. Finally, our ambition is also to briefly assess the impact of the analyzed frameworks for higher education institutions, staff, teachers, and students, according to different studies and reports available in the literature or in the responsible organizations' websites.

Tables 2 and 3 summarise the analysis regarding the eight reviewed frameworks.

The selected frameworks were published during the two last decades, from 1995 to 2018. AQF and Tuning were the earliest and influenced the development of others (e.g., QF-EHEA, DQP). Most frameworks have been periodically reviewed and updated along the years. Although the published documents of these efforts come from a single entity (e.g., governmental, academic), most frameworks were developed in collaboration with multiple stakeholders from different organisations and sectors (e.g., project consortiums, university associations, business companies) using different research designs (e.g., case studies, longitudinal research, survey research) and data collection methodologies (e.g., questionnaires, interviews, working groups). Only three frameworks represent national initiatives, purposely deployed within the higher education system of a country or nation (i.e., USA or Australia), while the other six constitute transnational efforts involving higher education actors from different countries or nations (e.g., Europe, North America).

Table 2. Summary of the frameworks regarding the learning outcomes – scope, purpose orientation, learning orientation and definitions of learning outcome[1]

Framework	Acronym	Year(s)	Authorship	Region	Scope	Purpose orientation (Prøitz, 2010)	Learning orientation and definitions of learning outcome (Prøitz, 2010)
Tuning Learning Outcomes and Competences	Tuning	2000	Tuning project/ European Commission	Worldwide	**Formal learning;** Both holistic/cross-disciplinary and subject-specific framework for learning outcomes (i.e., common to any degree or specific to a field of study) Up to 42 subject areas were covered.	**Accountability Educational, instructional planning and curriculum development** Transnational transparency, comparability, and mobility of learner's experience; Emphasis on 'learning' and 'student-centered approach'; Specific approaches to learning, teaching, and assessment Clear methodologies for design, delivery, maintenance, and evaluation of curricula, programmes and courses.	**Established definition Result-oriented, full-ended, and measurable** Learning outcomes viewed as 'statements of what a learner is expected to know, understand and be able to demonstrate after completion of a learning experience'. Expressed in terms of competencies (i.e., a combination of cognitive and meta-cognitive skills, knowledge and understanding, interpersonal, intellectual and practical skills, and ethical values) Two sequential cycle levels - i.e., bachelor and master – related in a common credit system, a specific expected workload and degrees Four intermediate levels in each cycle – i.e., basic, intermediate, advanced and specialized.

Framework	Acronym	Year(s)	Authorship	Region	Scope	Purpose orientation (Proitz, 2010)	Learning orientation and definitions of learning outcome (Proitz, 2010)
Student Student Learning and Development Outcomes	CAS	2003 2015	Council for the Advancement of Standards in Higher Education	North America	**Formal learning;** Meta, holistic and cross-disciplinary framework of generic descriptors of learning outcomes (i.e., translation device to higher education institutions mission, programs, and services);	**Accountability** **Educational, instructional planning and curriculum development** Advisory tool to programmes and services. To identify relevant student learning and development outcomes and encourage their achievement; It encourages program review, learning assessment and evaluation procedures focused on student learning and development continuingly for each learning domain. They include theoretical perspectives, standards, tools, variables and indicators, assessment examples and methodologies, recommended readings, among others.	**Established definition** **Result-oriented, full-ended, and measurable** Learning outcomes are foreseen as particular levels of knowledge, skills, and abilities to be attained by students at the end of a particular set of collegiate experiences; Six broad and independent learning domains – i.e., knowledge acquisition, construction, integration and application, cognitive complexity, intrapersonal development, interpersonal competence, humanitarianism and civic engagement, and practical competence. Twenty-eight outcomes dimensions are associated with the six domains.

Table 2. (Continued).

Framework	Acronym	Year(s)	Authorship	Region	Scope	Purpose orientation (Proitz, 2010)	Learning orientation and definitions of learning outcome (Proitz, 2010)
Framework for Qualifications of The European Higher Education Area	QF-EHEA	2005 2018	Bologna Working Group/ European Higher Education Area/ European Commission	Europe	**Formal learning;** Holistic and cross-disciplinary framework with generic qualifications and learning outcomes (i.e., translation device to national frameworks).	**Accountability** International transparency, recognition, and mobility of people's qualifications.	**Established definition** **Result-oriented, full-ended, and measurable** Learning outcomes as *'statements of what a learner is expected to know, understand and be able to do at the end of a period of learning'*. Expressed as knowledge and understanding, applying knowledge and understanding, making judgements, communication skills, and learning skills; Four sequential cycle levels - i.e., short, bachelor, master, and doctorate – related to a common credit system, a specific expected workload, and degrees.
Essential Learning Outcomes of Liberal Education and America's Promise	LEAP	2005	Association of American Colleges and Universities	United States of America	**Formal learning;** Meta, holistic and cross-disciplinary framework of generic descriptors of learning outcomes (i.e., translation device to schools and higher education institutions mission, programs, and services);	**Accountability** **Educational, instructional planning and curriculum development** Provide a common framework and a shared sense of direction for students' accomplishment across school and college;	**Alternative definition** **Process-oriented, open-ended, limited measurability** Learning outcomes are intended to build students' working understanding of the world and to foster capacities to be practiced in a continuum. They provide a framework to guide students' cumulative progress and curricular alignment, Outcomes can be achieved in many

Framework	Acronym	Year(s)	Authorship	Region	Scope	Purpose orientation (Proitz, 2010)	Learning orientation and definitions of learning outcome (Proitz, 2010)
						different ways, programmes of study and types of institutions; Learning outcomes are rooted on a 'liberal education' approach – i.e., seeking to empower and prepare individuals to deal with complexity, diversity, and change. Four main dimensions identified: knowledge of human cultures and the physical and natural world, intellectual and practical skills, personal and social responsibility, and integrative learning.	Provide a baseline set of reference points for what students should know and be able to do for the award of higher education degrees; Provides seven general principles of excellence for institutions and educators on effective educational practices on how to help students to achieve the essential learning outcomes.	
European Qualifications Framework for Lifelong Learning	EQF-LLL	2008 2017	European Commission	Europe	**Formal, non-formal and informal learning;** A holistic and cross-disciplinary framework of general qualifications and learning outcomes (i.e., translation device to national frameworks).	**Accountability** International transparency, comparability, and portability of people's qualifications.	**Established definition** **Result-oriented, full-ended, and measurable** Learning outcomes described in terms of *'knowledge, skills and attributes, and their application'*. Make explicit what graduates can *'do, be and know'* on completion of the qualification; Eight sequential levels – the last four levels correspond to the QF-EHEA cycle levels – related to specific credit systems, expected workload and degrees.

Table 2. (Continued)

Framework	Acronym	Year(s)	Authorship	Region	Scope	Purpose orientation (Proitz, 2010)	Learning orientation and definitions of learning outcome (Proitz, 2010)
New Zealand Qualifications Framework	NZQF	2010	New Zealand Qualifications Authority/ New Zealand Government	New Zealand	**Formal learning;** A holistic and cross-disciplinary framework of general qualifications and learning outcomes (i.e., translation device to national frameworks).	**Accountability** Support of national qualification outcomes, recognition, international comparability, and mobility.	**Established definition** **Result-oriented, full-ended, and measurable** Learning outcomes as a taxonomy of what graduates are expected to know, understand and be able to do as a result of learning. They are expressed in terms of knowledge, skills, and application of knowledge and skills; Ten sequential levels – the last four levels correspond to the higher education degrees – related to specific credit systems, expected workload and degrees.
Australian Qualifications Framework	AQF	2011 2013	Australian Qualifications Framework Council/ Australian Government	Australia	**Formal, non-formal and informal learning;** A holistic and cross-disciplinary framework of generic qualifications and learning outcomes (i.e., national qualification framework).	**Accountability** Support for national qualification outcomes, recognition, mobility and underpins regulatory and quality assurance arrangement for education and training.	
Degree Qualifications Profile	DQP	2011	Lumina Foundation	United States of America	**Formal learning;** Meta-, holistic and cross-disciplinary framework of generic descriptors of learning	**Accountability Educational, instructional planning and curriculum development**	**Established definition** **Result-oriented, full-ended, and measurable** Learning outcomes established according to proficiency descriptions expected from

Framework	Acronym	Year(s)	Authorship	Region	Scope	Purpose orientation (Proitz, 2010)	Learning orientation and definitions of learning outcome (Proitz, 2010)
					outcomes (i.e., translation device to higher education institutions mission, programs, and services).	Provides a baseline set of reference points for what students should know and be able to do for the award of higher education degrees; Guide faculty members to articulate and better align institutional student learning outcomes with departmental objects; Guide students in explaining the structure and coherence of the curriculum with a particular emphasis on the interdependence of general education and the major.	a graduate; It is organized in terms of student 'proficiency,' emphasizing the commitment that a student shows to further learning, not merely the attainment of particular knowledge or skill within a specific course or learning experience. Unlike competences, none of the proficiencies can be developed in a single learning experience (e.g., course), but it is a progressive and cumulative deployment of the knowledge and skills that have been practiced and developed across multiple learning experiences and assignments; Organizes learning outcomes into five broad, interrelated categories (i.e., specialized knowledge, broad and integrative knowledge, intellectual skills, applied and collaborative learning, and civic and global learning) within three main degrees (i.e., associate's, bachelor's and master's).

Table 2. (Continued)

Framework	Acronym	Year(s)	Authorship	Region	Scope	Purpose orientation (Prøitz, 2010)	Learning orientation and definitions of learning outcome (Prøitz, 2010)
Knowledge, Skills, and Attitudes, Values and Ethics Framework	KSAVE	2012	Assessment & Teaching of 21st Century Skills/ University of Melbourne, Cisco, Intel and Microsoft	Australia, Finland, Singapore, United States of America, Costa Rica and the Netherlands	**Formal learning;** Meta-, holistic and cross-disciplinary framework of generic descriptors of learning outcomes (i.e., translation device to higher education institutions mission, programs, and services).	**Accountability Educational, instructional planning and curriculum development** Mobilize international educational, political and business communities to transform educational assessment and instructional practice for the twenty-first century as a global priority; Generic recommendations and possible examples to support a large-scale assessment of twenty-first-century learning outcomes.	**Alternative definition Process-oriented, open-ended, limited measurability** Learning outcomes established as knowledge (i.e., the specific knowledge or understanding requirements for each skill), skills (i.e., the abilities, skills and processes that curriculum frameworks are designed to develop in students and which are a focus for learning), and attitudes, values and ethics (i.e., the behaviors and attitudes that students exhibit in relation to each skill); Organizes learning outcomes into four broad, interrelated categories (i.e., ways of thinking, ways of working, tools for working, and ways of living the world); Learning outcomes are seen as progressive and cumulative process within a continuum through school, academic and beyond (e.g., labor market), in which some of them has proven to be difficult to assess.

Framework	Acronym	Year(s)	Authorship	Region	Scope	Purpose orientation (Proitz, 2010)	Learning orientation and definitions of learning outcome (Proitz, 2010)
European Reference Framework of the Key Competences for Lifelong Learning	ERF-LLL	2018	European Commission	Europe	**Formal, non-formal and informal learning;** A holistic and cross-disciplinary framework of generic qualifications and learning outcomes (i.e., translation device to national frameworks).	**Accountability** Educational, instructional planning and curriculum development A reference tool to foster competence development in a lifelong learning perspective. Emphasis on '*learning*' and '*student-centered approach*'; Generic recommendations to support the development of key-competencies regarding learning approaches and environments, support for educational staff and assessment and validation of competence development.	**Alternative definition** Process-oriented, open-ended, limited measurability Competencies are defined as a combination of knowledge (i.e., facts and figures, concepts, ideas or theories already established and supporting the knowledge in a area/subject), skills (i.e., the ability and capacity to carry out processes and use existing knowledge to reach outcomes), and attitudes (i.e., the disposition and mind-sets to act or react to ideas, persons or situations). Competencies are to be translated into frameworks of learning outcomes. Eight key competencies with a flexible understanding, equally important, that overlap and interlock and can be applied in many different contexts and a variety of combinations within a lifelong learning perspective.

For a comprehensive understanding of these categories, please see: Proitz, T. S. (2010). Learning outcomes: What are they? Who defines them? When and where are they defined?. *Educational assessment, evaluation and accountability*, 22(2), 119-137. Available at https://link.springer.com/content/pdf/10.1007%2Fs11092-010-9097-8.pdf.

Table 3. Summary of the Frameworks regarding the Learning Outcomes – Targeted competences and learning outcomes, implementation, and impact

Framework Acronym	Targeted competences and learning outcomes	Implementation	Impact
Tuning	*Instrumental competencies* as cognitive, methodological, technological and linguistic abilities (e.g., analysis and synthesis abilities; organization and planning; oral and written communication; computing skills; information management skills, problem-solving and decision-making) *Interpersonal competencies*, as individual abilities relating to social interaction and cooperation (e.g., critical and self-critical abilities; teamwork; intra- and interprofessional skills; awareness of diversity and multiculturality; and ethical commitment) *Systemic competencies* as abilities and skills concerning whole systems (e.g., capacity for applying knowledge in practice, research skills, capacity to learn; adaptability; creativity; leadership; autonomy; project design and management; initiative and entrepreneurial spirit; concern for quality, and will to succeed)	Approaches to teaching, learning, and assessment of competences based on degree programmes: *teaching* – according to different typologies (e.g., seminar, exercise or laboratory classes or courses; workshops; problem-solving sessions; internship/traineeship); online/distance or e-learning; *learning* – focusing in multiple self-learning activities of different levels of difficulty/complexity, including teamwork problem-solving; oral presentations; peer-assess the work of colleagues; working under time constraints to meet a deadline; communicate questions and findings with other using a variety of media; learn to criticize their work; *assessment* – based on both the material produced by students (e.g., essays, manuscripts of portfolios, knowledge or skill testing, oral presentations;	*In Europe and the USA* (c.f. Birtwistle, Brown & Wagenaar, 2016) General limited progress has been made, and critical expectations have yet to be met. Good practices have been identified albeit the actual implementation of student-centered approach remains elusive. Failure to convince the on-setting players about the necessity and advantages of this paradigm shift Teachers struggle to adjust to new concepts of "learning facilitators" Most teachers make few investments in pedagogical development while when it happens is often too focused on the process Risk of failure of the reform if no additional and continued support is provided to teachers. *In Latin America* (c.f. Beneitone & Yarosh, 2015) Most institutions used this framework to revise and create their curricula, but very few

Framework Acronym	Targeted competences and learning outcomes	Implementation	Impact
		performance of procedures in working settings. *Specific guidelines to teach, learn and assess generic competencies*, namely: a capacity for analyses and synthesis, capacity for applying knowledge in practice, basic general knowledge in the field of study, information management skills, interpersonal skills, ability to work autonomously, elementary computer skills, research skills; *Key-guiding questions for programme design* (e.g., degree profile; learning outcomes; competencies; level; credits and workload; resources), *delivery, maintenance and evaluation* (e.g., monitoring; updating; sustainability and responsibility; organization and information) according to the Bologna reform, *and a checklist for curriculum evaluation* (e.g., educational process; educational outcomes; means and facilities required for program delivery).	implemented the competency-based, student-centered learning cross-university. Most participants do not have a system of credits to assess student's workload Positive attitudes from teachers and students, but unequal perceptions of the degree of implementation regarding assessment (formative vs. summative) and calculation of student's workload (c.f. Buchanan, Yu, Wheelahan, Keating & Marginson, 2010; c.f. Wheelahan, 2011)

Table 3. (Continued)

Framework Acronym	Targeted competences and learning outcomes	Implementation	Impact
CAS	***Knowledge acquisition, construction, integration, and application*** – understanding knowledge from a range of disciplines; connect different knowledge, ideas, and experiences; relating knowledge to daily life; ***Cognitive complexity*** – critical and reflective thinking; effective reasoning; creativity; ***Intrapersonal development*** – realistic self-appraisal, self-understanding, and self-respect; identity development; commitment to ethics and integrity; spiritual awareness; ***Interpersonal competence*** – meaningful relationships; interdependence; collaboration; effective leadership; ***Humanitarianism and civic engagement*** – appreciation of cultural and human difference; a global perspective; social responsibility; a sense of civic responsibility; ***Practical competence*** – pursuing goals; communicating effectively; technological competence; managing personal affairs; managing career development; demonstrating professionalism; maintaining health and wellness; living a purposeful and satisfying life.	Provision of ***Frameworks for Assessing Learning and Development Outcomes*** (FALDOs), designed to enable the assessment and evaluation procedures focusing on student learning and development in each domain or dimension. The framework elements include: ***Theoretical context*** (i.e., theories and theoretical discussions supporting a particular domain or dimension); ***Relevant variables and indicators*** (i.e., specific outcomes, knowledge, skills, abilities, behaviors, and attitudes related to each outcome domain or dimension and useful to measure such learning and development); ***Assessment examples including both quantitative and qualitative methodologies*** (i.e., which quantitative and qualitative methodologies may be used to assess college impacts on specific outcomes, attending to different research/assessment questions, samples, data collection tools, and data analyses techniques); ***Assessment, evaluation, and research tools available in the public domain***	Not applied (i.e., non-existence of studies or reports regarding its impact and implementation results)

Framework Acronym	Targeted competences and learning outcomes	Implementation	Impact
QF-EHEA	**Knowledge and understanding** - theoretical core knowledge in a given academic field; the ability to understand and explain, develop or apply original ideas, master the skills and methods of research associated with that field. *Applying knowledge and understanding* - operationalization of knowledge application in particular settings, and a fluency in the use of increasingly complex data and information; *Making judgments* - within a social and professional context; the ability to identify and use data to formulate responses to well-defined or ill-defined problems; the ability to gather and interpret relevant data to inform judgments considering social, scientific or ethical issues; critical analysis, evaluation, and synthesis of new and complex ideas; *Communication skills* - to adjust the communication to the topics and the audience (i.e., to communicate information, ideas, problems and solutions to both specialist and non-specialist audiences); to clearly communicate their understanding, skills, and activities, to peers, supervisors, and clients; *Learning skills* – engagement in autonomous, lifelong learning; to be able to promote, within academic and professional contexts, technological, social or cultural advancement in a knowledge-based society.	***Assessment of the compatibility of national frameworks with the QF-EHEA:*** By a body(ies) responding to the national ministry for higher education; A transparent link between the national framework qualifications and the cycle qualifications descriptors of the QF-EHEA; The national qualifications are transposed into learning outcomes and linked to ECTS or ECTS compatible credits; The national quality assurance system for higher education refers to the national framework of qualifications and are consistent with the communiqués within the Bologna Process; The national framework and any alignment with the European framework is referenced in all Diploma Supplements; Clear and public identification of the responsibilities of each domestic party in the national framework; Each country should publically certify the compatibility of its framework with the QF-EHEA; The national qualifications should be subject to appropriate systems of quality assurance;	By 2010 only a few EU countries had established a national qualifications framework for higher education, and self-certified it to the QF-EHEA By 2015, only about half of the participating countries (n=39) accomplished it. Some challenges remain, namely regarding the issuing of diplomas, inclusion of non-formal qualifications in national frameworks self-certified against the QF-EHEA, evaluation and recognition process of foreign qualifications (c.f. CEU, 2018)

Table 3. (Continued)

Framework Acronym	Targeted competences and learning outcomes	Implementation	Impact
LEAP	***Knowledge of human cultures and the physical and natural world*** – through the study in the sciences and mathematics, social sciences, humanities, history, languages, and the arts. ***Intellectual and practical skills*** – namely, inquiry and analysis, critical and creative thinking, written and oral communication, quantitative literacy, information literacy, teamwork, and problem-solving. Practiced extensively, across the curriculum, in the context of progressively more challenging problems, projects, and standards for performance; ***Personal and social responsibility*** – a civic knowledge and engagement (local and global), intercultural knowledge and competence, ethical reasoning and action, foundations and skills for lifelong learning. Anchored through active involvement with diverse communities and real-world challenges; ***Integrative learning*** – synthesis and advanced accomplishment across general and specialized studies. Demonstrated through the application of knowledge, skills, and responsibilities to new settings and complex problems.	***Principles for Excellence*** ***Aim high – and make excellence inclusive***: framing the entire educational experience, connecting school, college, work, and life; ***Give students a compass***: focusing each student's plan of study on achieving the essential learning outcomes, and assess progress; ***Teach the arts of inquiry and innovation***: immersing students in analysis, discovery, problem-solving, and communication. Beginning in school and advancing in college; ***Engage the big questions***: driving in the curriculum far-reaching issues – contemporary and enduring – in science and society, cultures and values, global interdependence, the changing economy, and human dignity and freedom; ***Connect knowledge with choices and actions***: preparing for citizenship and work linking learning to real-world problems; ***Foster civic, intercultural, and ethical learning***: emphasizing personal and social responsibility; ***Assess student's ability to apply knowledge***	Not applied (i.e., non-existence of studies or reports regarding its impact and implementation results);

Framework Acronym	Targeted competences and learning outcomes	Implementation	Impact
		to complex problems: use assessment to deepen learning and to establish a culture of shared purpose and continuous improvement; Provision of multiple tools (e.g., case studies, best practices, practical recommendations) to implement and assess the learning outcomes.	
DQP	***Specialized Knowledge*** - what students in any specialization should demonstrate regarding the specialization, beyond the vocabularies, theories, and skills of particular fields of study; ***Broad and Integrative Knowledge*** - asks students to consolidate learning from different broad fields of study (e.g., the humanities, arts, sciences and social sciences); to discover and explore concepts and questions bridging essential areas of learning; ***Intellectual Skills*** - analytic inquiry, use of information resources, engagement with diverse perspectives, ethical reasoning, quantitative and communicative fluency, to make, confront and interpret ideas and arguments from different points of reference (e.g., cultural, technological, political); ***Applied and Collaborative Learning*** - what students can do with their knowledge; to demonstrate their learning by addressing	Several ***testimonials, resources and illustrations of how institutions have been experimenting with the implementation of DQP***. They cover a range of approaches within different categories: Discussion and vetting of the DQP; Clarification and review of learning outcomes; Curriculum mapping; Review of degree proficiencies; Transfer and articulation; Assessment of student learning; Accreditation and strategic planning; Guiding questions, matrixes, rubrics and diagrams for curricular evaluation, planning, assignment development, and assessment.	Provides a systemic view of the educational landscape, because it helps those involved in supporting students to think more concretely about how students move through higher education as a different system. DQP presents a broad and deep impact when implemented as a large-scale change effort, requesting a collaborative effort to reach effectiveness. Presents a broad and deep impact when implemented as a larger-scale change effort, requesting a collaborative effort to reach effectiveness. DQP positive effects expand when the work is connected and builds to existing initiatives, structures, and processes, and when students and their learning are the major focus of the work (c.f. Jankowski & Giffin, 2016).

Table 3. (Continued)

Framework Acronym	Targeted competences and learning outcomes	Implementation	Impact
	unscripted problems in different settings in- and outside the classroom; includes research and creative activities involving both individual and group effort and may include practical skills crucial to the application of expertise; ***Civic and Global Learning*** - recognizes higher education's responsibilities both to democracy and the global community, evidenced through the integration of knowledge and skills concerning public, social, environmental, and economic challenges.		It has the potential to build trust across educational sectors, help foster cohesive educational experiences, and present new ways of thinking about teaching, learning, and assessment (c.f. Marshall, Jankowski & Vaughan III, 2017).
AQF	***Knowledge*** - what a graduate knows and understands, encompassing different dimensions (e.g., depth and broadness of knowledge; the range from concrete to abstract, from segmented to cumulative; and the complexity of knowledge; ***Skills*** - what a graduate can do. Are described in terms of the kinds and complexity of skills and include: cognitive and creative skills involving the use of intuitive, logical and critical thinking; technical skills involving dexterity and the use of methods, materials, tools and instruments; communication skills involving written, oral, literacy and numeracy skills; interpersonal skills and generic skills;	***The implementation handbook with guidelines and monitoring recommendations include:*** ***AQF Qualifications Issuance Policy*** - covering all AQF qualifications and, through the issuance of a statement of attainment, accredited units regardless of where and how they are delivered. ***AQF Qualifications Pathways Policy*** - covering all education and training sectors that issue AQF qualifications and the responsibilities for making qualification pathways accessible to students. ***AQF Qualifications Register Policy*** - covering	***Institutional perception of loss of autonomy*** - Institutional engagement and trust is limited by the framework ambiguity or over prescription; some Institutions prioritize strong relationships with professional/disciplinary bodies to the preserve standards for professional qualifications despite following AQF as a reference point for legitimizing their qualifications; ***Articulation and pathways*** - no improvement expected unless credit policies incorporate considerations of syllabi, assessment, teaching and

Framework Acronym	Targeted competences and learning outcomes	Implementation	Impact
	Application of knowledge and skills - the context in which a graduate applies knowledge and skills (e.g., autonomy, responsibility, and accountability in a predictable/unpredictable context and routine/non-routine tasks; ***Generic learning outcomes*** - the transferrable, non-discipline specific skills a graduate may achieve through learning which have application in a study, work and life contexts. Namely: fundamental skills, such as literacy and numeracy appropriate to the level and qualification type; people skills, such as working with others and communication skills; thinking skills, such as learning to learn, decision making and problem-solving; personal skills, such as self-direction and acting with integrity.	all education and training sectors that issue AQF qualifications and the responsibilities for the provision and management of registers of AQF qualifications and the organizations that issue them. ***AQF Qualifications Type Addition and Removal Policy*** - covering all the education and training sectors that issue AQF qualifications.	learning processes; requirements for a minimum amount of credits to be granted for prior qualifications may lead to institutions' reluctance to provide pathways; there is no requirement for Institutions to demonstrate their active implementation. ***Interaction with a national quality agency*** - increased scrutiny of Masters degrees is likely; which may trigger a change in offerings to improve consistency in content and duration of learning time associated with this qualification; Compliance with AQF qualifications' titles, levels and descriptors may be a greater focus of institutional audits and compliance requirements for self-accrediting higher education institutions than hitherto, thus contributing to a stronger regulatory environment. Learning outcomes descriptors in AQF are highly specified, instead of establishing hierarchies and of qualifications and relationships between them. This requires high contextual

Table 3. (Continued)

Framework Acronym	Targeted competences and learning outcomes	Implementation	Impact
			knowledge of the educational and professional field and technical understanding of the way that outcomes and standards are expressed. (c.f. Buchanan, Yu, Wheelahan, Keating & Marginson, 2010; c.f. Wheelahan, 2011)
KSAVE	*Ways of thinking* - emphasizes the thinking-related knowledge, skills, attitudes, values, and ethics, required for creative, innovative critical, problem-solving and decision-making processes, as well as for metacognition. It comprehends creativity, innovation, relevant reasoning, problem resolution, critical thinking reasoning, self-assessment and self-regulation of the thinking process; *Ways of working* - focus on the communication and teamwork settings that illustrate today's globalized world and workplace needs. It associates knowledge, skills, attitudes, values, and ethics, in interpersonal communication in different settings and forms, including teamwork management and leadership; *Tools for working* - entails the knowledge, skills, attitudes, values, and ethics, that makes possible for individuals to compete, connect and	*Assessment examples and case studies of how the skills might be measured*: creativity and innovation; critical thinking, problem-solving and decision making; learning to learn and metacognition; communication; collaboration and teamwork; information literacy; ICT literacy; local and global citizenship; life and career; personal and social responsibility; *Key challenges and recommendations to assess twenty-first century skills*, including: *to* address models for skill development and new kinds/forms of assessment of those skills; to make students' thinking visible; to ensure accessibility; to account for new ways to communicate (e.g., visual, aesthetic, social media); to foster collaboration and teamwork; to include local and global citizenship (i.e., attend to cultural differences and sensitivities); to ensure the	Not applied (i.e., non-existence of studies or reports regarding its impact and implementation results);

Framework Acronym	Targeted competences and learning outcomes	Implementation	Impact
	collaborate in technology and knowledge-based world market (i.e., information and ICT literacy); *Living the world* - incorporates the knowledge, skills, attitudes, values, and ethics, to manage life and career issues, including global and local citizenship, cultural awareness and competence.	validity and accessibility; to consider the cost and feasibility.	
ERF-LLL	*Literacy competence* - to be able to find, read, understand and interpret information or feelings in both oral and written forms, using visual, sound/audio and digital materials across disciplines and contexts; *Multilingual competence* - to use different languages appropriately and effectively for communication and understanding, with different levels of proficiency in different languages, according to the individual's needs; to use tools appropriately and learn languages throughout life; *Mathematical competence and competence in science, technology, engineering* - including to develop and apply mathematical thinking and insight to solve a range of everyday problems, to use observation and experimentation to explain, identify questions and to draw evidence-based conclusions;	***Example and good practices on how to support the development of key competencies, according to three major challenges***, using a variety of: *Learning approaches and environments:* Developing cross-discipline learning, partnerships between different education levels, training, and learning actors; Fostering early competence development by systematically complementing academic learning with social and emotional learning, arts, and health-enhancing physical activities; To increase learning motivation and engagement; Encouraging learners, teachers, and learning providers to use digital technologies; Developing specific opportunities for entrepreneurial experiences; Developing multilingual competence;	Not applied (i.e., non-existence of studies or reports regarding its impact and implementation results);

Table 3. (Continued)

Framework Acronym	Targeted competences and learning outcomes	Implementation	Impact
	Digital competence - the confident, critical and responsible use of digital technologies for learning, at work, and for participation in society; ***Personal, social and learning to learn competence*** - tackling self-reflection, time management, resiliency, self-learning, supporting physical and emotional wellbeing, and leading to a health-conscious, future-oriented life, empathize and manage conflict in an inclusive context; ***Citizenship competence*** - to act as responsible citizens and to fully participate in civic and social life, based on an understanding of social, economic, legal and political concepts and structures, as well as global developments and sustainability. ***Entrepreneurship competence*** - to act upon opportunities and ideas, and to transform them into values for others; to work collaboratively in order to plan and manage projects that are of cultural, social or financial value. ***Cultural awareness and expression competence*** - understanding and respecting the way ideas and meaning are creatively expressed and communicated in different cultures and through a range of arts and other cultural forms, as well as to have a sense of place or role in society in a variety of ways and contexts.	***Support for educational staff***, namely embedding competence-oriented approaches to education, training and learning; promoting the exchange of experiences, establishing networks, collaboration, and communities of practice; creating innovative practices, taking part in research and making appropriate use of new technologies; fostering the access to innovative tools and materials to enhance the quality. ***Assessment and validation of competence development:*** To translate key competence descriptions into frameworks of learning outcomes and identify suitable tools for diagnostic, formative and summative assessment and validation at appropriate levels; Use digital technologies to capture the multiple dimensions of learner progression); Develop different approaches to assessment and validate non-formal and informal learning	

2.1. Scope

All the frameworks are holistic in nature. They provide cross-disciplinary and general descriptions of learning outcomes for higher education or lifelong learning settings. They serve as a translation device to national qualifications frameworks and university systems. Only Tuning, covering up to 42 subject areas, provides both generic and subject-specific learning outcomes. Some frameworks are structured in sequential and interrelated levels (e.g., bachelor, master and doctorate), the prior learning giving access to the subsequent, while others simply present broad learning domains or dimensions without a predefined sequence or order. Only three frameworks encompass formal, non-formal and informal learning, the formal delivery of education being the most focused on by higher education or university institutions.

2.2. Purpose Orientation

All the frameworks somehow intend to responsibilize higher education institutions in a variety of accountability forms (e.g., political, legal, educational), being purposed in a rationale of transnational or national transparency, recognition, comparability and mobility of learners' experience, qualifications and competencies. That is the essential focus in two frameworks deployed by governmental bodies (e.g., QF-EHEA, AQF), which are constrained to list a set of learning outcomes attending to different cycles or degrees, within a common credit system comprising a specific expected workload or volume of learning (e.g., ECTS) but without an explicit guidance on how to support teaching and learning. Notwithstanding, six frameworks establish this link, providing several recommendations and guidelines for educational, instructional planning and curriculum development (e.g., principles, best practices, approaches to learning, teaching and assessment, support for educational staff).

2.3. Learning Orientation

Six of the frameworks are result-oriented, full-ended, and measurable. That is, they present explicit, predefined and established definitions or statements on what is intended by learning outcomes or competencies at the end of the educational experience, cycle or degree. For example, in the Tuning framework learning outcomes are viewed as "statements of what a learner is expected to know, understand and be able to demonstrate after completion of a learning experience". They are expressed in terms of competencies, presuming a combination of well-defined cognitive and meta-cognitive skills, knowledge and understanding, interpersonal, intellectual and practical skills, and ethical values, set in two sequential cycle levels - bachelor and master -, and four intermediate levels - basic, intermediate, advanced and specialized. Two of the frameworks (i.e., LEAP and ERF-LLL) are process-oriented, open-ended, and with limited measurability. That is, rather than presenting clear and explicit statements about the learning outcomes targeted at the end of the experience, cycle, degree or level, they provide a broad set of competencies or outcomes that overlap and interlock, focusing on the learning process, with a flexible understanding, and without a specific way or form to measure their acquisition. For instance, in the LEAP Framework the learning outcomes intent to *"build students' working understanding of the world and to foster capacities to be practiced in a continuum, from school to college and beyond"* (AAC&U, 2007, 27). Although it provides general indications to guide students' cumulative progress and curricular alignment, the outcomes can be achieved and assessed in many different ways, programmes of study and types of institutions. In LEAP, the learning outcomes are rooted in a 'liberal education' approach, that seeks to empower and prepare individuals to deal with complexity, diversity, and change. The framework does not provide a set of predefined outcomes but presents four broad dimensions which give space for different interpretations and understandings by those who intend to implement it.

2.4. Targeted Competencies and Learning Outcomes

Even though the analyzed frameworks proposed different terminologies and categorizations of competencies and learning outcomes, as well as a variety of prioritization, they reflect mainly (and can be grouped into) four main dimensions: *cognitive, personal, interpersonal* and *citizenship*. All the frameworks embrace the three first dimensions, but fewer give a clear emphasis to the latter (i.e., CAS, LEAP, DQP, KSAVE, ERF-LLL). The *cognitive dimension* encompasses the competencies related to knowledge acquisition and construction, integration, and application processes (in a specific domain, e.g., QF-EHEA, DQP - or broadly, e.g., CAS, LEAP), being translated into skills, attitudes or values, such as (but not limited to) critical, reflective and mathematical thinking, information and digital literacy, creativity, problem solving, ethical reasoning. The *personal dimension* addresses the competencies needed for self-development and lifelong learning, including self-regulation, self-reflection, time management, resiliency, dealing with uncertainty, emotional intelligence, autonomy, responsibility, the capacity to learn, integrity, initiative, and entrepreneurial spirit. The *interpersonal dimension* expresses the competencies involved in relationships and working with others, e.g., written, oral and multilingual communication skills, teamwork, leadership. The *citizenship dimension* is highlighted in some frameworks, clearly as humanitarian and civic engagement competencies, social responsibility, civic and global learning. It implies students to act and be able to appreciate cultural and human differences, to have a sense of civic responsibility, engage with diverse communities, real-world political, civic, social, environmental and economic challenges. On this respect, ERF-LLL is the only framework emphasizing cultural awareness, and specifically on the importance of *"how ideas and meaning are creatively expressed and communicated in different cultures and through a range of arts and other cultural forms"* (CEU, 2018, 12).

2.5. Implementation

This category is strongly related to the purpose orientation (section 2.2.) of each framework. Frameworks focusing into accountability (i.e., QF-EHEA, AQF) more likely provide policy-based recommendations to guide higher education institutions or national bodies during the implementation or assessment of compatibility between these institutions and the national or institutional frameworks. The majority of the frameworks, whose main purpose is to support educational, instructional planning and curriculum development, present a more practical and evidence-based set of guidelines allowing players (staff, teachers and students) to develop effectively (through teaching, learning and assessing) the competencies at stake. However, these guidelines present a variable level of detail across frameworks. There are frameworks providing examples, principles, pathways, implications and good practices (e.g., ERF-LLL, DQP, LEAP, Tuning) directed to the implementation of the whole framework in a general way. Conversely, other frameworks assist with specific theoretical rationale, tools, and standards to implement, teach and assess each domain or dimension of the targeted competencies and learning outcomes (e.g., CAS, KSAVE).

It was not possible to get a perspective on the impact for higher education institutions, staff, teachers, and students that resulted from the implementation of each framework. Even searching in different scientific databases or within the responsible organizations' websites, no studies or reports were found regarding the impact and implementation results of two frameworks (i.e., ERF-LLL, KSAVE). Regarding Tuning, QF-EHEA, DQP, AQF frameworks, the identified factors contributing to a successful implementation included the presence of a policy favorable for change and accountability, with specific indications for higher education; the existence of a monitoring system, institutional guidelines, support and documentation for academics; and financial support. The factors associated with an unsuccessful framework implementation included the resistance from teaching staff or students; the lack of teacher's training; and the complexity of the approach (Beneitone and Yarosh 2015; Birtwistle,

Brown, and Wagenaar, 2016). Despite the positive impact and usefulness of the frameworks acknowledged by educational actors and institutions, specifically by providing a common language for educational actors, a systemic view of the higher education landscape, or in changing teachers and students' attitudes towards the learning (Jankowski and Giffin, 2016; Marshall, Jankowski, and Vaughan III 2017), different levels of implementation were reported and some challenges remain.

In the case of QF-EHEA, those challenges are related to the issuing of diplomas, inclusion of non-formal qualifications in national frameworks, self-certification, evaluation and recognition processes of foreign qualifications (CEU 2018). Other frameworks (i.e., AQF) report problems regarding the institutional perception of loss of autonomy (resulting from ambiguity and over prescription), articulation and pathways (resulting from a no obligation to demonstrate active implementation of pathway policies), and the interaction with national quality agencies (lack of consistency, requirements and regulation) (Buchanan et al. 2010). This requires a high contextual knowledge of the educational and professional field, and technical understanding of the way that outcomes and standards are expressed (Wheelahan 2011). It is not, therefore accessible for all educational communities to build a common understanding.

3. CURRENT STATE AND FUTURE DIRECTIONS TO CLOSE THE COMPETENCE GAP

As seen in the previous section, there has been a continuous and remarkable deployment of learning outcomes frameworks worldwide over the years. Their elaboration reflects a major shift in higher education from a traditional 'teaching paradigm' to a 'learning paradigm'. Benefits of these frameworks include transparency and benchmarking against national and international established standards applied by governmental, professional or regulatory bodies. Besides, they help to link the world of education to the labor market by establishing standards associated with particular qualifications easier to understand by all stakeholders through a common language.

Conversely, different limitations and criticisms have been pointed out to the way these frameworks are currently used. For instance, they are more aligned to satisfy managerial and quality assurance needs, than to serve educational purposes, as it can be featured when looking to their overall purpose and learning orientation. Most frameworks were developed to meet accountability, seeing learning outcomes as result-oriented, full-ended, and measurable with a sense of precision and clarity that could be narrow, and insensitive to students' learning, teaching practices, or different contexts and disciplines. That is, this view of rigorous predefined learning outcomes is somehow opposite to the open, creative and dynamic nature of the learning process and contrary to match the ever-evolving skills demand. For instance, creativity in learning (i.e., students pursuing their own unique and original outcomes) may be threatened when learning outcomes are prescribed even before the learning process has started. Furthermore, students struggle to understand the level of learning required to cover their topic area or to pass assessments. They even might to seek for more detailed learning outcomes in order to know what they should learn precisely to ensure they achieve the targeted grade (i.e., accountability). For more discussion on this topic, see for example the works of Buss (2008), Hussey and Smith (2010), Brooks et al. (2014), or Havnes and Prøitz (2016).

Results from other studies (Lai and Vierring 2012; OECD 2013) suggest that the acquisition of academic competencies may vary across domains, institutions and countries. They are more successfully acquired in some specific contexts than others. Still, the knowledge of the determinants and conditions of these differences has been scarcely analyzed, without giving them the importance they deserve. Instead of investing in standardized measurement for comparability (Altbach 2015), key-questions should focus on how and into what extent academic competencies can be taught and acquired in various fields, types of institutions, and countries. For example, competencies like critical thinking, creativity, domain-specific knowledge are listed as expected learning outcomes in a general way, but the interpretation and assessment behind their meaning may be different between teachers of different countries and cultures (Bali 2015). Also, countries with a strong liberal arts tradition of education, where those competencies have been historically embedded in the curriculum (e.g., USA) may more easily continue teaching and assessing them. The same applies to institutional diversity. Institutions with a more applied or polytechnic nature may have different statements of expected learning outcomes and qualifications (Skolnik 2016).

Some frameworks start to prioritize the development of students' attitudes and dispositions (i.e., not only knowledge and skills). However, the measurement of non-cognitive outcomes is complex and still under-researched. Similarly, the 'citizenship' dimension of learning outcomes has been increasingly valued, but there is a lack of measuring instruments to assess those competencies in higher education, their alignment, transferability, and generalizability to daily life and labor market (Zlatkin-Troitschanskaia, Shavelson, and Kuhn 2015). These issues arise because institutions keep assuming that the function of learning assessment is to determine whether the students have obtained the required credits to graduate, rather than to focus on students' development and follow-up to social and professional contexts. Even among those institutions which offer internships as a commonly used teaching strategy to better prepare students for entering the labor market, most commonly seem to consider these internships as a summative way of assessment (i.e., as a final moment of the educational programme) (Koenen, Dochy, and Berghmans 2015).

Finally, teachers face several difficulties in implementing the learning approaches and methods recommended by the frameworks. Current frameworks provide a wide range of tools, guidelines, recommendations, and support for institutional management, teaching and learning, but most of them fail to anticipate challenges and barriers during implementation (e.g., time pressure, resistance to change, staff development, costs, students' characteristics) (Dragoo and Barrows 2016). For instance, teachers are still resisting and defending their freedom in teaching and, in some institutions, they are more focused on research. On the other hand, the massification of higher education allowed a growing number of students who are not always motivated to learn (but to obtain a final diploma) to access formal education (Serbati 2015).

In an attempt to provide further directions to the successful design, implementation and assessment of learning outcomes frameworks and in order to better build competencies until graduation, we outline different research questions that should be addressed by educational actors:

- How can learning outcomes be more process-oriented and open-ended, and attend to the complex and dynamic nature of learning and of societal changes, serving as insightful teaching and learning resources?
- What are the contextual patterns for an effective institutional change towards a competency-based educational approach?
- How can the transferability and generalizability of learning outcomes be promoted and assessed?
- To which extent can the difficulties and challenges expressed by teachers be minimized and better supported?

REFERENCES

AAC&U (Association of American Colleges and Universities) 2007. *College Learning of the New Global Century.* Washington: AAC&U.

Altbach, P. G. 2015. "AHELO: the Myth of Measurement and Comparability". *International Higher Education* 82: 2–3. doi: 10.6017/ihe.2015.82.8861.

Bali, Maha. 2015. "Critical thinking through a multicultural lens: Cultural challenges of teaching critical thinking" In *The Palgrave Handbook of Critical Thinking in Higher Education*, edited by Martin Davies and Ronald Barnett, 317-334. New York: Palgrave Macmillan.

Beneitone, P., and M. Yarosh. 2015. "Tuning impact in Latin America: Is there implementation beyond design?" *Tuning Journal for Higher Education* 3(1): 187–216. doi: 10.18543/tjhe-3(1)-2015pp187-216.

Birtwistle, T., C., Brown, and R. Wagenaar. 2016. "A long way to go… A study on the implementation of the learning-outcomes based approach in the EU". *Tuning Journal for Higher Education* 3(2): 429–463. doi: 10.18543/tjhe-3(2)-2016pp429-463.

Brooks, S., K. Dobbins, J. J. Scott, M. Rawlinson, and R. I. Norman. 2014. "Learning about learning outcomes: the student perspective". *Teaching in Higher Education* 19: 721–733. doi: 10.1080/13562517. 2014. 901964.

Buchanan, J., S. Yu, L. Wheelahan, J. Keating, and S. Marginson. 2017. *Impact analysis of the proposed strengthened Australian qualifications framework*. Adelaide: Australian Qualifications Framework Council.

Burnette, D. M. 2016. "The renewal of competency-based education: A review of the literature". *The Journal of Continuing Higher Education* 64(2): 84–93. doi: 10.1080/07377363.2016.1177704.

Buss, D. 2008. "Secret destinations". *Innovation in Education and Teaching International* 45: 303–308. doi: 10.1080/14703290802 176246.

Cedefop (European Centre for the Development of Vocational Training). 2015. *Skill shortages and gaps in European enterprises: Striking a balance between vocational education and training and the labour market*. Luxembourg: Publications Office of the European Union. doi: 10.2801/042499.

Cedefop (European Centre for the Development of Vocational Training) 2018. *Insights into skill shortages and skill mismatch: Learning from Cedefop's European skills and jobs survey*. Luxembourg: Publications Office of the European Union. doi: 10.2801/645011.

CEU (Council of the European Union) 2018. "Council Recommendation of 22 May 2018 on key competences for lifelong learning". *Official Journal of the European Union* 61.

Domingues, Caroline (coord.). 2018. *Critical Thinking across European Higher Education Curricula. A European Collection of the Critical Thinking Skills and Dispositions Needed in Different Professional Fields for the 21st Century*. Vila Real: UTAD. http://crithinkedu.utad.pt/en/intellectual-outputs/.

Dobbs, R., A. Madgavkar, D. Barton, E. Labaye, J. Manyika, C. Roxburgh, S. Lund, and S. Madhhav. 2012. *The world at work: Jobs, pay, and skills for 3.5 billion people*. New York: McKinsey & Company.

Dragoo, A., and R. Barrow. 2016. "Implementing competency-based education: Challenges, strategies, and a decision-making framework". *The Journal of Continuing Higher Education* 64(2): 73–83. doi: 10.1080/07377363.2016.1172193.

Eisner, E. W. 1979. *The education imagination. On the design and evaluation of school programs*. New York: Macmillan.

European Commission. 2016. *A new skills agenda for Europe: Working together to strengthen human capital, employability and competitiveness*. Luxembourg: Publications Office of the European Union.

Gagné, R. M. 1974. *Essentials of Learning for Instruction*. Illinois: The Dryden Press Hinsdale.

Havnes, A., and T. S. Prøitz. 2016. "Why use learning outcomes in higher education? Exploring the grounds for academic resistance and reclaiming the value of unexpected learning.". *Educational Assessment, Evaluation and Accountability* 28(3): 205–223. doi: 10.1007/s11092-016-9243-z.

Hussey, T., and P. Smith. 2012. *The trouble with higher education: A critical examination of our universities*. New York: Routledge.

Jankowsky, N. A., and L. Giffin. 2016. *Using the Degree Qualifications Profile to Foster Meaningful Change*. Illinois: National Institute for Learning Outcomes Assessment.

Koenen, A-K., F. Dochy, and I. Berghmans. 2015. "A phenomenographic analysis of the implementation of competence-based education in higher education". *Teaching and Teacher Education* 50: 1–12. doi: 10.1016/j.tate.2015.04.001.

Lai, E. R., and M. Viering. 2012. *Assessing 21st Century Skills: Integrating Research Findings*. New Jersey: Pearson.

ManpowerGroup. 2013. *2013 Talent Shortage Survey: Research Results*. http://bit.ly/ManPower_2SG5Ar5.

Marshall, D. W., N. A. Jankowsky, and T. Vaughan III. 2017. *Tuning Impact Study: Developing Faculty Consensus to Strengthen Student Learning*. Illinois: National Institute for Learning Outcomes Assessment.

Mourshed, M., D. Farrell, and D. Barton. 2013. *Education to Employment: Designing a System that Works*. New York: McKinsey & Company.

OECD (Organisation for Economic Co-operation and Development) 2013. *AHELO feasibility report, volume 2*. Paris: OECD.

Prøitz, T. S. 2010. "Learning outcomes: What are they? Who defines them? When and where are they defined?". *Educational Assessment, Evaluation and Accountability* 22: 119–137. doi: 10.1007/s11092-010-9097-8.

Serbati, A. 2015. "Implementation of Competence-Based Learning Approach: stories of practices and the Tuning contribution to academic innovation". *Tuning Journal for Higher Education* 3(1): 19–56. doi: 10.18543/tjhe-3(1)-2015pp19-56.

Shavelson, R. J. 2013. "On an Approach to Testing and Modeling Competence". *Educational Psychologist* 48(2): 73–86. doi: 10.1080/00461520.2013.779483.

Skolnik, M. L. 2016. "How do quality assurance systems accommodate the differences between academic and applied higher education?". *Higher Education* 71(3): 361–378. doi: 10.1007/s10734-015-9908-4.

Wheelahan, L. 2011. "From old to new: the Australian qualifications framework". *Journal of Education and Work* 24(3-4): 323–342. doi: 10.1080/13639080.2011.584689.

Zlatkin-Troitschanskaia. O., R. J. Shavelson, C. Kuhn. 2015. "The international state of research on measurement of competency in higher education". *Studies in Higher Education* 40(3): 393–411. doi: 10.1080/03075079.2015.1004241.

List of Frameworks

Australian Qualifications Framework (AQF). 2013. https://bit.ly/2tgtvEX.
Degree Qualifications Profile (DQP). 2011. https://bit.ly/29pUtwQ.
Essential Learning Outcomes of Liberal Education and America's Promise (LEAP). 2005. https://bit.ly/2sjg1EW.
European Reference Framework of the Key Competences for Lifelong Learning (ERF-LLL). 2018. https://bit.ly/2W8PkAN.
Framework for Qualifications of the European Higher Education Area (QF-EHEA). 2018. https://bit.ly/2TDrWhU.
Knowledge, Skills, and Attitudes, Values and Ethics Framework (KSAVE). 2012. https://bit.ly/2HngtfS.
Student Learning and Development Outcomes (CAS). 2003. https://bit.ly/2EZVAUc.
Tuning Learning Outcomes and Competences (Tuning). 2000. https://bit.ly/2sLot03.

In: Higher Education Institutions
Editor: Joe Maxwell

ISBN: 978-1-53615-717-8
© 2019 Nova Science Publishers, Inc.

Chapter 3

THE VALIDATION OF THE TOTAL QUALITY MANAGEMENT CONSTRUCT USING CONFIRMATORY FACTOR ANALYSIS

Farooq Miiro[1,*] *and Azam Othman*[2]
[1]Department of Educational Management, Faculty of Education,
Islamic University in Uganda, Uganda
[2]International Islamic University Malaysia, Selangor, Malaysia

ABSTRACT

Purpose: The empirical study sought to validate the structure of total quality management construct with an objective of identifying the current TQM practices employed as perceived by the staff of Islamic University in Uganda.

Design/methodology: A cross sectional survey was employed to solicit data from 361 respondents. This was done through randomization and a confirmatory factor analysis of structural equation modelling technique was employed for data analysis.

---

[*] Corresponding Author's E-mail: miirofarooq@gmail.com.

Findings: The results are in congruent with the earlier findings whereby focus on clients, focus on satisfaction of the workers' needs, process improvement, administrative and technological need were found as sound sub-dimensions of TQM. However the research tool merged with on 17 items compared to the earlier tools used.

Practical implications: The major implication is that enhancement of a survey tool with 17 items which other universities in future studies at the same level can apply to examine the levels of TQM practices at higher education institutions especially in Uganda. University managers and administrators can employ this tool often to examine how well they can reposition themselves in TQM practices. This kind of approach can lead to creation of a more impressing and interesting environment of teaching and learning and at the same time attract high quality personnel from both students and staff at international levels. The four subcontract tool of TQM is imperative for universities to employ since the current times are more emphatic on customer demands and value for money.

Keywords: total quality management, focus on client, workers' needs, process improvement, administrative and technological need, university management

INTRODUCTION

With increased competition for customers in higher education institutions (HEIs) and the influence of globalization tendencies which acts as a back born for shaping world market, the philosophy of total quality management (TMQ) has gained high attention in the recent past due to its significant results towards corporate service and improved organizational performance. It is alluded that organizations that put TMQ into consideration have not only gained reputable positions on the world market but have also given satisfactory results towards their customers (Ali & Shastri, 2010). The objective of TMQ is to help organization towards achievement and provision of continuous rightful services beyond customer expectations and satisfaction.

For instance in higher education institutions there is need for formation of performance indicators, accreditation, quality audit measurement and assessment of programs plus facilities management (Rosa, Sarrico, & Alberto, 2012). However, these efforts cannot be gained if these institutions do not in cooperate into their culture a practice of staff training and systematic review of both the performance and facilities management. Organizations from business sectors that employ similar approaches towards customer satisfaction are normally able to attract employees of standard performance and high qualification. Meanwhile, quality is the cornerstone for survival in the era of competition and this is coupled with the cost and performance in terms of services rendered by these institutions (Singh & Kumar, 2014). TQM is viewed as a multidimensional management aspect with interesting macabre situations to managers and researchers. So if TQM is to be implemented in an academic institution for instance; it poses to resonate that administration would of course need to contemplate on manifold tactics for inspiring its application. Alternatively, if it is a unidimensional, then it should be embedded in a culture with set values with the best choice to apply. The objective of this study is to empirically survey the validity of the views related to TMQ practices. The paper structure is as follows, it starts with the introduction of the forces shaping institutional management style, followed by literature review discussing extensively scholarly views on TQM, hence leading to the articulation of the research problem, followed by conceptual framework of the study. Methodology, sample, data collection and analysis tool using structural equation modelling (SEM). Lastly, discussion of the results is offered, tailed with conclusion, limitation and recommendation for future studies in the area. In addition many organizations seem to be implementing TMQ however due to its complex nature they seem not to be doing it in the best ways hence gaining zero results (Jancikova, 2009). It is upon this basis that this study was designed to examine the literature pertaining to total quality management and at the same time validate its theory and implementation at the Islamic university in Uganda.

LITERATURE

Total quality management can mean translating and understanding customer concerns and needs (Singh & Kumar, 2014). It can also be taken as a management tool used in all processes and functions of organization for the betterment and improvement of quality products and services with an aim of reducing the cost to customer satisfaction (Prajogo & McDermott, 2005). Also Panuwatwanich & Nguyen, (2017) state that for an organization to achieve TQM, there should be focus on customer care, continuous improvement, process orientation, teamwork and empowerment, visionary leadership and management by fact. It is therefore important for HEIs' management to understand that achievement of quality services and products is not something achievable without customer satisfaction. In this case customers play a significant role in shaping the mode of operation and business management in TQM implementation. Thus doing more than customer expectation should be the steering of all institutional activities since these are the people that market the institution to the external forces. For TQM to be implemented smoothly and effectively, it needs institutions to have clear and functioning structure, strategy and culture (Farooq, 2018; Roldán, Leal-Rodríguez, & Leal, 2012) Meanwhile, a study done in India on 600 post graduate (PG) students in a across sectional survey manner by Singh & Kumar, (2014) found out that staff behavior coupled with faculty influence, attitude, tangibles and delivery were the key significant cursor towards quality service delivery in HEIs. In addition, a study done in Vietnam on 104 respondents by Panuwatwanich & Nguyen, (2017) established that TQM has a lot of influence on organizational performance if organizations employ clan and hierarchy rather than marketing culture and adhocracy they would compete favorably on world market especially if clan and adhocracy are given superior attention while laying a conducive environment for TQM implementation. Conversely, in a similar study done in Spain by Roldán, Leal-Rodríguez, & Leal, (2012) on 113 Spanish companies realized that organizations should come up with innovative cultures in order to exceed performance and expected standards to please their customers. It is important for managers of HEIs to adjudicate to themselves that even though HEIs are expensive to run the basic needs and facilities must be provided if they are to continue flourishing on the world market. And this should be done by regular training session and modelling of the staff to show their students the best examples by teaching them accordingly, and at the same time provide guidance for re-sharpening their minds to avoid selfishness and cope with the demands of time. Today many institutions are in a protective manner whereby they emphasize laws to their customers which are also not trained to them often that without caring so much on the environment under which their customers are living. The world gives freedom to customers (students) to think logically and at the same time zoom the solutions that can save humanity from the mega challenges they are facing. For instance; change in values, technological advancement and globalization are some of the determinants that HEIs must study critically and help their citizens understand the dynamics and the ways of getting the best scores out of them for shaping both their lives and their societies (Farooq Miiro, Othman, Sahari Nordin, & Burhan Ibrahim, 2017; Farooq Miiro, 2017; Singh & Kumar, 2014). Managers of higher education should also understand that customers expect their institutions to have highly qualified faculty talented staff with best facilities and infrastructure so as to attain the conducive teaching and learning process (Miiro, Othman, Sahari, & Burhan, 2016). Through these efforts HEIs will be in position to improve on the level of civility and at the same time change the mind set and send well prepared change agents to the community (Zabadi, 2013). Since administrators play a key important role in provision of TQM HEIs authorities should always have quality days and sessions for reminding their staff and other employees on this aspect of management such that they move as coordinated troops towards the change of institutions corporate image, and the general society without therefore such strategies, some institutions will remain insular and useless to the development of their countries (Erturgut & Soyşekerci, 2009; Rosa, Sarrico, & Alberto, 2012; Singh & Kumar, 2014; Zabadi, 2013). Furthermore, in turbulent times managers of HEIs should not give any room for poor services in their institution due to the fact that some customers may not talk against what affects them but in the long run it will cause amenity towards the institutions and in future its graduates may not have the love to bring in their children. Worse still the image of the university will be tainted due to slow handling of some sensitive issues of which their results still may ruin the future existence of the institutional reputation. This can be backed by the view that private institutions are still mushrooming in many parts of the country and at the same time foreign institutions are still set to bridge the gap (Miiro, Othman, Sahari, & Burhan, 2017; Miiro, 2018; Singh & Kumar, 2014). Given to the spectrum of the stiff competition that HEIs are facing today and they are yet to face, it is most likely that institutions with competent talented staff without rigidity coupled with open mindset, with clear direction defined, ready for criticism, swift and flexible in nature and at the same time offer the best services at an affordable cost will survive. It is important to note that in the era when universities are still trusted as service industries, they must be sensitive with the mechanisms that enhance assessment, measurement methods, revenue streams in order to address students concerns and also remain steady first towards shucking the new trends of management (Ambrož & Praprotnik, 2008). Since TQM is a must do HEIs especially in Uganda must cope with the needs of the time for instance; a study done on 190 countries by World Bank revealed that quality products are a must products of higher education since they play a vital role in changing trends in the society (Al-Shobaki, Fouad, & Al-Bashir, 2010). The study examined three sub-constructs of TQM model by using requirements, action, results and the findings reflected that evaluating the systems and approaches used in the management of students' affairs is very important and reflects the level of devotion from management towards provision of high quality services. For the contemporary customer satisfaction, it is important for HEIs to employ dimensions that bring on board positive services and experience that can help achieve efficiently and zoom the image of self-development and while constructing a future developmental plan. Such customers do not require workers who are just enjoying offering services rather they need innovative workforce to show them how to go about certain things in life (Ambrož & Praprotnik, 2008). Also Singh & Kumar, (2014) used faculty, facilities, delivery, reliability, responsiveness, assurance and empathy as dimension for quality services and found that four dimensions were the key impetus for quality performance in HEIs in India. Equally Zabadi, (2013) in his write up employed fitness for the purpose, value for money, transformation, place and accountability, delivery mechanism, tangible elements and physical appearance and raising awareness of TQM practices. And recommended that for credibility purposes, HEIs must reshape themselves and maintain their strength to have weaknesses addressed so as to fit in the new social world order with an intention of addressing the national needs and at the same time respond to the demands of the new realities and opportunities in order to remain relevant. Nevertheless, Al-Bourini, Al-Abdallah, & Abou-Moghli, (2013) employed focus on client, focus on satisfaction of the workers' needs, process improvement and administrative and technological need for competitive advantage and the results revealed that TQM is achievable as long as the culture and direction of the organization are of standard. Gharakhani, Rahmati, Farrokhi, & Farahmandian, (2013) revealed that TQM enhances institutional improvement, stability, this can be done through strategic roadmap and customer satisfaction. Since TQM is a contentious management aspect whose real scale is of different perception among scholars, the current study is designed to establish the current practice of TQM as perceived by the staff at the Islamic university.

From the literature, it can be deduced that TQM is an aspect of management that puts a lot of emphasis on administrative and technological, focus on client needs and satisfaction, satisfaction of the workers' needs, process improvement with sound structures, systems and strategies to enable an organization, its clients and workers feel at home while executing and provision of services. It is therefore important for the management of HE is to ensure that its systems, structures, facilities and their employees are good enough to please the available customers and at the same time work as a basis to attract more from both national and international levels.

Problem Statement

Today TQM has received serious concern and interest from among researchers and managers of organizations both in business and education sectors. Yet, there is no agreed position and clarity on what should be embedded in the concept definition and dimensions. Even though numerous studies have been done on TQM with the objective of establishing the level of its implementation especially in HEIs. For instance; (Al-Bourini et al., 2013; Al-Shobaki et al., 2010, 2010; Ambrož & Praprotnik, 2008; Gharakhani et al., 2013). Nonetheless, their studies pose mixed results that raise more concern on what TQM is and whether institutions are committed to its relevance depending on the location and the dimensions used for its implementation. Meanwhile, in Uganda HEIs and National council for higher education are emphasizing more of quality assurance implementation. However there is scanty information about this particular concept of TQM in HEIs especially in Uganda whereas at the same time things seem not to be working as required (Kayongo, 2010; NCHE, 2010, 2011). Universities in Uganda seem to be working towards this aspect For instance; staff development programs, technology advancement, staff talent development, infrastructural development and ideal means of admission and graduation, meeting with students and their leadership (Basheka, 2008; Bunoti, 2011; Kasozi, Musisi, Nakayiwa, 2003; Kasozi, 2014; Miiro, 2018; Mpaata, 2010; Zeelen, 2012). However, little seems to be achieved due to rigidity, traditional management of students affairs, discontinuation of students, poor facilities management, staff moonlighting, brain drain, unpleasant teaching and learning environment and the dwindling number of students (Beuren & Teixeira, 2014;Escrigas, & Polak, 2011; Miiro, Othman, Sahari, & Burhan, 2016; Miiro, Othman, Sahari Nordin, et al., 2017; Miiro, 2017, 2018; NCHE, 2010). Thus on this basis the current study was designed to establish whether focus on client, focus on satisfaction of the workers' needs, process improvement and administrative and technological need for competitive advantage are implemented as the four-sub dimensions of TQM at Islamic university in Uganda in reference to staff perception.

PURPOSE OF THE STUDY

With increased internationalization and globalization of higher education, total quality management has become one of the imperatives and cornerstones that any university that is to survive in the era of unprecedented occurrences must give due attention and urgency towards its implementation. Universities have no room to continue operating the way they were in the past due to increased forces of demand and customer needs. Thus the purpose of this study was twofold. To survey the extent at which staff self-reported perceptions towards total quality management; and to find out whether the measurement model of TQM is suitable for use at university level.

RESEARCH QUESTIONS

1. Is the self-reported questionnaire of TQM a sub dimensional construct with interrelated factors which focus on the client, focus on satisfying the needs of the workers, process improving, administrative and technological needs of competitiveness?.
2. Is the four-sub-construct factor of TQM survey tool psychometrically plausible in terms of reliability, and valid for both convergent and discriminant validity?

METHOD

Population

The population of the study was composed of staff from both part time and full time staff across the four campuses of the university. However only three campuses were in reach of the study due to logistical issues. The number of staff at the University is 903 from both administrative and academic units.

Sample

The study sample was comprised of 361 staff from both academic and administrative units of the university. 850 questionnaires were dispatched to different campuses of the university however only 361 deemed plausible for further analysis after data screening and cleaning. From the sample 56.9% were male, 43.1% females, academicians were 55.3% administrators were 36.6% those who occupied both positions were 6.8% and office assistants were 1.8%. In terms of work experience less than one year were 10% 1-2 years were 10%, 17% as a percentage for staff who have been in the university for 3-5 years and 62% was a percentage for those who have served for 6 years and above. On age 12.5% was for staff between 20-25 years, 26-30 were 26.3%, 31-35 scored 20.3%, 36-40 were 20.6% and 20.3 were for staff with an age 41 and above. Since the study envisaged to use a robust mechanism of data analysis that is structural equation modelling with an emphasis on confirmatory factor analysis, the attained sample was reasonable enough to offer fit good indices (Albright & Park, 2009; Albright, 2008; Hooper, Coughlan, & Mullen, 2008; Prudon, 2015; Wang, French, & Clay, 2015).

Instrument

To attain a reasonable data, the study employed a self-reported questionnaire with 34 items to measure total quality management construct. The items were chosen from the previous studies and were adapted to fit the interest of the study. The items were segmented to sub-constructs of the hypothesized measurement model as shown below (focus on client with 8 items, focus on satisfying the workers' weeds with 8 items, focus on improving the processes with 5 items, focus on the administrative and technological needs for competitiveness with 15 items) were employed to address the objective of the study. Below Table 1 provides the details of the measurement of each of the construct and items used. A 5 Likert scale employed ranged between strongly disagree, to strongly agree.

DATA ANALYSIS PROCESS AND RESULTS

The study analyzed the data first using exploratory factor analysis with 100 respondents to establish the underlying structure of TQM depending on responses. The findings revealed that Kaiser-Meyer-Olkin Measure of Sampling Adequacy was .933, Bartlett's Test of Sphericity was significant with (χ^2 = 7374.060, df = 561, p = .000). The generated results suggested that further factor analysis was adequate and the sample used deemed reasonable for factorability.

UNDERLYING STRUCTURE OF TOTAL QUALITY MANAGEMENT

Rotation Matrix: Promax with Kaiser Normalization

The results above imply that the respondents' responses showed high levels of total quality management practices. This is because the total variance explained for the four multidimensional of the construct was 54.6% with internal consistency of index of the related items that were generated from the values of Cronbach's Alpha and at the same time exceeded the threshold of .50, the maximum was .884 and the minimum of .703 (Fan & Lê, 2011; Ghasemi & Zahediasl, 2012; Marnburg, 2014; Nunnally, Bernstein, & Berge, 1967; Pallant, 2007).

The four factors generated had no cross loadings and the variance explained by each of the factor was plausible where by focus on client had the highest Eigenvalue of 14.043, while for the focus on improving the processes was 1.853, focus on administrative and technological needs for competitiveness was 1.359 and 1.300 was the value for focus on satisfying the workers' needs respectively.

Table 1.

Code	Dimension/sub-construct	Alpha	Mean	SD	Factor loading
	Focus on Satisfying the Workers' Needs	.836			
FC1	The university works towards qualifying, training and motivating its workers.		3.40	1.31	.585
FC2	Opportunity is given to workers to show their views and constructive critiques		3.42	1.25	.615
FC3	Workers are delegated powers to change in their work performance styles		3.51	1.22	.754
FC4	Sufficient powers are vested in the workers to work for satisfying the clients' needs and desires		3.38	1.21	.706
FC5	Training in the university helps in applying the administrative concepts efficiently and effectively		3.31	1.31	.633
	Focus on Improving the Processes	.856			
FIP4	The university has a plan of reducing on the time of completing the transactions of customers' needs		3.27	1.08	.517
FIP5	University leadership is sensitive towards staff needs and attitudes towards work		2.89	1.35	.680
FIP6	The university has a system designated for studying the market and economical changes		2.81	1.35	.680
FAT2	The university sets a strategic plan and improves and amends it, if necessary		3.68	1.02	.527
FAT3	The university pays attention to the study of the competitors in order to improve its services		3.09	1.28	.731
FAT4	The university management has clear and accurate measurements for performance evaluation.		3.35	1.29	.553
FAT6	The communication means in the university are effective among the employees and clients		3.30	1.17	.555
	Focus on Administrative and Technological Needs for Competitiveness	.884			
FAT7	The university uses financial plans and indicators in quality control		3.32	1.22	.756
FAT8	The university continuously reviews and updates the control methods on quality standards		3.39	1.10	.738
FAT9	The statistical methods in the university contribute to quality control mechanisms		3.14	1.11	.784
FAT10	The university has specified times to complete the clients' transactions and needs		3.38	1.20	.690
FAT12	The university works with quality as a strategic goal seeking to achieve		3.48	3.48	.470
	Focus on Satisfying the Workers' Needs	.703			
FSW2	Opportunity is given to the workers to show their views and constructive critique		3.38	1.20	.744
FSW3	Workers are delegated powers to change in their work performance styles.		3.71	1.13	.621
FSW4	Sufficient powers are vested in the workers to work for satisfying the clients' needs and desires		3.19	1.21	.471

* Extracted from principal component analysis

The Validation of the Total Quality Management Construct ...

Furthermore to test the validity of the sub-constructs of TQM, a confirmatory factor analysis (CFA) was administered and the results of the hypothesized measurement model truly showed that the four-factor construct of TQM was reliable and adequate due to the good fit indices generated from the data of the study as showed in Figure 1 below. The model estimates were within the minimum standards and satisfactory in nature where CMIN 230.595, CFI = .940, RMSEA =.068, Chi-square = 2.713, df = 85. Hence the model of TQM was concordant with the required estimates (Matsunaga, 2010)

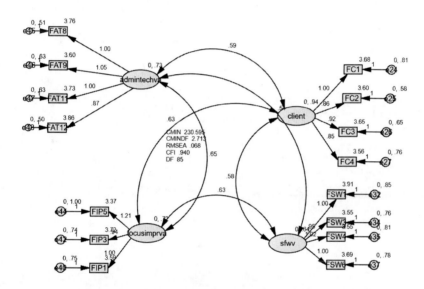

Figure 1. Results for the four-factor construct of TQM.

THE PSYCHOMETRIC OF THE FOUR-FACTOR CONSTRUCT OF TQM SURVEY TOOL

From the findings of the study the psychometric properties of TQM confirm that convergent and discriminant validity exist as shown in Table 2. Along the diagonal the statistics show the average amount of variation (AVE) that TQM explains through its indicators. Thus it is clearly indicated that there is convergent validity measurement. Also the AVE values of each the sub-dimension was higher than 0.5 hence reflecting the convergent validity. In addition, discriminant validity was evident due to the fact that most of the AVE values that correspond with shared values were above the figures in in the diagonal as showed in the table below. Furthermore the inter-correlation among the sub-construct of the construct is reflected that TQM is multidimensional with individual inter-related constructs. Finally, the results exhibited that the composite reliability of the constructs was plausible and ranged between 0.8 (focus on improving process) and Focus on Administrative and Technological Needs for Competitiveness 0.92.

Table 2.

Dimension	1	2	3	4
AD	0.71	0.5	0.86	0.69
CL	0.71	0.7	0.59	0.88
SFW	0.83	0.75	0.73	0.56
FOC	0.93	0.77	0.94	0.7
Composite Reliability	**0.92**	**0.74**	**0.82**	**0.8**

Note. Showed lengthways in the diagonals are average variance extracted (AVEs) of every sub-dimension; underneath the diagonal is the correlation matrix; and overhead the diagonal is the shared variance matrix.

DISCUSSION

From the results above it can be observed that TQM construct is unidimensional in nature in that it packages different practices for managers of institutions to use and for this reason, the study confirms and at the same time extends the previous findings to the level of university management in Uganda. This is evidenced with 54.6 total variance explained by the four inter-related factors of the TQM in reference to the self -reported questionnaire that examined the staff perceptions at the Islamic University in Uganda. The findings are in agreement with the Mosaad Saud Al-Otaibi, (2014) who used regression and found that training and education customers focus, information analysis, continuous improvement management of process and top management commitment are towards total quality achievement in education institutions. Furthermore the study found out that the reliability of the four constructs of the TQM construct were above the threshold of 0.5 and this is because the highest valued Cronbach alpha scored was .884 and the lowest was .703. The results from data analysis showed support for both convergent and discriminant valid of the TQM survey tool employed. This is attributed to the fact that the AVEs of all the four sub-dimensions were above the minimum requirement yet the inter-correlation among the unidimensional practices of TQM was satisfactory. Therefore, the survey tool employed was plausible and adequate enough for future use since 17 items emerged useful for measuring the four TQM practices at university level.

CONCLUSION

The study contributed practically by enhancing a survey tool with 17 items that others universities and future studies can apply to examine the levels of TQM practices at higher education institutions especially in Uganda. University managers and administrators can employ this tool often to examine how well they can reposition themselves in TQM practices so as to create a more impressing and interesting environment of teaching and learning and at the same time attractive high quality personnel from both students and staff at both national and international levels. The four subcontract tool of TQM is imperative for universities to employ since the current times are more emphatic on customer demands and value for money.

Despite the significant results of the study, there were limitations, first of all the sample was homogenous in nature and it was inclined on one university this means that if other studies are on conducted in other sister universities results may differ depending on the level and locality of the institution. Furthermore the study did not go deeper to examine the causal relationship of demographic factors due to time and technicalities involved in the whole process of the analysis.

In conclusion the study extends the readers understanding in relation to total quality management at university level. The findings therefore are imperative in reshaping the current practice of TQM at university level in order to help universities cope with the demand of the time.

LIMITATIONS OF THE STUDY

The study was a cross sectional survey in nature therefore it could not reach all the campuses and the target staff. However, another study can be done in a longitudinal manner to establish whether varying results can be attained.

The study was quantitative in nature therefore it could not go in depth and dig out some issues related to TQM practices at Islamic University in Uganda.

REFERENCES

Al-Bourini, F. A., Al-Abdallah, G. M. & Abou-Moghli, A. A. (2013). Organizational Culture and Total Quality Management (TQM). *International Journal of Business and Management*, *8*(24), 95–106. https://doi.org/10.5539/ijbm.v8n24p95.

Albright, J. J. (2008). *Confirmatory Factor Analysis using Amos*, LISREL, AND MPLUS.

Albright, J. J. & Park, H. M. (2009). *Confirmatory Factor Analysis using Amos, LISREL, Mplus, SAS/STAT CALIS**, *4724*(812).

Ali, M. & Shastri, R. (2010). Implementation of total quality management in higher education. *Asian Journal of Business Management*, *2*(1), 9–16.

Al-Shobaki, S. D., Fouad, R. H. & Al-Bashir, A. (2010). The Implementation of Total Quality Management (TQM) for The Banking Sector in Jordan. *Jordan Journal of Mechanical and Industrial Engineering*, *4*(2), 304–313. https://doi.org/10.5296/ijim.v1i1.771.

Ambrož, M. & Praprotnik, M. (2008). Organisational Effectiveness and Customer Satisfaction. *Organizacija, 41*(5), 161–173. https://doi.org/10.2478/v10051-008-0018-2.

Basheka, B. C. (2008). *"Value for Money and Efficiency in Higher Education": Resources Management and Management of Higher Education in Uganda and its Implications for Quality Education Outcomes*, (September).

Beuren, I. M. & Teixeira, S. A. (2014). Evaluation of Management Control Systems in a Higher Education Institution with the Performance Management and Control. *Journal of Information Systems and Technology Management, 11*(1), 169–192. https://doi.org/10.4301/S1807-17752014000100010.

Bunoti, S. (2011). The Quality of Higher Education in Developing Countries Needs Professional Support. *22nd International Conference on Higher Education.* ..., (Okwakol 2009). Retrieved from http://www.intconfhighered.org/FINAL Sarah Bunoti.pdf.

Cristina, Escrigas. & Eva Egron Polak, O. J. (2011). *Development By Higher Education Institutions In Sub-Saharan Africa Survey Report*.

Erturgut, R. & Soyşekerci, S. (2009). The problem of sustainability of organizational success in public educational institutions: a research on the education administrators in Turkey. *Procedia - Social and Behavioral Sciences, 1*(1), 2092–2102. https://doi.org/10.1016/j.sbspro.2009.01.368.

Fan, S. & Lê, Q. (2011). Developing a Valid and Reliable Instrument to Evaluate Users' Perception of Web-Based Learning in an Australian University Context. *Journal of Online Learning and Teaching, 7*(3), 366–379. https://doi.org/10.2427/13.

Farooq, M., Othman, A., Nordin, M. S. & Ibrahim, M. B. (2016). A Measurement Model of Talent Management Practices Among University Staff in Central. *Journal of Positive Management, 7*(3), 3–19.

Gharakhani, D., Rahmati, H., Farrokhi, M. R. & Farahmandian, A. (2013). Total Quality Management and Organizational Performance. *American*

Journal of Industrial Engineering, 1(3), 46–50. https://doi.org/10.12691/ajie-1-3-2.

Ghasemi, A. & Zahediasl, S. (2012). Normality tests for statistical analysis: A guide for non-statisticians. *International Journal of Endocrinology and Metabolism*, 10(2), 486–489. https://doi.org/10.5812/ijem.3505.

Hooper, D., Coughlan, J. & Mullen, M. R. (2008). " Structural Equation Modelling: Guidelines for Determining Model Fit Structural Equation Modelling: Guidelines for Determining Model Fit. *The Electronic Journal of Business Research Methods*, 6(1), 53–60. https://doi.org/10.1037/1082-989X.12.1.58.

Hoyle, R. H. (2000). ANALYSIS.

Jancikova, A. (2009). Tqm and Organizational Culture As Significant Factors in Ensuring Competitive Advantage : a Theoretical Perspective. *Economics and Sociology*, 2(1), 80–95.

Kasozi, A. B. K., Musisi, N. B., Nakayiwa, F. A. B. & S. K. (2003). *The Uganda Tertiary/Higher Education Unit Cost study*. Kampala: Makerere Institute of Social Research.

Kasozi, A. B. K. (2014). Trends in Higher Education Regulation in sub-Saharan Africa. *International Higher Education*, 75(75), 1–5.

Kayongo, P. M. (2010). *E - Learning Services vs. Physical Education Institutions; Which way to go in financial terms . NCHE*.

Maria, J. Rosa., Claudia, S. Sarrico. & Alberto, A. (2012). *Implementing Quality Management systems in Higher Education Institutions*. Slavka Krautzeka.

Marnburg, E. (2014). Testing the Validity and Reliability of the Levels of Self-Concept Scale in the Hospitality Industry. *Journal of Tourism and Recreation*, 1(1), 37–50. https://doi.org/10.12735/jotr.v1i1p37.

Matsunaga, M. (2010). How to Factor-Analyze Your Data Right: Do's, Don'ts, and How-To's. *International Journal of Psychological Research*, 3(1), 97–110. https://doi.org/10.4090/juee.2008.v2n2.033040.

Miiro F, Othman, A., Sahari, M. & Burhan, M. (2016). A Measurement Model of Talent Management Practices Among University Staff in Central. *Journal of Positive Management*, 7(3), 3–19.

Miiro, F. (2017). Holistic Personality Development of Youth Through Higher Education Using The Prophetic Practices. *Australian Journal of Humanities and Islamic Studies Research (AJHISR)*, 3(1), 1–5.

Miiro, F. (2018). An Exploratory Factor Analysis for Validation of a Measurement of Organizational Excellence Construct among Universities in the Central Region of Uganda. *Interdisciplinary Journal of Education*, Vol. *1*, No. 1, May 2018, *1*(1), 40–61. https://doi.org/ISSN 2616-9096. Available at: <http://journals.iuiu.ac.ug/index.php/ije/article/view/37.

Miiro, F., Othman, A., Sahari, M. & Burhan, M. (2016). A Measurement Model Of Talent Management Practices Among University Staff In Central. *Journal of Positive Management*, 3–19.

Miiro, F., Othman, A., Sahari, M. & Burhan, M. (2017). Examining Organizational Health Practices Among Universities. *Journal of Positive Management, Vol. 8*, (No. 2, 2017), 69–86.

Miiro, F., Othman, A., Sahari Nordin, M. & Burhan Ibrahim, M. (2017). *Analysing the Relationship Between Sustainable Leadership, Talent Management and Organization Health As Predictors of University Transformation*, *32*(1), 32–50. https://doi.org/10.12775/JPM.2017.003.

Mosaad Saud Al-Otaibi, F. (2014). Role of Exploratory Factor Analysis Applicability of TQM Practices on the Items of Quality Culture in the Kingdom of Saudi Arabia. *International Journal of Business and Management*, *10*(1), 136–143. https://doi.org/10.5539/ijbm.v10n1p 136.

Mpaata, A. K. (2010). *University competitiveness through quality assurance: The challenging battle for intellectuals*. Kampal.

Multivariate Data Analysis. (2010). (7th ed.). Prentice Hall, Upper Saddle River, New Jersey. Retrieved from http://studentsrepo.um.edu.my/3216/6/Chapter_3.pdf.

NCHE. (2010). *The state of higher education and training in Uganda 2011: a report on higher education delivery and institutions*. Kampala.

Retrieved from http://www.unche.or.ug/wp-content/uploads/2014/04/The-State-of-Higher-Education-2011.pdf.
NCHE. (2011). *National Council for Higher Education.*
Nunnally, J. C., Bernstein, I. H. & Berge, J. M. T. (1967). (1967). *Psychometric theory.* New York: McGraw-Hill., *226.* https://doi.org/10.5014/ajot.2013.007625.
Pallant, J. (2007). SPSS survival manual. *Journal of Advanced Nursing, 36*(3), 478–478. https://doi.org/10.1046/j.1365-2648.2001.2027c.x.
Panuwatwanich, K. & Nguyen, T. T. (2017). Influence of Organisational Culture on Total Quality Management Implementation and Firm Performance: Evidence from the Vietnamese Construction Industry. *Management and Production Engineering Review, 8*(1), 5–15. https://doi.org/10.1515/mper-2017-0001.
Prajogo, D. I. & McDermott, C. M. (2005). The relationship between total quality management practices and organizational culture. *International Journal of Operations & Production Management, 25*(11), 1101–1122. https://doi.org/10.1108/01443570510626916.
Prudon, P. (2015). *Confirmatory factor analysis: a brief introduction and critique,* (August 2013).
Roldán, J. L., Leal-Rodríguez, A. L. & Leal, A. G. (2012). The influence of organisational culture on the total quality management programme performance. *Investigaciones Europeas de Direccion Y Economia de La Empresa, 18*(3), 183–189. https://doi.org/10.1016/j.iedee.2012.05.005.
Singh, G. & Kumar, M. (2014). Exploratory Factor Analysis of Service Quality. *GE-International Journal of Management Research, 14*(8), 2–11.
Suhr, D. D. Ph, D. (n.d.). *Exploratory or Confirmatory Factor Analysis?,* 1–17.
Wang, X., French, B. F. & Clay, P. F. (2015). Convergent and Discriminant Validity with Formative Measurement: A Mediator Perspective. *Journal of Modern Applied Statistical Methods, 14*(1), 83–106. https://doi.org/10.22237/jmasm/1430453400.
Woman, Y. (n.d.). Visit to. *Homo.*

Zabadi, A. M. A. (2013). Implementing Total Quality Management (TQM) on the Higher Education Institutions – A Conceptual Model. *Journal of Finance and Economics*, *1*(1), 42–60.

Zeelen, J. (2012). Universities in Africa: Working on Excellence for Whom? Reflections on Teaching, Research, and Outreach Activities at African Universities. *International Journal of Higher Education*, *1*(2), 157–165. https://doi.org/10.5430/ijhe.v1n2p157.

In: Higher Education Institutions
Editor: Joe Maxwell

ISBN: 978-1-53615-717-8
© 2019 Nova Science Publishers, Inc.

Chapter 4

MEASURING AND EXPLAINING THE PRODUCTION EFFICIENCY OF HIGHER EDUCATION INSTITUTIONS WITH AN APPLICATION TO THE PUBLIC UNIVERSITIES OF SPAIN

Manuel Salas-Velasco[*]
University of Granada, Department of Applied Economics
Campus Cartuja, Granada, Spain

ABSTRACT

Increasing efficiency and productivity in the higher education systems should be at the core of the governments' policy agendas in this time of constrained resources. Expenditure on higher education in the OECD countries accounts for a significant share of public spending. Knowing whether or not public higher education institutions optimize

---
[*] Corresponding Author's E-mail: msalas@ugr.es.

their resources in production is, therefore, an important education policy issue. This chapter begins by exploring the methodology for measuring efficiency in the higher education context. By using several inputs and outputs at the institutional level, we can identify the most technically efficient institutions that may work as a benchmark in the sector. Next, the chapter focuses on a deeper understanding of the efficiency measurement and its determinants of the higher education institutions of Spain.

1. INTRODUCTION

The evaluation of activities of higher education institutions (HEIs) is vital for judging the degree to which resources made available to the higher education sector are being used efficiently to obtain desired outcomes. However, the evaluation of HEIs' activities is complex, and the perspective adopted depends on the aims of the assessment (Palomares-Montero & García-Aracil, 2011). To assess institutional performance, considerable efforts have been undertaken to produce quantitative measures of achievement called performance indicators (Ball & Halwachi, 1987). Although it is difficult to obtain valid and reliable data, and the results of evaluation processes depend on the quality of the information available (Palomares-Montero & García-Aracil, 2011).

The use of performance indicators for assessing the efficiency of public services is continuously increasing (Propper & Wilson, 2003). Citizens are demanding that governments be made more accountable for what they achieve with taxpayers' money (Curristine et al., 2007). As a means of encouraging accountability, performance indicators and rankings in higher education is one approach to trying to achieve more efficient use of taxpayers' money (Johnes, 2016). Furthermore, governments around the world have been faced with increasing pressure on their finances, giving rise to the need to operate universities with a higher degree of efficiency (Abbott & Doucouliagos, 2003). In the UK, the use of performance indicators in the higher education sector — such as labor market destinations, completion rates, or achievement rates — has long been recognized, and they have served as the basis for resource allocation to the

UK higher education sector (Johnes, 2016). Australia has also used performance-based schemes to fund research and research training.[1] The idea of linking resource allocation to performance is that universities that are efficient at transforming educational inputs into results should receive more resources than those that are inefficient.

The literature has proposed several methods for evaluating the activities of universities, but there is intense debate over which are the most appropriate ones. From an economic point of view, discussions on performance have focused on outputs and how inputs and processes produce them (Hazelkorn et al., 2018). However, HEIs are multi-product firms with complex production processes, so that indicators based on simple ratios (and rankings which utilize these ratios) are unlikely to capture the accurate picture of performance (Johnes, 2016). As techniques have developed to capture performance in a multi-output multi-input production framework, it has become possible to develop more sophisticated indicators. Performance indicators should ideally represent the efficiency with which HEIs transform inputs into outputs. For example, how much output universities could produce from given inputs (known as an output-oriented approach). In practice, Data Envelopment Analysis (DEA) and other related non-parametric techniques have been the most used methodologies for measuring the efficiency in the context of higher education (e.g., Abbott & Doucouliagos, 2003; Agasisti & Dal Bianco, 2009; Agasisti & Wolszczak-Derlacz, 2015; Halkos et al., 2012; Johnes, 2006; Tyagi et al., 2009; Wolszczak-Derlacz & Parteka, 2011). By using several inputs and outputs at the institutional level, we can identify the most (technically) efficient institutions that may work as a benchmark in the sector. DEA gives efficiency scores as summary efficiency measures of individual performance and those institutions that reach a score equal to 1 are considered (technically) efficient.

Performance indicators have also been used in higher education to rank universities. With the emergence of international rankings, such as *the*

---

[1] See https://education.gov.au/research-block-grants.

Shanghai academic ranking of world universities,[2] HEIs around the world are now worried about improving their worldwide reputation and positioning themselves well in those rankings. Making efforts to compete for a top place in these "world-class" league tables has affected, for example, how universities in the Asian countries are governed (e.g., Yang, 2003). The National University of Singapore (NUS) presents itself as a model case study of how emerging universities successfully construct global identities to position themselves as world-class (Xavier & Alsagoff, 2013).[3] Also, previous studies of the impact of global rankings have found that Australian universities attach great importance to them and are among the most likely in the world to want to improve their position (Sheil, 2016). A high rank enhances visibility and helps create a brand (Hazelkorn, 2015b). Being international leaders assure universities not only higher revenues from research contracts but also graduate degrees. As tuition fees and research grants are the most significant income streams in universities' budgets, having top academics and outstanding reputation has become a prerequisite for financial sustainability (Koryakina et al., 2015). Exporting higher education services by recruiting overseas students is an integral facet of internationalization of higher education (Ng, 2011). International students continue to rate reputation and position in rankings as decisive determinants in their choices of the institution, program, and country (Hazelkorn, 2015a). This is particularly true for Asian students who may seek employment in their home country upon graduation (Hazelkorn, 2015b). Also, a policy of merging HEIs is being rolled out in China in the belief that global rankings of domestic HEIs can be favorably affected (Shin & Toutkoushian, 2011).

This chapter focuses on DEA as a valuable technique for efficiency measurement of HEIs; a technique that also yields a valid ranking of HEIs. Previous studies such as Bougnol and Dulá (2006) have demonstrated that DEA produces an assessment that matches closely the one provided by

---

[2] Academic Ranking of World Universities (ARWU), Shanghai Jiao Tong University, China, 2003.
[3] Position #85 in ARWU 2018.

acknowledged experts; DEA, however, minimizes the amount of subjectivity needed for the analysis. In the next section, we describe the production process of HEIs and we define the concept of efficiency. Next, we explain a two-stage methodology for measuring (first stage) and explaining (second stage) the efficiency of HEIs; in particular, a non-parametric approach (first stage) and a bootstrapped-truncated regression (second stage). Although the theoretical developments of this methodology have been substantial in the last two decades since Simar and Wilson's (2007) work, its practical implementation has not been possible until recently thanks to programs such as STATA. The fourth section applies the previous methodology to the Spanish public universities as a practical illustration. The article ends with a section of conclusions.

2. EXPLAINING THE PRODUCTION PROCESS OF HIGHER EDUCATION INSTITUTIONS

The economic theory of production looks at the activity of an organization mainly as a production process that transforms inputs (such as capital and labor) into outputs (products). The input-output approach applied to education production is a simplified conceptual framework that views higher education as a process that transforms educational inputs into educational outputs (Cave, 1997). Figure 1 shows this approach. Universities are multi-product firms that produce multiple outputs from multiple inputs (Cohn et al., 1989). Let us focus first on the entries into the higher education system. Typically, as educational inputs we have:

- Labor input (academic and non-academic staff).
- Capital input (buildings and grounds…).
- The total number of (under)graduate students.
- Library books, lab equipment, computers, …

Second, even though outputs in higher education may be ill-specified and poorly measured, the outputs of HEIs are broadly grouped into teaching, research, and services (Ahn & Seiford, 1993). In Figure 1, universities' traditional missions of teaching and research have been considered along with universities' third mission activities (consultancy to public and private organizations, etc.). In this regard, we should clarify that there is no singular definition of what "third mission" means. It can be broadly defined as the third role beyond teaching and research that centers specifically on the contribution to regional development or as a wide range of activities involving the generation, application and exploitation of knowledge and other university capabilities outside academic environments (Koryakina et al., 2015). The engagement of universities in entrepreneurship and business-related activities might be seen as one of the primary strategies adopted by universities in recent years (Gulbrandsen & Slipersæer, 2007).

In this framework of educational production, it is essential to measure and explain the efficiency of the higher education system. The term "efficiency" is a concept of economic analysis indicating no waste of resources in economic activity. A common approach distinguishes between internal and external efficiency. Internal or production efficiency refers to how resources are used in production. In turn, internal efficiency can be technical or economic. Technical efficiency reflects the ability of the firm to produce the maximum amount of output (product) from a set of resource inputs, given the technology (output-orientation).[4] A production process is also efficient if a given quantity of output cannot be produced with fewer inputs (input-orientation); it is said to be inefficient when another feasible process exists which, for any given output, uses fewer inputs (Rodríguez-Ferrero et al., 2010). In the evaluation of the efficiency of the higher education system, if HEIs are achieving the best possible production (outputs) in a given period, with existing technology and using all available inputs – and resources are at their best use – then the system makes

---

[4] Technology, in the sense of the economic theory, refers to the known ways of transforming inputs into outputs.

efficient use of scarce resources. For example, technically efficient universities are not able to deliver more teaching plus research output (without reducing quality) given its current capital, labor, and other inputs (Abbott & Doucouliagos, 2003).[5] Again, this is the efficiency in production or internal efficiency from the technical point of view.[6] On the other hand, external efficiency is achieved if the goods and services produced efficiently in the economy are valued by society. In the case of HEIs, external efficiency implies that the results of educational processes are desirable for society (social utility).[7] Sound management should be based not only on efficient use of resources but also on the impact of results achieved: the outcomes from higher education most valued by society.

Why are some universities more efficient than others converting resources into results? The influence of process and contextual (environmental) variables on production efficiency has been a significant topic of economic research especially for managers and policy makers (e.g., Banker & Natarajan, 2008). In principle, the process variables are under the control of the HEIs. Graduation rates, for example, can be improved by more effective teaching delivery or by lowering standards (so-called "grade inflation") (Johnes, 2016). On the other hand, environmental variables refer to those factors over which HEIs have little or no control to increase the efficiency of the educational production process such as the introduction/increase of undergraduate tuition fees. For example, Beneito et al. (2016), using data from a sample of Spanish students at the University of Valencia, showed that students reacted to the increase in regional tuition fees with a more considerable effort that translated into better grades and a drop in repetition rate.[8]

---

[5] Efficiency requires a knowledge of the outputs of universities, inputs going into those outputs, and the production relationship between them (Johnes & Taylor, 1990).

[6] Closely related to the analysis of education production is the study of education costs. However, the study of the production process from an economic point of view is outside the scope of this paper.

[7] For example, it would be useless to produce many theoretical physicists efficiently if society does not need them.

[8] In Spain, the educational policy is decentralized at the level of *Comunidades Autónomas* that are regions with one or more provinces. An important feature of the Spanish system of

Finally, it is worth highlighting two situations of inefficiency that the higher education systems must face and eliminate, especially in the public sector. On the one hand, when the duration of the education production process is longer than planned. In other words, when students need more time than scheduled to finish their studies. In this regard, Lassibille and Navarro (2011) found that less than 40% of graduates at the University of Málaga (Spain) completed their degrees within the minimum degree period. On the other hand, the dropouts of (under)graduate students. Research is now increasingly focused on student persistence and completion both for equity and efficiency reasons. Poor academic productivity is the prelude of dropouts at HEIs.

3. EFFICIENCY MEASUREMENT AND ITS DETERMINANTS: A TWO-STAGE METHODOLOGY

As we said in the introduction, this chapter aimed to measure the efficiency of universities as a performance indicator in higher education. For this purpose, we need to summarize first in a performance measure the production process which was described in Figure 1.[9] Non-parametric techniques such as DEA allowed us to do that. According to Nunamaker (1985, p. 51), the principal strength of DEA "lies in its ability to combine multiple inputs and outputs into a single summary measure of efficiency without requiring specification of any a priori weights." In our study, the efficiency score given by DEA for each university of a sample is an indicator of how well a university is transforming its resources into results. If the score is different than 1.0, the unit under evaluation is inefficient. A university is efficient if its efficiency score is 1 and all slacks are zero.

---

higher education is that public universities can charge tuition fees, which are the same for all public universities in the same region.

[9] Internal or production efficiency.

An advantage of DEA compared to the parametric alternatives is the wealth of managerial information provided by the technique (Johnes, 2006).[10] The outcome of any DEA, in addition to efficiency scores, is a list of the "peers" which each inefficient producer should ideally emulate to become efficient. Moreover, the efficiency scores given by DEA for each university are incorporated as a dependent variable in a regression to identify those factors that may influence the efficiency with which universities use resources to produce outputs.

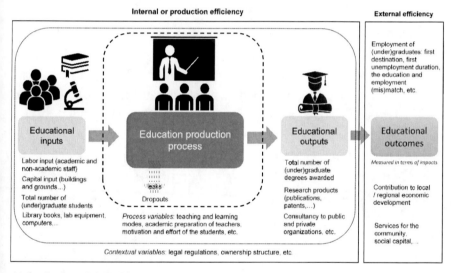

Author's own elaboration.

Figure 1. The higher education production process.

The identification of factors that explain differences in efficiency across HEIs is essential for improving universities' results.

---

[10] In order to measure the efficiency of the higher education sector, we must consider multiple inputs and multiple outputs. The latter is not possible with parametric methods such as stochastic frontier analysis (SFA).

On the one hand, we should think about those factors under control by the decision-makers (management variables).[11] On the other hand, we should take into account the impact of variables beyond their control, that is, environmental factors.[12] Generally, the actual inputs and outputs belong in the DEA (first stage) while factors explaining the efficiency with which inputs produce outputs belong in the regression (second stage) (McMillan & Datta, 1998). Unfortunately, the division between resource inputs and management/environmental variables is not always distinct.

3.1. First Stage: Measuring the (in)Efficiency

In Microeconomics, a production function is a mathematical relationship that indicates the highest output that a firm can produce for every specified combination of inputs — the physical relationship between inputs and output — while holding technology constant at some predetermined state. The microeconomic analysis assumes that the firm operates on its production possibility frontier. However, in practice, this ideal frontier is not observed. What the analyst does is build a production frontier based on the "best practices" observed for a sample of producers. The efficient units in DEA are the most efficient of those observed, not in comparison to some ideal; thus, the DEA efficient group is that subset demonstrating the "best practices" among a group of operating units (McMillan & Datta, 1998).

DEA was introduced by Farell (1957) and extended by Charnes et al. (1978), Färe et al. (1994) and Färe and Primont (1995), among others. DEA estimates a piece-wise linear production function relative to which the efficiency of each firm or decision-making unit (DMU) can be measured.[13] In practice, we need data on input and output quantities of the

---

[11] Process variables in Figure 1.
[12] Contextual variables in Figure 1.
[13] We would like to avoid the exposition of the technical details involved since DEA is well established in the literature. See, among others, Emrouznejad et al. (2008), Liu et al. (2013), Seiford (1997), and Zhu (2016).

DMUs in our sample to construct this frontier surface. This frontier surface is constructed by the solution of a sequence of linear programming problems — one for each institution in the sample —. The degree of technical inefficiency of each DMU is measured by the distance between the observed data and the frontier.

DEA can be either input-orientated or output-orientated. In the input-orientated case, DEA looks for the maximum possible proportional decrease in input usage, with production levels held constant. In the output-orientated case, DEA seeks the maximum proportional increase in production with input levels held fixed. The two measures offer the same technical efficiency scores when constant returns to scale (CRS) technology applies, but scores are different when variable returns to scale (VRS) are assumed. In the context of higher education, we can use DEA to measure how efficiently educational inputs are being used by universities to maximize their teaching and research outputs. Since universities are financed mainly by governments, it seems reasonable to assume that the objective of the institutions is orientated towards obtaining the best results by the resources available to them (and technology).

DEA has the ability not only of taking into account multiple inputs and outputs, which is the crucial consideration in choosing this methodology, but also: i) it does not require an explicit a priori determination of the production function, and ii) it does not necessarily require information on prices. In short, the programming approach is non-parametric; this enables it to avoid confounding the effects of misspecification of the functional form (of both technology and inefficiency) with those of inefficiency.[14] Under variable returns to scale (output-oriented), the following linear programming problem must be solved n times (once for each DMU)

---

[14] Some weaknesses of DEA should also be mentioned, and include: i) it is deterministic, and attributes all deviations from the frontier to inefficiencies; and ii) its efficiency scores are relative to the study sample; data from additional entities may thus affect the sample efficiency scores.

maximize ϕ_k

subject to

$$\phi_k y_{rk} - \sum_{j=1}^{n} \lambda_j y_{rj} \leq 0 \quad r = 1, \ldots, s$$

$$x_{ik} - \sum_{j=1}^{n} \lambda_j x_{ij} \geq 0 \quad i = 1, \ldots, m \quad (1)$$

$$\sum_{j=1}^{n} \lambda_j = 1$$

$$\lambda_j \geq 0 \quad \forall j = 1, \ldots, n$$

where there are s outputs and m inputs; yrk is the amount of output r produced by university k; xik is the amount of input i used by DMU k.

Technical efficiency provides a signal of how well (efficiently) DMUs are using their physical inputs to produce outputs. The symbol φ is used to denote the efficiency measure (score). In an output-orientation, φ will take a value greater than or equal to one for each producer. With $\varphi > 1$ the decision unit under evaluation is inside the frontier (i.e., it is inefficient), while $\varphi = 1$ implies that the decision unit is on the frontier (i.e., it is efficient). Under output-orientation, a score greater than 1 corresponds to the required production expansion to make a DMU efficient, keeping input levels fixed.[15]

3.1.1. Inputs and Outputs, and Their Measurement in Higher Education

Universities are multi-product organizations which produce at least two different outputs (research and teaching) using multiple inputs. In the first stage, therefore, we must identify the relevant inputs and outputs in the higher education sector.

---

[15] [(φ – 1) 100] is the percentage increase in outputs that could be achieved by the DMU under study with input quantities held constant.

There is no consensus on which output measures to use and, in many cases, output selection is driven by the availability of reliable data. Commonly accepted outputs of the university production process are the number of graduates as a proxy for teaching and the number of publications as a proxy for research. In numerous applied studies of efficiency measurement of HEIs, scientific production is proxied by the research income obtained by a university (e.g., Johnes, 2006).[16] On the contrary, university inputs are more readily measurable. Workers are typically incorporated in full-time equivalent numbers or as salary expenses. This may be extended to include all academic staff or even non-academic staff, again in numbers or costs. Abbott and Doucouliagos (2003), Johnes (2006), and Flegg et al. (2004) considered staff in numbers and Warning (2004) in costs. Other separately designated inputs are the full-time equivalent number of students (Flegg et al., 2004; Johnes, 2006), expenditure on inputs other than labor inputs, and proxies for the university's capital stock. Johnes (2006) for instance, used the value of interest payments and depreciation as a measure of the capital stock.

3.2. Second Stage: Explaining the (in)Efficiency Scores

The determinants of (in)efficiency are usually identified in a second-stage parametric regression of the DEA efficiency scores on explanatory variables that are expected to influence efficiency. The functional form of regression depends on the structure of the hypothesized relationship between the scores and the process/context variables. Some studies have used ordinary least squares regression (OLS). The relationship between the efficiency scores and the explanatory variables is evaluated based on the results of this regression.

---

[16] Funds for research depend on the number of publications and quality of these publications.

However, the bounded nature of DEA (efficiency scores bounded at 1) prompted researchers to use other models that can take this into account. Numerous existent papers (e.g., Banker & Natarajan, 2008; Gillen & Lall, 1997) applied Tobit regression for this purpose, which assumes a censored normal distribution. The literature is not, however, clear whether the efficiency distribution is censored at 1, in which case a Tobit model can be preferred or whether the distribution is truncated at one, in which case a truncated regression may be used.

Simar and Wilson (2007) argued that the application of Tobit regression is erroneous because it ignores the data generating process (DGP). The argument of Simar and Wilson (2007) was that DEA generates a complex (unknown) pattern of correlation between the estimated efficiency scores with i = 1, ..., n by construction not independent. To cope with this shortfall, Simar and Wilson (2007) proposed a bootstrapped-truncated regression to improve the reliability of estimates. The merit of this technique was acknowledged in recent studies (e.g., Chang et al., 2017). In short, since the scores are not observable but have been already determined, and they are censored at 1, to guarantee the statistical accuracy of the analysis Simar and Wilson (2007) recommended a bootstrapped-truncated regression. Their procedure can be undertaken in STATA — through a user-contributed package called *simarwilson* (Tauchmann, 2016) — to estimate the following model

$$DEA_i = \alpha + \sum_k \beta_k X_{ki} + \varepsilon_i \qquad (2)$$

where: i refers to a single DMU; X_i is a matrix of potential determinants of the previously estimated efficiency scores DEA_i; and ε_i is an error term.[17] This method allows us to obtain unbiased regression's coefficients and valid confidence intervals.

---

[17] We treat the efficiency scores DEA_i previously estimated in the first stage as the dependent variable in regression equation (2).

4. EFFICIENCY ASSESSMENT OF SPANISH PUBLIC UNIVERSITIES THROUGH DATA ENVELOPMENT ANALYSIS AND BOOTSTRAPPED-TRUNCATED REGRESSION

4.1. Data and Variables

The Spanish university system is made up of two types of universities: public and private ones which offer a broad-ranging, highly-regarded variety of degrees at undergraduate, graduate and doctoral levels. There are 79 universities, 50 public and 29 private. The majority of students (around 88%) are registered at public universities. To work with a homogeneous sample of producers (HEIs), we considered in the analysis only face-to-face Spanish public universities; we excluded private universities and distance/on-learning universities.[18] In total, there are 47 traditional or face-to-face public universities. We worked only with 45 HEIs because we did not have information on one input and one output for Universidad Complutense and Universidad Rey Juan Carlos.

We should highlight that Figure 1 showed the ideal information on inputs/outputs and process/contextual variables to achieve an efficiency study of the higher education system. In practice, nevertheless, we have several limitations. First, it is hard to find suitable information in official sources. Data for the academic year 2008/09 form the basis of our analysis, published by the Conference of Rectors of Spanish Universities (CRUE) in *La universidad española en cifras*.[19] Second, the distinction between input variables and process variables is more straightforward in theory than in practice. We made the distinction shown in Table 1, and we verified that there was no correlation between input variables (first-stage variables) and process/contextual variables (second-stage variables). Finally, the excessive use of inputs and outputs in an efficiency study results in many

---

[18] It is likely that production technology is different for the latter.
[19] Unfortunately, CRUE stopped providing researchers with this detailed information so we do not have more up-to-date figures. Anyhow, the case of Spain is used only to illustrate the proposed methodology.

efficiency scores equal to 1 because many institutions end up comparing themselves. A rule of thumb was given by Banker et al. (1984) as

$$s + m \leq \frac{n}{3}$$

where s is the number of outputs, m the number of inputs, and n the number of HEIs. In this chapter, the number of input and output measures, 7, is less than one-third of the number of universities considered.

In relation to the educational inputs, instead of using the total number of students enrolled in university degrees, we used for each university the *total number of enrolled credits* by the students in short-cycle and long-cycle university studies.[20] The choice of this variable supposes an innovation in comparison with previous papers that have appeared in the literature. Among other advantages, we avoid the problem of having full-time and part-time students. In addition, for each university, we considered the *weight of technical degrees* to take into account the difficulty involved in technical university studies such as engineering, computer science, etc. For each HEI, the weight was defined as the quotient between the enrolled credits in technical degrees over the total of enrolled credits.[21] Second, we considered the *total of full-time equivalent faculty* at public universities on July 31, 2008. The number of academic staff is used to reflect academic labor input. Finally, we included *administration and services personnel* on July 31, 2008. Administration and services staff measures the non-academic labor factor.

Concerning the educational outputs, universities are multi-output organizations producing research, teaching, and community services.

---

[20] The data shown in Table 1 are before the university reform of 2010 (called Bologna reform). University degrees in Spain were simultaneously made up of short-cycle university studies (3 years, equivalent to undergraduate studies), and long-cycle university studies (4 or 5 years, equivalent to graduate studies).

[21] In this paper, we considered the contribution of a variable to the total efficiency as determined by its level (of input or output) times the weight. See Angulo-Meza and Lins (2002) for further details.

The focus of this study was on outputs of teaching and research of the Spanish public universities.[22] As an output variable of the instructional component of higher education, we used for each university the *total number of exceeded or passed credits* by university students.[23] We added the results of the investigation approximated by the *liquidated income of applied research*. Income received for research purposes was included to reflect research output. It is a potentially controversial measure of research output. Nevertheless, it provides an up- to- date measure of both the quantity and quality of research because it is related to past research records of the academic staff (Abbott & Doucouliagos, 2003; Flegg & Allen, 2007a, 2007b; Flegg et al., 2004; Worthington & Lee, 2008). We also took into account the *weight of the degrees in Health Sciences* (such as Medicine or Pharmacy) in each university as the departments linked to those degrees have the most potential to get money for research.[24] For each HEI, we divided the enrolled credits in Health Sciences degrees over the total of enrolled credits.

Let's focus finally on the process/contextual variables. The choice of the explanatory or independent variables to incorporate in the regression (2) was driven mainly by our general interest in factors that might determine the efficiency of HEIs determined by previous studies and data availability. We used finally for each university:

- Current spending per student.[25]
- Percentage of international students.[26]
- Percentage of grantees.[27]
- Percentage of students from other regions.[28]

---

[22] We have no information to measure the so-called third mission of universities.
[23] Outputs of the education system typically include some measure of examination success.
[24] Not all universities offer Health university degrees in Medicine and Pharmacy.
[25] Quotient between current operating expenses in 2008 (Euros) and the total number of students enrolled in the 2008/09 academic year (AY).
[26] Percentage of international students studying at Spanish public universities in the 2008/09 AY.
[27] Spanish Ministry of Education, 2008/09 AY.

We want to clarify that many previous tests were done using different second-stage variables. The four variables finally used were those that showed the best results. Concerning the current expenditure per student, it mainly captures the salaries of the academic staff. A greater human capital of a university should be reflected in higher salaries of its faculty.[29] For example, a university with a higher number of professors with tenure — which means a greater current expenditure — may suggest a priori higher teaching quality and better academic results, and greater scientific productivity, and therefore more efficient production processes.[30] About grant recipients, it is demonstrated that students who receive financial support to funding their university studies have a better academic performance (e.g., Lassibille & Navarro-Gómez, 2011; Santelices et al., 2016). Our initial hypothesis was that the higher the percentage of recipients of public aids the better the academic results and, therefore, the more efficient the education production process. Finally, we took into account the mobility of students. On the one hand, international students who study at Spanish universities, usually for one year, in exchange programs. On the other hand, students who graduated from high school in a region and enrolled in a university in a different region. Greater mobility of students — between countries or between Spanish regions — is associated with greater educational choices of individuals and, hypothetically, an increase in competition for students between HEIs. And research results have suggested that the higher the degree of competition between institutions the more efficient they are (e.g., Bradley et al., 2001).

Table 1 showed the description of the inputs, outputs, and second-stage variables.

---

[28] Spain is divided into 17 regions called *Comunidades Autónomas*. Regional mobility captures the percentage of students enrolled at HEIs in 2008/09 outside their region of high-school graduation.

[29] For example, Mulligan and Sala-i-Martin (1997) developed a human capital index based on wage incomes. The idea was that the volume of human capital of a person is reflected in what s/he earns.

[30] Research quality is positively related to teaching quality (Cadez et al., 2017).

Table 1. Variables (and descriptive statistics) in a two-stage DEA model to evaluate the overall performance of Spanish HEIs

	Obs.	Mean	Std. Dev.	Min	Max
First-stage variables					
Output variables					
Total number of exceeded or passed credits in 2008/09	45	813431.8	478410.8	155559	2072620
Liquidated income of applied research in 2008 (in Euros)	45	1.13E + 07	1.60E + 07	638751.6	9.03E + 07
Weight of the degrees in Health Sciences	45	0.102615	0.077958	1.00E-10	0.307675
Input variables					
Total number of enrolled credits in 2008/09	45	1271348	772450.6	263430	3428148
Weight of technical degrees	45	0.281748	0.225297	0.014089	0.969238
Total of full-time equivalent faculty on July 31, 2008	45	1696.889	999.4602	400	4495
Administration and services personnel on July 31, 2008	45	1005.044	616.4831	252	2399
Second-stage variables					
Explanatory variables of efficiency					
Current spending per student	45	6959.606	1250.823	4933.789	9671.607
Percentage of international students	45	1.518138	2.019196	0.047710	7.697642
Percentage of grantees	45	18.25244	5.861927	1.890696	29.09
Percentage of students from other regions	45	11.78465	8.684688	1.223736	43.28358

4.2. Measuring the Productive Efficiency: Results of the First Stage

The statistical software STATA was used to run a DEA with output orientation, allowing variable returns to scale, based on the assumption that all the defined inputs affect the amount of product obtained.[31] The efficiency scores are presented in Table 2. First, we focus on a model that evaluates only the efficiency of teaching. The information on academic performance rates — what percentage of the enrolled credits a student can pass in one academic year — traditionally shows a relatively low students' academic productivity at Spanish public universities (Salas-Velasco, 2018). If students do not pass all the credits they enroll, the higher education production process is not efficient. Table 2 (second column) displays the technical efficiency scores. In this case, it is correct to speak of technical efficiency in the strict sense because both the output considered (total number of passed credits) and the three inputs incorporated (those defined in Table 1 except non-academic staff) are measured in non-monetary units. Only ten Spanish public universities achieve efficiency in teaching. The average efficiency is 1.1145 meaning that students' academic performance in public universities should rise by 11.45%.

Table 2 (third column) shows the efficiency scores when all the inputs and outputs defined in Table 1 are considered. Now, twenty-one universities achieve efficiency. It is noteworthy that, even considering the weight of technical careers, universities specialized in engineering,... appear less efficient in teaching; for example, the Polytechnic University of Cartagena, the Polytechnic University of Madrid or the Polytechnic University of Valencia. However, by jointly evaluating teaching and research, these universities achieve efficiency. But, overall, the higher education sector in Spain is performing well. The average efficiency among Spanish public universities is 1.0562. There is still room for improvement. To operate efficiently, Spanish universities should simultaneously expand their outputs by around 6%, keeping their inputs fixed. The apparent high level of efficiency in this and other studies of the efficiency of the higher education sector warrants further discussion given

---

[31] In a parametric approach such as SFA, we can know which inputs affect the output, looking at the significance of the coefficients in the estimation of the production function. This is not possible with DEA.

that this is a sector where there is no profit motive. One probable explanation for this result is that DEA produces a measure of efficiency relative to that achieved by the other producers or DMUs in the sample. Thus, the production frontier estimated by DEA may not be the true frontier that could be achieved if the sector were truly efficient; it is merely the observed production frontier for the industry. If this is the case, then overall levels of efficiency are overestimated by DEA, but rankings of and comparisons between the DMUs are likely still to be valid (Johnes, 2006). In Table 2 (column 3), universities are ranked based on the evaluation of their efficiencies in teaching and research. We obtain 21 efficient universities, and half of them are among the best research universities according to SIR National Rank (penultimate column).[32] The SCImago-Institutions Rankings (SIR), developed by the SCImago LAB research group, is a resource for the evaluation of universities and scientific research institutions around the world, which generates ranking information to analyze the results of research using the Scopus database. For purposes of classification, the calculation is generated each year from the results obtained during a five-year interval whose last year corresponds to two years before the edition of the ranking.[33] To test the robustness of the efficiency scores obtained from DEA, we compute the **Spearman's rank correlation** among DEA efficiency scores (teaching & research) and SIR (2012) National Rank. Spearman's rank correlation coefficient or Spearman's rho assesses the statistical dependence between the rankings of two variables

H_0: rankings from DEA-scores and SIR-national-rank are independent

H_1: rankings from DEA-scores and SIR-national-rank are directly related

---

[32] National ranking including only universities.
[33] We have chosen the classification of 2012.

Spearman's rho = 0.4349
Prob > |t| = 0.0028

Since the p-value for this test is 0.0028, we have solid evidence to believe H_1.

**Table 2. Productive efficiency-based ranking:
The case of Spanish public universities**

University (U.)	DEA efficiency scores (Teaching)[a]	DEA efficiency scores (Teaching & Research)[a]	SIR National Rank[b]	SIR Global Rank[b]
U. de BARCELONA	1	1	1	206
U. AUTONOMA de BARCELONA	1	1	2	289
U. AUTONOMA de MADRID	1.0136	1	3	299
U. POLITECNICA de VALENCIA	1.1849	1	6	366
U. de VALENCIA (ESTUDI GENERAL)	1	1	7	375
U. de SEVILLA	1	1	8	398
U. de GRANADA	1	1	10	446
U. POLITECNICA de MADRID	1.1958	1	12	459
U. de SANTIAGO de COMPOSTELA	1.0747	1	13	460
U. POMPEU FABRA	1	1	15	484
U. ROVIRA I VIRGILI	1	1	16	495
U. de VIGO	1.0269	1	19	520
U. MIGUEL HERNANdeZ de ELCHE	1.0704	1	21	529
U. CARLOS III de MADRID	1	1	23	544
U. de MURCIA	1.1358	1	24	548
U. de LLEIDA	1.0342	1	27	561
U. de CANTABRIA	1.2538	1	36	608
U. PABLO de OLAVIde	1	1	39	627
U. POLITECNICA de CARTAGENA	1.3150	1	41	642

University (U.)	DEA efficiency scores (Teaching)[a]	DEA efficiency scores (Teaching & Research)[a]	SIR National Rank[b]	SIR Global Rank[b]
U. de JAEN	1.0589	1	42	649
U. de LA RIOJA	1	1	46	673
U. de CASTILLA-LA MANCHA	1.0129	1.0008	18	515
U. POLITECNICA de CATALUNA	1.0722	1.0021	4	317
U. de ZARAGOZA	1.0737	1.0220	9	408
U. del PAIS VASCO	1.1415	1.0269	11	454
U. de CORDOBA	1.0853	1.0334	20	524
U. de EXTREMADURA	1.0942	1.0360	33	599
U. de SALAMANCA	1.0843	1.0388	24	548
U. PUBLICA de NAVARRA	1.0988	1.0458	30	572
U. de CADIZ	1.1057	1.0474	39	627
U. de MALAGA	1.0975	1.0768	22	537
U. de ALCALA de HENARES	1.2114	1.0788	29	566
U. de LEON	1.1017	1.0822	40	634
U. de GIRONA	1.1457	1.1104	28	563
U. de VALLADOLID	1.1475	1.1127	33	599
U. de BURGOS	1.2788	1.1337	37	609
U. de ALMERIA	1.1601	1.1527	34	601
U. de HUELVA	1.2335	1.1542	35	603
U. de LA CORUNA	1.1687	1.1571	45	659
U. de OVIEDO	1.2344	1.1584	17	501
U. de LA LAGUNA	1.2380	1.1610	38	623
U. de ALICANTE	1.1692	1.1692	25	554
U. de las ISLAS BALEARES	1.2548	1.1895	31	575
U. de LAS PALMAS de GRAN CANARIA	1.2526	1.2320	43	650
U. JAUME I de CASTELLON	1.3265	1.3063	26	557
Average Efficiency	*1.1145*	*1.0562*		

[a]Efficiency scores under variable returns to scale—output-oriented. Universities achieving a score of 1 are efficient, while inefficiency is indicated by the values greater than 1.

[b]The SCImago-Institutions Rankings (SIR), 2012.

4.3. Results of the Second Stage: Explaining the Productive Efficiency

Table 3 presents the results of a bootstrapped-truncated regression based on the procedure of Simar and Wilson (2007).[34] Since the values of efficiency scores are larger than or equal to one, negative (positive) regression's coefficients would mean that due to the rise of the independent variable, inefficiency decreases (increases). First, the higher the spending per student in a university, the lower its inefficiency (or the higher its efficiency). Our result makes sense in the context of the public higher education in Spain. As we anticipated, this variable basically includes the salary mass of the faculty of a university. Universities with a high percentage of professors with tenure tend to have higher payrolls. And, to get tenure, academics must show high scientific productivity. In short, higher payrolls are related to academic staff with greater scientific productivity and affects university efficiency. This result is in line with research works that have shown that HEIs with a greater share of full professors are more efficient (e.g., Agasisti & Wolszczak-Derlacz, 2014). Also, professors with more teaching experience tend to earn more. It is expected that this academic staff, with substantial teaching experience, will also have a positive effect on quality teaching and an increase in academic performance. Second, HEIs with a greater percentage of grantees tend to be less inefficient. Thus, a greater percentage of grantees has positive effects on stimulating effort and academic performance. In this regard, Dynarski (2003) finds that offering grant aid increases college attendance and completion. Lastly, the higher the percentage of international students in a university, the lower the inefficiency. This result is in line with some works published in the literature. For example, Abbott and Doucouliagos (2009) show that competition for overseas students has led to increased efficiency in Australian universities.

---

[34] In the regression, the efficiency scores of the third column in Table 2 are included as the dependent variable following algorithm #1 proposed by Simar and Wilson (2007).

Table 3. Simar and Wilson (2007) analysis of DEA efficiency scores

	Observed Coef.	Bootstrap Std. Err.	z	P > |z|
Current spending per student	-8.87E-05**	0.00002	-3.67	0.000
Percentage of international students	-0.01363*	0.00753	-1.81	0.070
Percentage of grantees	-0.01251**	0.00453	-2.76	0.006
Percentage of students from other regions	-0.00264	0.00222	-1.19	0.235
Constant	1.97522**	0.23486	8.41	0.000
/sigma	0.06659**	0.01290	5.16	0.000
Number of DMUs	45			
Number of inefficient DMUs	24			
Number of efficient DMUs	21			
Number of bootstr. reps	2000			
Wald chi2(4)	14.41			
Prob > chi2(4)	0.0061			

** Represents 5% level of significance.
* Represents 10% level of significance.

CONCLUSION

This chapter relies on the idea of productive efficiency, meaning the ability of a university to transform inputs into outputs. We recommend an output-oriented DEA in which efficiency is measured about a non-parametric frontier estimation of efficient units. The output-orientation version is defined as the capacity of universities to generate the maximum output given the number of resources they use. Using a sample of Spanish public universities, the results reveal that the higher education sector in Spain is performing well, although there is still room for improvement. To operate efficiently, Spanish universities should simultaneously expand their outputs (teaching and research) by around 6%, keeping their inputs fixed.

Why are some universities more efficient than others at providing higher education to students and producing research at the same time? It is common to explore the determinants of (in)efficiency in a second stage. As determinants of efficiency, this chapter finds that universities with a higher percentage of grantees tend to be less inefficient, and the competition for overseas students leads to increased efficiency in Spanish universities. However, Spanish public universities still have problems of serious inefficiencies that they must solve, mainly the important number of dropouts in the first years of studies, and the relatively low academic performance of students who take longer to finish their studies than those officially established.

REFERENCES

Abbott, M. & Doucouliagos, C. (2003). The efficiency of Australian universities: A data envelopment analysis. *Economics of Education Review*, 22(1), 89–97.

Abbott, M. & Doucouliagos, C. (2009). Competition and efficiency: Overseas students and technical efficiency in Australian and New Zealand universities. *Education Economics*, 17(1), 31–57.

Agasisti, T. & Dal Bianco, A. (2009). Reforming the university sector: Effects on teaching efficiency—evidence from Italy. *Higher Education*, 57(4), 477–498.

Agasisti, T. & Wolszczak-Derlacz, J. (2015). Exploring efficiency differentials between Italian and Polish universities, 2001-11. *Science and Public Policy*, 43(1), 128–142.

Ahn, T. & Seiford, L. M. (1993). Sensitivity of DEA to models and variable sets in a hypothesis test setting: The efficiency of university operations. *Creative and Innovative Approaches to the Science of Management*, 6, 191–208.

Angulo-Meza, L. & Lins, M. P. E. (2002). Review of methods for increasing discrimination in data envelopment analysis. *Annals of Operations Research*, 116(1-4), 225–242.

Ball, R. & Halwachi, J. (1987). Performance indicators in higher education. *Higher education*, 16(4), 393–405.

Banker, T. & Natarajan, R. (2008). Evaluating contextual variables affecting productivity using data envelopment analysis. *Operations Research*, *56*(1), 48–58.

Banker, R. D., Charnes, A. & Cooper, W. W. (1984). Some models for estimating technical and scale inefficiencies in data envelopment analysis. *Management Science*, *30*, 1078–1092.

Beneito, P., Boscá, J. E. & Ferri, J. (2016). *Tuition fees and student effort at university* (FEDEA Policy Papers No. 2016-23).

Bougnol, M. L. & Dulá, J. H. (2006). Validating DEA as a ranking tool: An application of DEA to assess performance in higher education. *Annals of Operations Research*, *145*(1), 339–365.

Bradley, S., Johnes, G. & Millington, J. (2001). The effect of competition on the efficiency of secondary schools in England. *European Journal of Operational Research*, *135*(3), 545–568.

Cadez, S., Dimovski, V. & Zaman Groff, M. (2017). Research, teaching and performance evaluation in academia: The salience of quality. *Studies in Higher Education*, *42*(8), 1455–1473.

Cave, M. (1997). *The use of performance indicators in higher education: A critical analysis of developing practice*. London: Kingsley.

Chang, Y. T., Lee, S. & Park, H. K. (2017). Efficiency analysis of major cruise lines. *Tourism Management*, *58*, 78–88.

Charnes, A., Cooper, W. W. & Rhodes, E. (1978). Measuring the efficiency of decision making units. *European Journal of Operational Research*, *2*, 429–444.

Cohn, E., Rhine, S. & Santos, M. (1989). Institutions of higher education as multi-product firms: Economies of scale and scope. *Review of Economics and Statistics*, *71*(2), 284–290.

Curristine, T., Lonti, Z. & Joumard, I. (2007). Improving public sector efficiency: Challenges and opportunities. *OECD Journal on Budgeting*, *7*(1), 1–41.

Dynarski, S. M. (2003). Does aid matter? Measuring the effect of student aid on college attendance and completion. *American Economic Review*, *93*(1), 279–288.

Emrouznejad, A., Parker, B. R. & Tavares, G. (2008). Evaluation of research in efficiency and productivity: A survey and analysis of the first 30 years of scholarly literature in DEA. *Journal of Socio-Economics Planning Science, 42*(3), 151–157.

Färe, R. & Primont, D. (1995). *Multi-output production and duality: Theory and applications*. Boston: Kluwer Academic Publishers.

Färe, R., Grosskopf, S., Norris, M. & Zhongyang, Z. (1994). Productivity growth, technical progress and efficiency change in industrialized countries. *American Economic Review, 84*(1), 66–83.

Farrell, M. (1957). The measurement of productive efficiency. *Journal of the Royal Statistical Society (Series A), 120*, 253–281.

Flegg, T. & Allen, D. (2007a). Does expansion cause congestion? The case of the older British universities, 1994-2004. *Education Economics, 15*(1), 75–102.

Flegg, T. & Allen, D. (2007b). Using Cooper's approach to explore the extent of congestion in the New British universities. *Economics Issues, 12*(2), 47–81.

Flegg, T., Allen, D., Field, K. & Thurlow, T. W. (2004). Measuring the efficiency of British universities: A multi-period data envelopment analysis. *Education Economics, 12*(3), 231–249.

Gillen, D. & Lall, A. (1997). Developing measures of airport productivity and performance: An application of data envelopment analysis. *Transportation Research Part E: Logistics and Transportation Review, 33*(4), 261–273.

Gulbrandsen, M. & Slipersæer, S. (2007). The third mission and the entrepreneurial university model. In A. Bonaccorsi & C. Daraio, *Universities and strategic knowledge creation. Specialization and performance in Europe* (pp. 112–143). Cheltenham, UK: Edward Elgar.

Halkos, G., Tzeremes, N. G. & Kourtzidis, S. A. (2012). Measuring public owned university departments' efficiency: A bootstrapped DEA approach. *Journal of Economics and Econometrics, 55*(2), 1–24.

Hazelkorn, E. (2015a). *Rankings and the reshaping of higher education: The battle for world-class excellence*, 2nd edn. London: Palgrave Macmillan.

Hazelkorn, E. (2015b). Globalization, internationalization and rankings. *International Higher Education*, 53, 8–10.

Hazelkorn, E., Coates, H. & McCormick, A. C. (2018). Quality, performance and accountability: Emergent challenges in the global era. In E. Hazelkorn, H. Coates, & A. C. McCormick (Eds.), *Research handbook on quality, performance and accountability in higher education*. Cheltenham: Edward Elgar Publishing Ltd.

Johnes, J. (2006). Data envelopment analysis and its application to the measurement of efficiency in higher education. *Economics of Education Review*, 25(3), 273–288.

Johnes, J. (2016). Performance indicators and rankings in higher education. In R. Barnett, P. Temple & P. Scott (Eds.), *Valuing higher education: An appreciation of the work of Gareth Williams* (Ch. 4). London: UCL IOE Press.

Johnes, J. & Taylor, J. (1990). *Performance indicators in higher education*. Buckingham: Society for Research into Higher Education and Open University Press.

Koryakina, T., Sarrico, C. S. & Teixeira P. N. (2015). Universities' third mission activities. Challenges to extending boundaries. In E. Reale & E. Primeri (Eds.), *The transformation of university institutional and organizational boundarie*s (pp. 63–82). Rotterdam: Sense Publishers.

Lassibille, G. & Navarro-Gómez, M. L. (2011). How long does it take to earn a higher education degree in Spain? *Research in Higher Education*, 52(1), 63–80.

Liu, J. S., Lu, L. Y. Y., Lu, W. M. & Lin, B. J. Y. (2013). A survey of DEA applications. *Omega*, 41, 893–902.

McMillan, M. L. & Datta, D. (1998). The relative efficiencies of Canadian universities: A DEA perspective. *Canadian Public Policy/Analyse de Politiques*, 24(4), 485–511.

Mulligan, C. B. & Sala-i-Martin, X. (1997). A labor income-based measure of the value of human capital: An application to the states of the United States. *Japan and the World Economy, 9*(2), 159-191.

Ng, S. W. (2011). Can Hong Kong export its higher education services to the Asian markets? *Educational Research for Policy and Practice, 10*(2), 115–131.

Nunamaker, T. R. (1985). Using data envelopment analysis to measure the efficiency of non-profit organizations: A critical evaluation. *Managerial and Decision Economics, 6,* 50–58.

Palomares-Montero, D. & García-Aracil, A. (2011). What are the key indicators for evaluating the activities of universities? *Research Evaluation, 20*(5), 353-363.

Propper, C. & Wilson, D. (2003). The use and usefulness of performance measures in the public sector. *Oxford Review of Economic Policy, 19*(2), 250–267.

Rodríguez-Ferrero, N., Salas-Velasco, M. & Sánchez-Martínez, M. T. (2010). Assessment of productive efficiency in irrigated areas of Andalusia. *International Journal of Water Resources Development, 26*(3), 365–379.

Salas-Velasco, M. (2018). Can educational laws improve efficiency in education production? Assessing students' academic performance at Spanish public universities, 2008–2014. *Higher Education* (forthcoming). DOI: https://doi.org/10.1007/s10734-018-0322-6.

Santelices, M. V., Catalán, X., Kruger, D. & Horn, C. (2016). Determinants of persistence and the role of financial aid: Lessons from Chile. *Higher Education, 71*(3), 323–342.

Seiford, L. M. (1997). A bibliography for data envelopment analysis (1978-1996). *Annals of Operations Research, 73,* 393–438.

Sheil, T. (2016). Managing expectations. An Australian perspective on the impact and challenges of adopting a university rankings narrative. In M. Yudkevich, P. G. Altbach, & L. E. Rumbley (Eds.), *The global academic rankings game. Changing Institutional policy, practice, and academic life,* 1st edn. London: Routledge.

Shin, J. C. & Toutkoushian, R. K. (2011). The past, present, and future of university rankings. In J. C. Shin, R. K. Toutkoushian & U. Teichler (Eds), *University rankings: Theoretical basis, methodology and impacts on global higher education* (pp. 1–18). Dordrecht, The Netherlands: Springer.

Simar, L. & Wilson, P. (2007). Estimation and inference in two-stage, semi-parametric models of production processes. *Journal of Econometrics, 136*(1), 31–64.

Tauchmann, H. (2016). SIMARWILSON: Stata module to perform Simar & Wilson efficiency analysis. *Statistical Software Components.* Retrieved from https://ideas.repec.org/c/boc/bocode/s458156.html.

Tyagi, P., Yadav, S. P. & Singh, S. P. (2009). Relative performance of academic departments using DEA with sensitivity analysis. *Evaluation and Program Planning, 32*(2), 168–177.

Warning, S. (2004). Performance differences in German higher education: Empirical analysis of strategic groups. *Review of Industrial Organization, 24*(4), 393–408.

Wolszczak-Derlacz, J. & Parteka, A. (2011). Efficiency of European public higher education institutions: A two-stage multicountry approach. *Scientometrics, 89*(3), 887–917.

Worthington, A. C. & Lee, B. L. (2008). Efficiency, technology and productivity change in Australian universities 1998-2003. *Economics of Education Review, 27*(3), 285–298.

Xavier, C. A. & Alsagoff, L. (2013). Constructing "world-class" as "global:" A case study of the National University of Singapore. *Educational Research for Policy and Practice, 12*(3), 225–238.

Yang, R. (2003). Globalization and higher education development: A critical analysis. *International Review of Education, 49*(3/4), 269–291.

Zhu, J. (Ed.) (2016). *Data envelopment analysis: A handbook of empirical studies and applications.* New York: Springer.

In: Higher Education Institutions
Editor: Joe Maxwell

ISBN: 978-1-53615-717-8
© 2019 Nova Science Publishers, Inc.

Chapter 5

EVOLVING ENTREPRENEURIAL ACTIVITIES AT POST-SOVIET UNIVERSITIES

Radzivon Marozau[1], Maribel Guerrero[2,3],*,
David Urbano[4],† and Asunción Ibañez[5]

[1]Belarusian Economic Research and Outreach Center (BEROC), Minsk, Belarus

[2] School of Business and Economics at Universidad del Desarrollo, Chile

[3]Newcastle Business School, Northumbria University, Newcastle upon Tyne, UK

[4]Department of Business, Universitat Autònoma de Barcelona, Barcelona, Spain

[5]Deusto Business School, University of Deusto, Donostia-San-Sebastián, Spain

---

* Corresponding Author's E-mail: maribel.guerrero@northumbria.ac.uk.
† David Urbano acknowledges the financial support from the Spanish Ministry of Economy & Competitiveness [project ECO2017-87885-P], the Economy & Knowledge Department—Catalan Government [project 2017-SGR-1056] and the Catalan Government [ICREA-Academia Program]

ABSTRACT

Stimulating entrepreneurship inside universities and the consequent development of entrepreneurial universities against the backdrop of global reduction of governmental financial support is one of the current foci of academics, university authorities and policy makers from all around the world. These issues are more critical to post-Soviet economies where the level of the entrepreneurial activity and, as a consequence, of entrepreneurship within universities is lower in comparison with western market economies, while the majority of such countries are still trying to develop an entrepreneurship- and innovation-friendly environment.

In this regard, the aim of this chapter is to explore the influence of a university environment on entrepreneurial activities of students and alumni in the post-Soviet context. Methodologically, we combined the case study methodology and the regression analysis to embrace two levels of analysis: organizational (a university) and individual (students and alumni). Capitalizing on the nature and uniqueness of the Belarusian context, we contribute to the debate on factors shaping an entrepreneurial environment in the context of a post-Soviet university and demonstrate how a university environment influences the entrepreneurial behavior of students and alumni.

The general conclusion to be drawn from the study is that underdeveloped entrepreneurial and business competences and the Soviet heritage that is still visible in attitudes and values restrain employing the abundant human and physical resources of the Belarusian State University to contribute to economic development not only by educating job-seekers but by fostering job-creators and transforming research activity into economic value. However, as the regression analysis showed, existing formal business-related education does facilitate the entrepreneurial activity of alumni.

Keywords: entrepreneurial universities; entrepreneurial activities; post-Soviet Countries; Belorussia

INTRODUCTION

Going beyond the scope of teaching, knowledge generation and dissemination, universities transform themselves into entrepreneurial organizations and are expected to contribute to development of entrepreneurial thinking, values, action, and institutions (Gibb, 2012; Guerrero, Cunningham and Urbano, 2015). Therefore, stimulating entrepreneurship inside universities and the consequent formation of entrepreneurial universities against the backdrop of global reduction of governmental financial support (Kwiek, 2001) is one of the current foci of academics, university authorities and policy makers. Although many studies have advanced the understanding of university-level factors shaping a university entrepreneurial environment and thereby promoting entrepreneurial activities of the university community (Guerrero, Cunningham and Urbano, 2015; Markuerkiaga, Errasti and Igartua, 2014; O'Shea, Chugh and Allen, 2008; Wright et al., 2007), there are relatively few studies on these issues in the context of transition economies of Eastern Europe (see for example Marozau and Guerrero (2016)). At the same time, these countries have started planning and undertaking measures to reform universities and academic institutions, support entrepreneurial infrastructure, improve the environment for innovative start-ups and small- and medium-sized enterprises. It became evidential that such entrepreneurial transformation at universities is needed to respond to the challenges of the global knowledge economy (Uvarov and Perevodchikov, 2012).

Observing the role of universities in promoting entrepreneurship and creating entrepreneurship capital in the USA and Western Europe, policy makers in many countries with transition economies have realized that such entrepreneurial transformation at universities is needed to respond to the challenges of the global knowledge economy (Kwiek, 2008; Uvarov and Perevodchikov, 2012). However, unlike many Western higher education systems, universities in post-Soviet economies are being transformed not by state actions, but, paradoxically, by state inaction (Shattock, 2004). Therefore, responding to the changes in global and domestic post-Soviet socioeconomic conditions has required from universities new kinds of resources, capabilities, forms of management and approaches to teaching, research and entrepreneurial activities.

Hence, the aim of this chapter is to explore the influence of a university environment shaped by certain factors on entrepreneurial activities of students and alumni in the post-Soviet context. In this regard, we used prior research on the topic (Guerrero, Urbano and Fayolle, 2016; O'Shea, Chugh and Allen, 2008; Wright et al., 2007) and united management and entrepreneurship research domains, namely the resource-based theory, the institutional approach, the theory of planned behavior and the social cognitive theory in order to achieve this objective.

Capitalizing on the nature and uniqueness of the Belarusian context, we contribute to the debate on factors shaping an entrepreneurial environment in the context of a post-Soviet university and demonstrate how a university environment influences the entrepreneurial behavior of students and alumni. In addition, we expect to generate a competitive explanation of entrepreneurial activities at universities that may stimulate researchers to study different manifestation of this phenomenon in greater depth as well as to monitor how recent changes in the legal and economic environment will condition the ongoing processes.

Methodologically, we combined the case study methodology and the regression analysis to embrace two levels of analysis: organizational (a university) and individual (students and alumni). Based on the previous research, in this chapter we explored the entrepreneurial activities of the main members of a Belarusian university approximated by the entrepreneurial intentions of students and (ii) the entrepreneurial actions of alumni. In particular, we focused on the Belarusian State University (BSU) – one of the leading and most reputable classical universities in post-Soviet countries[1]. Its case seems to be relevant and interesting because, despite formal and informal institutions unsupportive of entrepreneurship in Belarus (Ivanova, 2005; Miazhevich, 2007), BSU demonstrates several characteristics – 'irreducible minimum' – of universities with an entrepreneurial environment such as an expanded developmental periphery and a diversified funding base (Clark, 1998) which should be pillars of the inevitable future transformation.

---

[1] According to the Interfax Rankings evaluating universities from the Commonwealth of Independent States, Georgia, Latvia, Lithuania and Estonia, BSU took the 2nd place in 2015. In 2017, BSU took the 334th place in the QS World University Rankings.

The chapter proceeds as follows: in Section 2, we discuss university-level factors influencing the entrepreneurial activities of universities. Section 3 describes the data collection and analysis methods, while, in Section 4, we provide results of the qualitative and quantitative analysis. Afterwards, Section 5 integrates and discusses main findings and propounds several initiatives to be implemented at BSU to develop entrepreneurship-friendly environment at the university level. The final section provides a conclusion and delineates future research lines.

THEORETICAL FRAMEWORK

Organizational Factors that Condition Entrepreneurial Activities at Universities

Given the tenets of the resource-based theory (Amit and Shoemaker, 1993) often used in the management domain, several critical types of resources and capabilities were identified in the literature that may influence entrepreneurial activities at universities (Guerrero, Urbano and Fayolle, 2016; O'Shea et al., 2007; Zhou and Peng, 2008). In the same vein, for the purpose of this chapter, we focused on (a) university resources, (b) university governance and leadership, and (c) entrepreneurship education.

Human resources with expert knowledge, managerial skills, talent, and characteristics of leaders, who are able to recognize market opportunities, to orchestrate resources and to manage multifunctional teams, lead to converting university competences, knowledge and technology into viable products and to closer university-industry interrelation (Guerrero, Urbano and Fayolle, 2016; Zhou and Peng, 2008). In addition, the availability of office spaces, labs, co-working areas, incubators, science parks and other entrepreneurship infrastructure, which are often regarded as physical resources (Clarysse et al., 2005; Urbano and Guerrero, 2013), creates an opportunity to link talent, technology, capital, and know-how. Diversified sources of financial resources are important to attain financial independence from state and, as a result, to be free in conducting an entrepreneurial policy and building links with the external environment (Clark, 1998; Subotzky, 1999). Simultaneously, the scarcity of financial resources and inability to obtain external funds retard entrepreneurial activities at universities, especially, in developing and transition economies (Nkamnebe, 2009; Uvarov and Perevodchikov, 2012) since there is a gap between knowledge and technology available at universities and those demanded by the business sectors. In addition, the importance of commercial resources (technology transfer offices and industrial liaison offices) for entrepreneurial activities within universities is justified by the need to make a bridge between suppliers of research results (academics and students) and customers (firms, entrepreneurs, business angels) who differ in their objectives, values, and environments (Gál and Ptaček, 2011; O'Shea, Chugh and Allen, 2008).

An appropriate no bureaucratic governance and leadership system of a university is believed to be a crucial factor connecting teaching, research and administration functions (Guerrero and Urbano, 2012). This allows for making adequate and quick decisions, implementing entrepreneurial strategy, maintaining university dynamism and facilitating incessant innovations (Clark, 2001). In the same vein, the level of decentralization of decision-making, operational and strategic responsibility, the power to innovate and take risks may create stimuli and facilitate entrepreneurial activities within universities (Gibb, 2012; Liu and Dubinsky, 2000).

Entrepreneurship education is charged with providing individuals with the ability to recognize opportunities; with knowledge and skills to act on them, as well as to increase the willingness of individuals to consider entrepreneurship as a career path (Jones and English, 2004; Kuratko, 2005). The rationale behind that is an expectation that more and better entrepreneurship courses and programs delivered by universities can result in both the number and the quality of entrepreneurs entering an economy (Matlay, 2008) and creating goods, services, and jobs (European Commission, 2015; Lange et al., 2011). Ideally, entrepreneurship education should be accompanied with role models (O'Shea et al., 2007; Toledano and Urbano, 2008) – fully fledged entrepreneurs from among academics, staff, students, and alumni. They may serve as role models and mentors to demonstrate the attractiveness of entrepreneurial activities (Siegel and Phan, 2005; Urbano and Guerrero, 2013) and be involved in the educational process and providing support in starting up a business (Hayter, 2013).

University Environment Conditioning Entrepreneurial Behavior

We analyzed the influence of a university environment on entrepreneurial activities approximated by the entrepreneurial behavior of undergraduate students and alumni.

Previous studies in the entrepreneurship domain recognized that one of the most adequate models to analyze the entrepreneurial behavior is the theory of planned behavior (TPB) (Guerrero, Rialp and Urbano, 2008; Fayolle, Gailly and Lassas-Clerc, 2006; Souitaris, Zerbinati and Al-Laham, 2007). According to this theory, intentions to pursue certain behaviors are impacted and shaped by three main factors (Ajzen, 1991): (a) the attitude towards behavior is the attractiveness of this activity or personal valuation about performing a behavior; (b) subjective norms refer to the perceived social pressures from family and friends to carry out an entrepreneurial activity, and (c) the perceived behavioral control measures the perceived easiness and ability of performing an activity. Several studies having the TPB as a framework included directly or indirectly some conditions associated with an environment (Aidis, Estrin and Mickiewicz, 2008; Liñán, Urbano and Guerrero, 2011). In this regard, this chapter explores how the university environment directly conditions the entrepreneurial behavior of students and alumni.

In terms of the TPB, the university environment may change attitudes and perceived behavioral control of students and thereby influence intention towards entrepreneurship (Fayolle, Gailly and Lassas-Clerc, 2006; Lüthje and Franke, 2003) through teaching, inspiring and developing a positive image of venture creators. In this connection, we proposed and tested on the data of BSU a conceptual model that integrates the framework of the TPB and the notion of the influence of university environment on students' entrepreneurial behavior. In addition, several studies that focused on the entrepreneurial behavior of a person and university context explored an entrepreneurial activity of alumni because they can provide important insights into the influence of a university on business creation (Hsu, Roberts and Eesley, 2007; Lange et al., 2011). The rationale behind this is a widely shared belief that it is important to gain some work experience as well as business contacts and the appropriate finance prior to start-up (Carter and Collinson, 1999). In this regard, in addition to TPB, we adopted the basis of the social cognitive theory (SCT) (Bandura, 1986). This theory helps to understand how individuals act based on their perceptions. Ideas of SCT have been applied to many areas of human functioning including the learning performance and entrepreneurial behavior (Hmieleski and Baron, 2009; Krueger Jr. and Brazeal, 1994; Lange et al., 2011). In general, the theory explained how decisions are influenced by three elements: (a) self-efficacy, (b) reward for a behavior, and (c) environment.

In compliance with SCT, the personal determinant reflects whether an individual has high or low self-efficacy towards a behavior or, in other words, reflects the individual's belief in his/her capabilities to organize and execute action required to manage prospective situations (Bandura, 1986) – that is to say – to perform the roles and tasks of an entrepreneur (Boyd and Vozikis, 1994). The behavioral determinant is the response an individual receives after he/she performs a behavior – reward for a behavior, while the environmental determinant reflects aspects of the environment or setting that influences the individual's ability to successfully complete a behavior (Bandura, 2001). From this perspective, contemporary universities can be a fertile and benevolent environment for developing positive image of venture creators, fostering business ideas and transforming them into new firms (Guerrero et al., 2014; Laukkanen, 2000). Therefore, drawing on the role of the university environment in promoting entrepreneurial behavior, we proposed that:

P1. Perceived university entrepreneurial environment is positively related to entrepreneurial behavior of students of BSU

P2. Perceived university entrepreneurial environment is positively related to entrepreneurial behavior of alumni of BSU.

The conceptual model is provided in Figure 1.

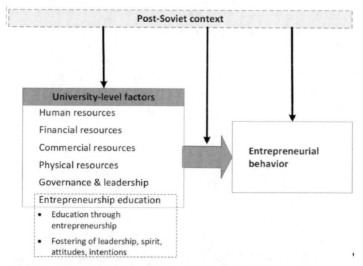

Source: Adapted from Guerrero and Urbano (2012).

Figure 1. Conceptual framework of the entrepreneurial behavior.

As emphasized in the model, the specific post-Soviet context influences the factors and relationships integrated into the model. It is worth noting that such context has a dual effect since it is characterized by factors that either facilitate or retard the entrepreneurial transformation of universities.

METHODOLOGY

Methodological Approach

Due to the complexity of the phenomenon under consideration as well as blurred boundaries between the phenomenons in the context of post-

Soviet economies, a case study methodology seemed to the most appropriate for our analysis (Eisenhardt, 1989). This approach allows collecting and analyzing in-depth data aimed at developing theory and thereby providing insights to our discussion (Yin, 2014). Specifically, a single case study method with a mixed data collection approach was selected to explore the environment that conditions entrepreneurial activities at the Belarusian State University (BSU). It was chosen as the case because it is the largest and the most diversified university in the Republic of Belarus and has relatively rich experience in promoting entrepreneurial activities. The research process consisted of two steps: qualitative and quantitative. In view of that, during the process of data collection, we gathered data using both qualitative and quantitative tools in order to maximize the full potential of a case study design.

Data Collection

Qualitative Data

We used different types of secondary data sources, such as annual reports, Rector's reports, press releases, project descriptions, statistical reports, as well as the websites of BSU and its organizational units[2]. In addition, face-to-face interviews with five anonymous top managers of BSU (Directors of an educational establishment and innovative enterprises, Dean, Chief of a main department) were conducted in Fall-Winter 2013. Each respondent was asked about university-level factors identified in the previous section as well as about BSU entrepreneurial environment in general and its potential impact on the entrepreneurial behavior of students and alumni.

---

[2] Qualitative data from secondary sources were obtained as of December 31, 2014 to juxtapose them with quantitative data obtained from the surveys.

Quantitative Data

For the purposes of our case study, we adapted a version of a questionnaire used in the 2013/2014 Global University Entrepreneurial Spirit Students' Survey (GUESSS)[3] (Sieger, Fueglistaller and Zellweger, 2014). The web-based survey was conducted in November and December of 2013 using the Google Drive platform because of the geographic dispersion of BSU's campuses and limited resources. Overall, emails were sent out twice to a population of 4,540 students (about 25% of the total number of students) whose email addresses were available. Of the 4,540 students initially invited to participate, we obtained 363 completed questionnaires. Thus, the resulting response rate of 8.0 percent was relatively high as compared to the average response rate of 5.5 percent in all countries of the 2013/2014 GUESSS (Sieger, Fueglistaller and Zellweger, 2014). After eliminating questionnaires with missing data and those filled by students who were running a business at the moment of the survey, the final sample included 316 university students with a sample error of ± 5.3% at a confidence level of 95%. General characteristics of the respondents are provided in Table 1. The description of dependent, independent and control variables used in the analysis of students' entrepreneurial behavior is provided in Table 2.

We tested the reliability of the scales of independent variable using Cronbach's alpha. The scales were found to be reliable because the values of Cronbach's alpha ranged from .810 to .951[4], while the widely acknowledged threshold level is .7 (Hair et al., 2010). In addition, to assess convergent validity of the independent variables we performed the factor analysis (Liñan and Chen, 2009). The appropriateness of the factor analysis was confirmed by the value of the Kaiser-Meyer-Olkin index of .885 and the significance of Barlett's test of sphericity at the .001 level. The factor analysis revealed the existence of four factors with an eigenvalue higher than 1, which accounted for 79.7% of the variance. These results

---

[3] Belarusian universities and BSU in particular did not participate in the survey.
[4] Rotated component matrix and reliability indicators are in Annex 1.

completely confirmed our expectations and measures used by GUESSS (Sieger, Fueglistaller and Zellweger, 2014).

Table 1. General characteristics of respondents

	Students		Alumni	
	N	%	N	%
Total number of valid responses	316	100%	257	100%
Gender:				
Male	124	39.2	83	32.3
Female	192	60.8[5]	174	67.7
Age (average)	19.41		25.2	
Parents entrepreneurs:				
Yes	109	34.5		
No	207	65.5		
Field of study:				
Agricultural science, forestry, and nutrition science	1	0.3		
Art, science of art	1	0.3	34	13.2
Business/Management	168	53.2	99	38.6
Economics	22	7.0	13	5.1
Engineering and architecture	1	0.3		
Information science/IT	62	19.6	23	8.9
Law	1	0.3		
Logistics	10	3.2	4	1.6
Mathematics and natural sciences	39	12.3	23	8.9
Medicine and health sciences	1	0.3		
Other social sciences (including education)	10	3.2	61	23.7
Attended at least one course on entrepreneurship:				
Yes	85	26.9	116	45.1
No	231	73.1	141	54.9
Student/alumnus of the School of Business and Management of Technology (SBMT):				
Yes	178	56.3	99	38.5
No	138	43.7	158	61.5
Regular job next to your studies:				
Yes	75	23.7		
No	241	76.3		

---

[5] Female are the majority in the population of Belarusian students. According to the Statistical Committee of Belarus, in 2012 female accounted for about 58% students. Seemingly, this percentage is higher if we consider classical (not technical) universities.

	Students		Alumni	
	N	%	N	%
Intention to become an entrepreneur/successor in a firm within five years after graduation:				
Yes	227	70.9		
No	96	29.1		
Years of work experience (average)			4.3	
Doing business:				
Yes			28	10.9
No			229	89.1
Income higher than an average salary in the country:				
Yes			146	56.8
No			111	43.2

In order to explore the entrepreneurial behavior of alumni, we applied a web-based survey using the Google Drive platform[6]. It was administered by the Career Development Center of the School of Business and Management of Technology of BSU (SBMT)[7] in July-June of 2014. The population included 8780 alumni graduated from 1999 to 2014. Thus, the link to the anonymous online questionnaire was sent out to 8780 BSU alumni. However, delivery problems occurred with 3548 addresses. In total, 268 (5.1%) questionnaire responses were received within the survey period. After eliminating questionnaires with missing data, the sample included 263 university alumni with a sample error of ± 6.0% at a confidence level of 95%. For the purposes of the study, we excluded six alumni who continued their study and who were on maternity leave. As a result, the final sample included 257 BSU alumni. General characteristics of the respondents are provided in Table 1.

The description of dependent, independent and control variables used in the analysis of alumni entrepreneurial actions is provided in Table 3.

In order to assess the convergent validity of this construct of the university environment, we performed the factor analysis. The value of

---

[6] The questionnaire is available in Annex 2.
[7] School of Business and Management of Technology of BSU was renamed in School of Business in April 2018.

Table 2. Description of variables used for the analysis of entrepreneurial intentions[44]

	Variable	Measure	References
Dependent	Entrepreneurial intention	1 – if a student wants to be either an entrepreneur or a successor in a firm of parents or another firm. 0 – otherwise	Lange et al. (2011); Sieger, Fueglistaller and Zellweger (2014).
Independent	Entrepreneurial environment at BSU (*Environment*)	1. 'The atmosphere at my university inspires me to develop ideas for new businesses'. 2 'There is a favorable climate for becoming an entrepreneur at my university'. 3 'At my university, students are encouraged to engage in entrepreneurial activities'. 1 – not at all; 7 – very much	Sieger, Fueglistaller and Zellweger (2014).
	Attitude towards entrepreneurship (*Attitude*)	1. 'Being an entrepreneur implies more advantages than disadvantages to me'. 2. 'A career as entrepreneur is attractive for me'. 3. 'If I had the opportunity and resources, I would become an entrepreneur'. 4. 'Being an entrepreneur would entail great satisfactions for me'. 5. 'Among various options, I would rather become an entrepreneur'. 1 – strongly disagree; 7 – strongly agree.	Liñan and Chen, (2009); Sieger, Fueglistaller and Zellweger (2014).
	Subjective norms (*Norms*)	1. 'How would react student's close family if a student became an entrepreneur'? 2. 'How would react student's friends if a student became an entrepreneur'? 3. 'How would react fellow students' friends if a student became an entrepreneur? 1 – very negatively; 7 – very positively.	Liñan and Chen, (2009); Sieger, Fueglistaller and Zellweger (2014).
	Perceived behavioral control (*PBC*)	1. 'For me, being self-employed would be very easy'. 2. 'If I wanted to, I could easily pursue a career as self-employed'. 3. 'As self-employed, I would have complete control over the situation'. 4. 'If I became self-employed, the chances of success would be very high'. 1 – strongly disagree; 7 – strongly agree.	Tkachev and Kolvereid (1999); Iakovleva, Kolvereid and Stephan, (2011); Sieger, Fueglistaller and Zellweger (2014).

[44] Descriptive statistics and a correlation table are provided in Annex 3.

	Variable	Measure	References
Control	Gender (*Male*)	1–male; 0–female	Karhunen and Ledyaeva (2010); Packham et al. (2010); Ertuna and Gurel (2011).
	Business/Economics specialties (*Business field*)	1 – Business/Economics students[45] 0 – students of other specialties	Sieger, Fueglistaller and Zellweger (2014); Souitaris, Zerbinati and Al-Laham (2007); Bae et al. (2014).
	Students of SBMT (*SBMT*)	1 – students of SBMT; 0 – students of other faculties.	
	Entrepreneurship courses (*Entrepr. course*)	1 – a student had attended at least one entrepreneurship course; 0 – otherwise.	Yar Hamidi, Wennberg and Berglund (2008); Packham et al. (2010); Zhang, Duysters and Cloodt (2014).
	Self-employed parents (*Self-empl. parents*)	1 – a student reported that at least one of parents was self-employed and 0 – otherwise	Toledano and Urbano (2008); Laspita et al. (2012); Dohse and Walter (2012).
	Age squared (*Age squared*)		Liñán and Chen (2009); Yar Hamidi et al. (2008).
	Employment (*Employment*)	1 – if a student was employed; 0 – otherwise	Lange et al. (2011); Liñán et al. (2011).

---

[45] We assigned to this group students who indicated as their field of study Business/Management, Economics, and Logistics.

Table 3. Description of variables used for the analysis of entrepreneurial actions[46]

	Variable	Measure	References
Dependent variable	Entrepreneurial action of alumni	1–if an alumnus reported that he/she was running a business; 0–otherwise.	Galloway and Brown (2002); Lange et al. (2011).
Independent variables	Entrepreneurial self-efficacy (*Personal: doing business skills*)	The level of doing business skills acquired at the university. 1–very low; 5–very high.	Galloway and Brown (2002).
	Reward for an entrepreneurial behavior (*Behavioral: higher income*)	Whether his/her monthly income is above an average monthly salary in Belarus. 1–yes; 0–no.	Bandura (2001).
	university environment (*Environmental: university*)	1. 'The atmosphere at my university inspired me to develop ideas for new businesses'. 2 'There was a favorable climate for becoming an entrepreneur at my university'. 3 'At my university, students were encouraged to engage in entrepreneurial activities'. 1 – not at all; 5 – very much	Coduras et al. (2008); Sieger, Fueglistaller and Zellweger (2014).
Control variables	Gender (*Male*)	1–male; 0–female	Karhunen and Ledyaeva (2010); Packham et al. (2010).
	Business/Economics specialties (*Business field*)	1–Business/Economics alumni 0–alumni of other specialties	Sieger, Fueglistaller and Zellweger (2014); Souitaris, Zerbinati and Al-Laham (2007); Bae et al. (2008).

[46] Descriptive statistics and a correlation table are provided in Annex 4.

Variable	Measure	References
Alumni of SBMT (*SBMT*)	1–alumni of SBMT; 0 – alumni of other faculties.	
Entrepreneurship courses (*Entrepr. course*)	1–alumni had attended at least one entrepreneurship course; 0–otherwise.	Toledano and Urbano (2008); Packham et al. (2010);
Self-employed parents (*Self-empl. parents*)		Zhang et al. (2014).
Age squared (*Age squared*)	1–alumni reported that at least one of parents was self-employed; 0–otherwise	Toledano and Urbano (2008); Laspita et al. (2012).
Years of work experience (*Work experience*)		Liñan and Chen (2009).
Years after graduation (*Years after graduation*)		Carter and Collinson (1999); Autio et al. (2001); Dohse and Walter (2012).

Kaiser-Meyer-Olkin index of .730 and the significance of Barlett's test of sphericity at the .001 level confirmed the appropriateness of the analysis. Three measures were loaded on one factor as we expected. We tested the reliability of the construct using Cronbach's alpha which appeared to be higher (.865) than the cut-off level of .7.

Data Analysis

The utilization of these sources of quantitative and qualitative data enabled methodological triangulation of the case findings and enhancing the validity of the study (Yin, 2014). Based on the existing literature, we predefined antecedents of an entrepreneurial environment at the university. This approach facilitated the systematic collection and analysis of relevant qualitative data. Since the dependent variables in both cases took on a value of 1 or 0, a binary logistic regression model was appropriate for the analysis. Regression scores for each factor obtained from the factor analysis and representing independent variables were introduced in the models. In order to test our propositions on the entrepreneurial behavior of students and alumni we ran two separate sets of models (Table 4 and Table 5).

RESULTS

The University-Level Factors of BSU

The social, political and cultural contexts of Belarus are characterized by significant government control, lack of transparency and isolation from the Western market economy and from the democratization processes (Miazhevich, 2007), while many management practices, especially in the higher education system, trace their roots to the Soviet times (Rees and Miazhevich, 2009). The higher education system remains rigid and unreformed creating a daunting policy challenge. The Ministry of

Education has considerable influence on student recruitment regulations, standards of teaching, the curriculum, awarding of qualifications, faculty hiring procedures, postgraduate and doctoral studies, licensing and certification of universities and educational programs (Kuznetsov and Yakavenka, 2005).

The Belarusian State University (BSU) – the largest educational and scientific center in Belarus – was founded in 1921 and is a flagship of the higher education sector. During the period of the sociopolitical transformations of the early 1990s, BSU has been able to develop its potential under new circumstances. Presently, BSU is an integral complex consisting of academic, research, production, social and cultural, and other units. The structure includes 17 educational faculties offering programs at bachelor, master and doctoral levels, 7 educational establishments, 6 R&D establishments, 6 scientific-production enterprises. It is worth noting that BSU is only Belarusian University that owns a business school – the School of Business and Management of Technology (SBMT).

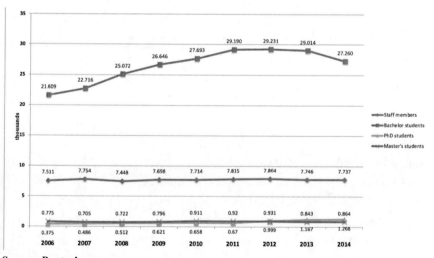

Source: Rector's report.

Figure 2. Human resources of BSU.

BSU employs approximately 7,740 staff members and enrolls over 27,000 bachelors, 860 Master's, 1268 PhD students (Figure 2). The research and innovative potential of BSU is corroborated by its leading position among all Belarusian universities in terms of scientific publications in international journals[47] and the third place in terms of patents granted[48]. Similarly to other post-Soviet countries, a massification of higher education took place without much increase in teaching staff or funding (Sangren, 2004). A considerable proportion of faculty does not conduct research, or at least not research close to the frontiers of knowledge production. Employment at BSU as well as at other Belarusian universities is not attractive to people with a business and entrepreneurial background due to a substantially lower level of salaries than in the private sector. Competences of such people are demanded only in the expensive advanced training and MBA programs. Therefore, their contribution to an entrepreneurial environment and to the fulfillment of the entrepreneurial mission is limited.

Noteworthy examples of physical resources devoted to idea and technology development are scientific laboratories and shared use research centers, which provide quite modern scientific equipment and render science-based services. Overall, activities of these units encompass only the first – research stage of the development of university-based enterprises and are not aimed at business incubation. After the breakdown of the Soviet Union, many leading universities in the region including BSU started developing entrepreneurial activities imitating Western universities, using various methods of income generation such as student fees, renting out of facilities, grants from international foundations, short-term courses (Sangren, 2004). Following these tendencies, BSU had managed to develop a diversified funding base. No budget sources accounted for about 45.4 percent of total revenues in 2014 (Figure 3). Tuition fees constituted a major part of revenues – 63 percent, while revenues from R&D activities

---

[47] According to the Scopus data base
[48] Data were obtained from the National Center for Intellectual Property.

and production activities accounted for 14.5 and 22.5 percent respectively (Figure 4).

At the same time, there are no special fundraising services or university funds for the financial support of innovative projects and new enterprises initiated by staff members, students or alumni. Every business initiative goes through a long chain of departments that are supposed to be involved in project realization but their participation is usually not rewarded. With respect to students' entrepreneurial initiatives, BSU does not provide any financial support or fundraising services.

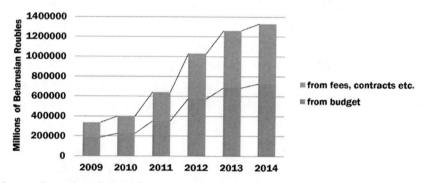

Source: Rector's report.

Figure 3. Sources of revenues of BSU[49].

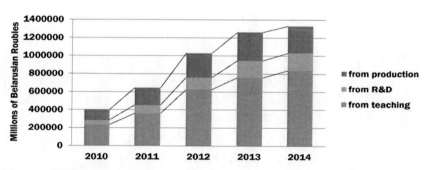

Source: Rector's report.

Figure 4. Distribution of revenues of BSU.

---

[49] The exchange rate of the Belarusian Rouble is volatile. At the end of 2014, 1 US dollar equaled 11,850 Belarusian Roubles

Specific organizational units – commercial resources – were set up at BSU to facilitate entrepreneurial activities related to knowledge transfer and commercialization. The Department for Maintenance of Innovative Projects is responsible for examination of business plans, innovative projects and agreements as well as consulting on the development and implementation of products and services. The Department for Intellectual Property Protection aims at revealing objects of intellectual property, preparing and submitting patent applications, providing intellectual property protection and consulting services on acquisition and transfer of intellectual property. This evidences that BSU has created a formal structure, which is expected to lead to the implementation of innovative projects and development of knowledge-based enterprise. However, the activities are focused mainly on consulting, patenting, and promotion, while such crucial functions as market research, evaluation of market value of knowledge and technology, developing strategy, attracting investors, and establishing university-industry networks are neglected. In addition, the aforementioned units tend to rely mainly on internal human resources and do not employ personnel with a business and entrepreneurial expertise and experience that are essential for university entrepreneurship (Chapple et al., 2005).

During the Soviet times, all universities were parts of the centralized state system and consequently were managed, funded and controlled through a uniform plan (Groudzinski, 2004). Universities were considered as servants of the state educating a defined number of specialists in certain fields and conducting research required by industries and according to state development plans. Therefore, in the 1990s, BSU was enforced to begin internal reforms towards new organizational structures aimed at promoting the development of educational and research activities. During the transition period, the universities, on the one hand, gained more freedom for their own decision-making. On the other hand, the need for self-development in the new conditions required changes in governance and organizational structure as well as high-quality management and an entrepreneurial style of work.

BSU is directly accountable to the Ministry of Education of the Republic of Belarus, while its Rector is appointed by the President of the Republic of Belarus. As a matter of fact, BSU has a rigid vertical organizational structure (central administration – faculties – chairs). At the same time, during the past two decades, BSU has developed "the expanded developmental periphery" (Clark, 1998) represented by educational establishments, R&D centers and institutes, as well as innovative enterprises which have a certain degree of autonomy in decision making and strategy implementing. Thus, they have separate bank accounts, can purchase and exercise property rights, found affiliated enterprises but have to form a centralized fund of BSU rendering not more than 25% of profit remained at the disposal after taxes. In this regard, entrepreneurial forms of management are most likely to be found at these units since they are empowered to keep a substantial part of their income and are enforced to be effective in taking and managing risks to develop or to survive. On the one hand, such decentralization contributes to efficiency through increasing quality and speed of decision making, stimulating local initiatives and promoting leadership. On the other hand, BSU and its peripheral units continue to suffer from the lack of highly qualified managers at all levels that is a common problem in many post-Soviet countries (Sangren, 2004). The vast majority of university managers are appointed from among academics that have no business or entrepreneurial background. Moreover, a Soviet style management still prevails.

An entrepreneurial vision is missing from the mission statement. An emphasis is put on the preservation of classical university traditions while neglecting contemporary processes in higher education and environmental challenges. Currently, BSU is mainly focused on executing plans and achieving goals that are set by the government. These circumstances can be explained by dominating traditional values and institutions inherited from the Soviet times and immature new market and social institutions (Aidis, Estrin and Mickiewicz, 2008; Uvarov and Perevodchikov, 2012).

In general, the remuneration and promotion system for academics of BSU does not go beyond teaching, research and publication criteria, whereas university managers are remunerated if plans developed by the state government and allocated by university authorities to organizational units are executed. Such a system substantially retards entrepreneurial initiative at the level of departments, educational establishments, research institutes and university-based enterprise.

In comparison with other Belarusian universities, BSU can be proud of the entrepreneurship and business education system, which has been developed during the past two decades. From this perspective, SBMT can be considered as a stronghold of entrepreneurship education, while some entrepreneurship and business-oriented courses are provided at the Faculty of Economics. However, the rigorous curricula of natural sciences and IT specialties are not supplemented with formal and experiential entrepreneurship education. Innovative methodologies and entrepreneurial approaches to teaching as well as faculty entrepreneurial role models are rare. Moreover, all changes in degree syllabuses need state approval that makes BSU and its educational units less flexible and nimble, while supporting entrepreneurial activity has not been an important part of the culture of the university.

THE IMPACT OF BSU ENVIRONMENT ON STUDENTS' AND ALUMNI'S ENTREPRENEURIAL BEHAVIOR

Table 4 depicts the results of seven models aimed at calculating the effects of the university-level factors on students' entrepreneurial behavior. The Hosmer-Lemeshow statistic indicated that the models adequately fitted the data since the significance value was substantially higher than .05 in all models (Hosmer and Lemeshow, 2004). The values of Nagelkerke R square, which were interpreted as reflecting the amount of variation accounted for by the binary logistic model (Hair et al., 2010), range from .153 to .164.

Table 4. Binary logistic regression

DV: Entrepreneurial intention (to become an entrepreneur/successor within 5 years after completion studies)							
	M1	M2	M3	M4	M5	M6	M7
Environment_factor	0.210	0.213	0.198	0.189	0.194	0.207	0.179
Attitude_factor	0.428***	0.422***	0.409**	0.398**	0.455**	0.402**	0.441**
Norms_factor	0.142	0.142	0.119	0.165	0.213	0.115	0.168
PBC_factor	0.507***	0.503***	0.491***	0.462***	0.562***	0.530***	0.582***
Norms x Attitude					0.055		0.060
Norms x PBC					0.269*		0.271*
Environment x Attitude						-0.067	-0.071
Environment x PBC						0.043	-0.007
Environment x Norms						-0.086	-0.089
Male (1/0)	-0.346	-0.356	-0.295	-0.350	-0.295	-0.358	-0.299
Business field	0.076	0.071	0.308		0.142	0.078	0.145
SBMT				0.737			
Entrep. Course							
Self-empl. parents	0.326	0.334	0.316	0.237	0.272	0.326	0.269
Age squared	0.001	-0.001	0.001	-0.001	0.001	-0.001	-0.001
Employment	-0.114						
Nagelkerke R Square	0.154	0.153	0.158	0.172	0.170	0.157	0.173
Hosmer and Lemeshow Test, p-value > .05	0.793	0.873	0.941	0.724	0.389	0.662	0.309

N = 316; *** Significant at the 0.001 level; ** Significant at the 0.01 level; * Significant at the 0.05 level.

The university environment was found not to be a significant predictor of students' entrepreneurial behavior at BSU. With respect to other predictors, the results provided evidence of the positive relationship between attitude towards entrepreneurship and entrepreneurial intention [.428; .001] as well as between perceived behavioral control and entrepreneurial intention [.507; .001] (M1). These findings confirmed TPB (Ajzen, 1991) and concurred with previous studies in the field (Iakovleva, Kolvereid and Stephan, 2011; Souitaris, Zerbinati and Al-Laham, 2007). However, subjective norms appeared insignificant that is at odds with results obtained even in another post-Soviet economy – Russia (Karhunen and Ledyaeva, 2010), which is characterized by hostile entrepreneurial environment (Aidis, Estrin and Mickiewicz, 2008).

Importantly, we can deduce that Business/Economics students (M2), students of SBMT (M3), and those attended at least one entrepreneurship course (M4) did not report higher entrepreneurial intention in comparison to other students of BSU. In addition, models with interaction terms (M5-M7) provided additional insights. Thus, a positive value of the interaction between social norms and perceived behavioral control (*Norms* × *PBC*) in M5 [.269; $p < .05$] and M7 [.271; $p < .05$] may imply that the higher a value of perceived social norms is, the greater the effect of perceived behavioral control on student's entrepreneurial intention is. Other interaction terms appeared insignificant. In general, there was no evidence to support the proposition P1 that perceived university entrepreneurial environment is positively related to entrepreneurial behavior of BSU students.

In Table 5, we provide the results of four models predicting the entrepreneurial behavior of BSU alumni on the basis of SCP. Although the models adequately fitted the data (the significance values of the Hosmer-Lemeshow statistic ranged between .208 and .897, Nagelkerke R square range between .196 and .258), personal, behavioral, and environmental determinants were found not to be significant antecedents of entrepreneurial actions. This means that a perceived level of doing business skills acquired at the university, income above average, a perceived university environment do not increase the probability of alumni being entrepreneurs.

We found evidence that graduation from both Business/Economics specialties [1.867; .001] (M1) and SBMT [1.070; .05] (M4) increases the probability of running a business by alumni. Drawing on exponentiated coefficients, alumni graduated from a Business/Economic specialty are 5.5 times more likely to become entrepreneurs than their counterparts graduated from other specialties, whereas SBMT graduates are 1.9 times more likely to be engaged in entrepreneurial activity (M4). Likewise, if an alumnus attended at least one entrepreneurship course [1.024; .05], the probability of running own business appeared to be 1.8 times higher (M5).

Table 5. Binary logistic regression

	DV: Doing Business				
	M1	M2	M3	M4	M5
Personal: doing business skills	-0.413	-0.400	-0.462	-0.313	-0.280
Reward for a behavior: higher income	0.409	0.351	0.441	0.551	0.562
Environmental: university factor	0.209	0.175	0.275	0.252	0.228
Male	1.712***	1.664***	1.771***	1.693***	1.723***
Business field (Business vs. others)	1.867***	1.973***	1.684**		
SBMT				1.070*	
Entrepr. course					1.024*
Age squared	-0.001			0.001	-0.001
Work experience		0.152			
Years after graduation			-0.120		
Nagelkerke R Square	0.252	0.257	0.258	0.196	0.198
Hosmer and Lemeshow Test, p-value > .05	0.208	0.897	0.609	0.459	0.450

257 alumni; *** Significant at the 0.001 level. * Significant at the 0.05 level.

To summarize, we did not find strong support for the proposition P2, which claimed that perceived university entrepreneurial environment is positively related to an entrepreneurial action of BSU alumni.

Discussion

Our qualitative study demonstrated that, being a leading Belarusian university, BSU has at its disposal the necessary human, physical, financial and commercial resources to create a benevolent entrepreneurial environment, but it is not capable and lacks role models to harness these resources for fostering of an entrepreneurial intention among students and faculty. Therefore, in terms of Kirby, Guerrero and Urbano (2011), the natural incubator does not work since there are no clear and generally accessible mechanisms, procedures and support measures and 'collective involvement' (Secundo et al., 2016) to transform abundant knowledge, ideas, networks and intention into entrepreneurial activities. This was confirmed by the results of our empirical analysis that the perceived environment is not predictive of the entrepreneurial behavior neither of students nor of alumni. BSU still enjoys its outstanding reputation and state resources mostly available to maintain the status quo – confirming the notion of Clark (1998) that flagships of higher education systems can be more unhurried in transforming their governance, culture and attitudes.

Notwithstanding the unsupportive BSU environment, serious institutional weakness and quite a hostile atmosphere for entrepreneurship in post-Soviet countries in general (Aidis, Estrin and Mickiewicz, 2008, Ivanova, 2005), students of BSU have a high level of entrepreneurial intention – 4.6 – if we compare with universities from other countries participating in GUESSS in 2013 (Sieger, Fueglistaller and Zellweger, 2014). If BSU represented Belarus in GUESSS, it would be ranked 5th or 6th among 34 countries, while the evaluated level of the entrepreneurial environment would be below average. Findings of the two sets of models may imply that, since curricula of the majority of BSU students do not include any formal entrepreneurship or business courses, the high proportion of potential entrepreneurs is not transformed into entrepreneurship capital (Audretsch, 2014). Therefore, the country loses potential entrepreneurs, who would be able to generate economic value and employment if they were exposed to entrepreneurship education at the university level (Lange et al., 2011; Todorovic and Ma, 2010).

In view of that, BSU, as with all Belarusian universities, needs to take serious strides to catch up with Western universities in terms of creating entrepreneurial ecosystems and thereby being contributors to the socioeconomic development (Bramwell and Wolfe, 2008). Our qualitative study has shown that BSU has two out of five characteristics of the entrepreneurial university proposed by Clark (1998) such as the expanded developmental periphery and the diversified funding base which should be pivots of the inevitable future transformation. Hence, we propose several initiatives to develop an entrepreneurship-friendly environment at the university level.

First and foremost, BSU needs to adopt and coordinate apparent and shared strategy across its critical activities: teaching, research, and production to integrate organizational units. A strategic plan should empower entrepreneurial actions, synergies and cooperation among individuals, organizational units as well as university-business relations. Next, peripheral units such as educational establishments and innovative enterprises – the nimblest structures – should be treated as contributors to the university development in the broad sense rather than income generators. The presence of the business school is a substantial advantage. As the formation of an entrepreneurial ecosystem and university transformation require skills, competences, attitudes not associated with a traditional university community (Siegel and Phan, 2005), BSU should utilize the potential of SBMT to provide consulting, training and mentoring to establish relationships with the business sector and to support activities targeted at developing university spin-outs and start-ups.

In the same vein, BSU should be concerned about the development of the periphery. Extensive support (IP management, business planning, marketing, PR) should be given to entrepreneurial teams attracting and motivating the participation of existing units. BSU should adopt and implement the Supportive model of spinning out new enterprises (Clarysse et al., 2005) securing sustainability of ventures by providing access to university resources and capabilities. University based enterprises can act as test beds for new ideas and technologies generated at BSU, as bases for fellowships and internships (Klofsten, 2000). Moreover, entrepreneurs and entrepreneurial teams could be the best role models for their counterparts (Schulte, 2004).

In addition, BSU should concentrate efforts on providing all members of the academic community with entrepreneurship-specific education to equip them with relevant knowledge and competences as well as with entrepreneurial alertness and risk-taking assets (Solesvik et al., 2013). More enterprising and action-oriented approaches and activities aimed at developing critical thinking, independence and readiness to assume responsibility (Toledano and Urbano, 2008) supplemented with cross-disciplinary projects should gradually supplant traditional passive methods of education aiming at "feeding" learning material to students (Kuznetsov and Yakavenka, 2005).

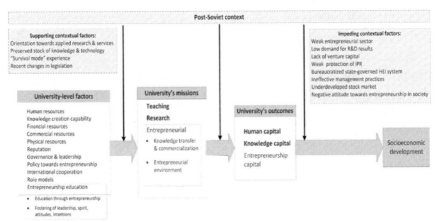

Source: Adapted from Guerrero and Urbano (2012).

Figure 5. Conceptual model for future research.

Another rudiment of the Soviet higher education system that should certainly be pruned is the promotion and remuneration system, which is still focused only on teaching and research activities. As a matter of fact, this system closes the door to people with a business background, while such people are of great importance in changing 'the hearts and minds' of students and colleagues and thereby creating an entrepreneurial environment within the university.

Drawing on the existing literature and our findings, we propose a conceptual model that embodies the entrepreneurial development of universities in post-Soviet economies and may be used by researchers focusing on this phenomenon (Figure 5). The model integrates university-level factors conditioning a fulfilment of the three missions as well as the outcomes of these missions contributing to the socioeconomic development. First-priority measures for the incorporating of the entrepreneurial mission should be focused on creating of a supportive entrepreneurial environment within universities as well as on promoting of effective knowledge transfer and commercialization.

The specific post-Soviet context moderates all the relationships integrated into the model. It is worth noting that such context has a dual effect since it is characterized by factors that either facilitate or retard the entrepreneurial transformation of universities.

CONCLUSION

The mandate of universities to play an active role in fostering entrepreneurial mindsets and intentions is arguably more critical in the context of post-Soviet economies which are characterized by the unsupportive institutional environment and underdeveloped entrepreneurial sector. At the same time, playing this role, the universities need to be flexible, entrepreneurial and innovative which is often at odds with their governance system, values and perceived missions. In this sense, the main contribution of this chapter consists in demonstrating how university-level factors shape a university entrepreneurial environment in the context of post-Soviet economies and how this environment influences the entrepreneurial behavior of students and alumni.

While the entrepreneurial environment and education at the majority of post-Soviet universities substantially lag behind Western developed economies, policy makers have started paying more attention to these issues to use potential of universities to create entrepreneurship capital. Thus, the State Program for Development of Higher Education the

Republic of Belarus for 2011-2015 stipulated the creation of business incubators in each university to promote a joint innovative and entrepreneurial activity. However, while, on the one hand, these plans appeared unrealistic, on the other hand, there were no clear measures targeted at the development of an entrepreneurial spirit and attitude among the university community. Consequently, entrepreneurship education appeared well out of the policy agenda. Later on, the State Program for Innovative Development of the Republic of Belarus for 2016-2020 stressed the need for involvement of faculty members in entrepreneurial activities; creation of technology transfer offices at all universities and development of entrepreneurial competences of the university community. The State Program "Education and Youth Policy" 2016-2020 echoed the previous one in defining involvement of youth in entrepreneurial activities as one of the policy priorities. Moreover, in autumn 2017, the Ministry of Education initiated the development and implementation of an experimental project "Formation of higher education institutions based on the University 3.0 model" that captured some facets of entrepreneurial transformation. However, some skepticism exists on whether some relevant measures will be undertaken against the backdrop of the lack of funding for such activities and absence of elaborate study in the field.

The general conclusion to be drawn from this single case study is that underdeveloped entrepreneurial and business competences and the Soviet heritage still visible in attitudes and values restrain employing the abundant human and physical resources of BSU to contribute to economic development not only by educating job seekers but by fostering job creators and transforming research activity into economic value (Kirby, Guerrero and Urbano, 2011). Nevertheless, as the regression analysis showed, existing formal business-related education does facilitate an entrepreneurial activity of alumni that is consistent with previous studies (Martin, McNally and Kay, 2013). Therefore, from a policy perspective, further efforts need to be made to extend entrepreneurship education or some facets of it to all specialties to equip university graduates with the competences, attitudes and motivation for being leaders in innovative development.

We acknowledge that the chapter has some limitations. Firstly, the economic and social environment that is external to the university (Dohse and Walter, 2012; MacKenzie and Zhang, 2014) and endemic to transition economies (Aidis, Estrin and Mickiewicz, 2008) remained mostly beyond the scope of our study. The university-government affinity, weak incentives for knowledge commercialization and reliance on personal networks are thought to be essential antecedents in the context of Belarus and other countries with transition economies. The impact of these factors could be explored by conducting a multiple case study.

Secondly, the size of the both samples used for the quantitative analysis was quite small for such studies. Thirdly, our samples did not match the proportions in the total population of BSU students and alumni in terms of the study field. Larger samples and proportional quota sampling should ideally be used. Fourthly, we estimated a direct effect of the university environment on entrepreneurial behavior to make a comparison between its influences on both the students' and alumni's entrepreneurial behavior. Finally, our quantitative analyses concentrated only on students and alumni as representatives of one university community. Therefore, future quantitative studies may focus on faculty's perceptions of an entrepreneurial environment at universities and their entrepreneurial behavior (Guerrero and Urbano, 2014) at universities of different profiles and at universities with the Soviet past and those established in the post-socialist era.

REFERENCES

Aidis, R., Estrin, S. and Mickiewicz, T. (2008). Institutions and entrepreneurship development in Russia: A comparative perspective. *Journal of Business Venturing*, 23: 656-672.

Ajzen, I. (1991). The theory of planned behavior. *Organizational behavior and human decision processes*, 50 (III): 179-211.

Amit, R. and Shoemaker, P. J. (1993). Strategic assets and organizational rent. *Strategic Management Journal*, 14 (II): 33-46.

Audretsch, D. B. (2014). From the entrepreneurial university to the university for the entrepreneurial society. *The Journal of Technology Transfer*, 39 (III): 313-321.

Autio, E., Keeley, R. H., Klofsten, M., Parker, G. G. and Hay, M. (2001). Entrepreneurial intent among students in Scandinavia and in the USA. *Enterprise and Innovation Management Studies*, 2 (II): 145-160.

Bae, T. J., Qian, S., Miao, C., and Fiet, J. O. (2014). The Relationship between Entrepreneurship Education and Entrepreneurial Intentions: A Meta–Analytic Review. *Entrepreneurship theory and practice*, 38 (II): 217-254.

Bandura, A. (1986). *Social foundations of thought and action: a social cognitive theory*. Englewood Cliffs: Prentice-Hall.

Bandura, A. (2001). Social cognitive theory of mass communications. *Media effects: Advances in theory and research* (2nd ed.) edited by Bryant, J. and Zillman D. 121-153. Hillsdale: Lawrence Erlbaum.

Boyd, N. G. and Vozikis, G. S. (1994). The influence of self-efficacy on the development of entrepreneurial intentions and actions. *Entrepreneurship Theory and Practice*, 18: 63-77.

Bramwell, A. and Wolfe, D. A. (2008). Universities and regional economic development: The entrepreneurial University of Waterloo. *Research Policy*, 37 (VIII): 1175-1187.

Carter, S. and Collinson, E. (1999). Entrepreneurship education: Alumni perceptions of the role of higher education institutions. *Journal of Small Business and Enterprise Development*, 6 (III): 229-239.

Chapple, W., Lockett, A., Siegel, D. and Wright, M. (2005). Assessing the relative performance of UK university technology transfer offices: parametric and non-parametric evidence. *Research Policy*, 34 (III): 369-384.

Clark, B. R. (1998). *Creating entrepreneurial universities*. Oxford: Pergamon.

Clark, B. R. (2001). The entrepreneurial university: new foundations for collegiality, autonomy and achievement. *Higher Education Management*, 13 (II): 9-24.

Clarysse, B., Wright, M., Lockett, A., Van de Velde, E. and Vohora, A. (2005). Spinning out new ventures: a typology of incubation strategies from European research institutions. *Journal of Business Venturing*, 20 (II): 183-216.

Coduras, A., Urbano, D., Rojas, Á. and Martínez, S. (2008). The relationship between university supports to entrepreneurship with entrepreneurial activity in Spain: A GEM data based analysis. *International Advances in Economic Research*, 14 (IV): 395-406.

Dohse, D. and Walter, S. G. (2012). Knowledge context and entrepreneurial intentions among students. *Small Business Economics*, 39 (IV): 877-895.

Eisenhardt, K. M. (1989). Building theories from case study research. *Academy of management review*, 14 (IV): 532-550.

Ertuna, I. Z. and Gurel, E. 2011. The moderating role of higher education on entrepreneurship. *Education+ training*, 53(V): 387-402.

European Commission. (2015). *Entrepreneurship Education: a Road to Success*. Luxembourg: Publications Office of the European Union.

Fayolle, A., Gailly, B. and Lassas-Clerc, N. (2006). Assessing the impact of entrepreneurship education programmes: a new methodology. *Journal of European Industrial Training*, 30 (IX): 701-720.

Gál, Z. and Ptaček, P. (2011). The role of mid-range universities in knowledge transfer in non-metropolitan regions in Central Eastern Europe. *European Planning Studies*, 19 (IX): 1669-1690.

Galloway, L. and Brown, W. (2002). Entrepreneurship education at university: a driver in the creation of high growth firms? *Education+ Training*, 44 (VIII-IX): 398-405.

Gibb, A. (2012). Exploring the synergistic potential in entrepreneurial university development: towards the building of a strategic framework. *Annals of Innovation & Entrepreneurship*, 3: 1-24.

Groudzinski, A. (2004). "A project-oriented approach to university management," In *Entrepreneurialism and the Transformation of Russian Universities* edited by Shattock M. 122-137. Paris: UNESCO/International Institute tor Educational Planning (IIEP).

Guerrero, M. and Urbano, D. (2012). The development of entrepreneurial university. *Journal of Technology Transfer*, 37 (I): 43-74.

Guerrero, M. and Urbano, D. (2014). Academics' start-up intentions and knowledge filters: an individual perspective of the knowledge spillover theory of entrepreneurship. *Small Business Economics*, 43 (I): 57-74.

Guerrero, M., Cunningham, J. A. and Urbano, D. (2015). Economic impact of entrepreneurial universities' activities: An exploratory study of the United Kingdom. *Research Policy*, 44 (III): 748-764.

Guerrero, M., Rialp, J. and Urbano, D. (2008). The impact of desirability and feasibility on entrepreneurial intentions: A structural equation model. *International Entrepreneurship and Management Journal*, 4 (I): 35-50.

Guerrero, M., Urbano, D., Cunningham, J. and Organ, D. (2014). Entrepreneurial universities in two European regions: a case study comparison. *The Journal of Technology Transfer*, 39 (III): 415-434.

Guerrero, M., Urbano, D. and Fayolle, A. (2016). Entrepreneurial activity and regional competitiveness: evidence from European entrepreneurial universities. *The Journal of Technology Transfer*, 41 (I): *105-131*

Hair, J. F., Black, W., Babin, B. and Anderson, R. (2010). *Multivariate Data Analysis. A Global Perspective.* New Jearsey: Pearson Prentice Hall.

Hayter, C. S. (2013). Harnessing university entrepreneurship for economic growth: Factors of success among university spin-offs. *Economic Development Quarterly*, 27 (I): 18-28.

Hmieleski, K. M. and Baron, R. A. (2009). Entrepreneurs' optimism and new venture performance: a social cognitive perspective. *Academy of management Journal*, 52 (III): 473-488.

Hosmer, D. W. and Lemeshow, S. (2004). *Applied Logistic Regression.* New York: John Wiley & Sons.

Hsu, D. H., Roberts, E. B. and Eesley, C. E. (2007). Entrepreneurs from technology-based universities: Evidence from MIT. *Research Policy*, 36 (V): 768-788.

Iakovleva, T., Kolvereid, L. and Stephan, U. (2011). Entrepreneurial intentions in developing and developed countries. *Education+Training*, 53 (V): 353-370.

Ivanova, Y. V. (2005). Belarus: entrepreneurial activities in an unfriendly environment. *Journal of East-West Business*, 10 (IV): 29-54.

Jones, C. and English, J. (2004). A contemporary approach to entrepreneurship education. *Education+Training*, 46 (VIII): 416-423.

Karhunen, P. and Ledyaeva, S. (2010). Determinants of entrepreneurial interest and risk tolerance among Russian university students: empirical study. *Journal of Enterprising Culture*, 18 (III): 229-263.

Kirby, D., Guerrero, M. and Urbano, D. (2011). The theoretical and empirical side of entrepreneurial universities: An institutional approach. *Canadian Journal of Administrative Sciences*, 28 (III): 302-316.

Klofsten, M. (2000). Training entrepreneurship at universities: a Swedish case. *Journal of European Industrial Training*, 24 (VI): 337-344.

Krueger Jr., N. F. and Brazeal, D. V. (1994). Entrepreneurial potential and potential entrepreneurs. *Entrepreneurship theory and practice*, 18 (III): 91-104.

Kuratko, D. F. (2005). The emergence of entrepreneurship education: Development, trends, and challenges. *Entrepreneurship Theory and Practice*, 29 (V): 577-597.

Kuznetsov, A. and Yakavenka, A. (2005). Barriers to the absorption of management knowledge in Belarus. *Journal of Managerial Psychology*, 20 (VII): 566-577.

Kwiek, M. (2001). Social and cultural dimensions of the transformation of higher education in Central and Eastern Europe. *Higher Education in Europe*, 26 (III): 399-410.

Kwiek, M. (2008). Academic entrepreneurship vs. changing governance and institutional management structures at European universities. *Policy Futures in Education*, 6 (VI): 757-770.

Lange, J. E., Marram, E., Jawahar, A. S., Yong, W. and Bygrave, W. (2011). Does an entrepreneurship education have lasting value? A study of careers of 4,000 alumni. *Frontiers of Entrepreneurship Research,* 31 (VI): 210-224.

Laspita, S., Breugst, N., Heblich, S. and Patzelt, H. (2012). Intergenerational transmission of entrepreneurial intentions. *Journal of Business Venturing,* 27 (IV): 414-435.

Laukkanen, M. (2000). Exploring alternative approaches in high-level entrepreneurship education: creating micromechanisms for endogenous regional growth. *Entrepreneurship & Regional Development,* 12 (I): 25-47.

Lazzeretti, L. and Tavoletti, E. (2005). Higher education excellence and local economic development: The case of the entrepreneurial university of Twente. *European Planning Studies,* 13 (III): 475–493.

Liñan, F. and Chen, Y.-W. (2009). Development and Cross- Cultural application of a specific instrument to measure entrepreneurial intentions. *Entrepreneurship Theory and Practice,* 33 (III): 593-617.

Liñán, F., Urbano, D. and Guerrero, M. (2011). Regional variations in entrepreneurial cognitions: Start-up intentions of university students in Spain. *Entrepreneurship and Regional Development,* 23 (III-IV): 187-215.

Liu, S. S. and Dubinsky, A. J. (2000). Institutional entrepreneurship - A panacea for universities-in-transition? *European Journal of Marketing,* 34 (XI/XII): 1315-1337.

Lüthje, C. and Franke, N. (2003). The 'making' of an entrepreneur: testing a model of entrepreneurial intent among engineering students at MIT. *R&D Management,* 33 (II): 135-147.

MacKenzie, N. G. and Zhang, Q. (2014). A regional perspective on the entrepreneurial university: Practices and policies. In *Handbook on the entrepreneurial university* edited by Fayolle, A. and Redford D. T. 188-206. Cheltenham: Edward Elgar Publishing.

Markuerkiaga, L., Errasti, N. and Igartua, J. I. (2014). Success factors for managing an entrepreneurial university: Developing an integrative framework. *Industry and Higher Education,* 28 (IV): 233-244.

Marozau, R. and Guerrero, M. (2016). Conditioning factors of knowledge transfer and commercialisation in the context of post-socialist economies: the case of Belarusian higher education institutions. *International Journal of Entrepreneurship and Small Business,* 27 (IV): 441-462.

Martin, B., McNally, J. J. and Kay, M. (2013). Examining the formation of human capital in entrepreneurship: A meta-analysis of entrepreneurship education outcomes. *Journal of Business Venturing,* 28 (II): 211-224.

Matlay, H. (2008). The impact of entrepreneurship education on entrepreneurial outcomes. *Journal of Small Business and Enterprise Development,* 15 (II): 382-396.

Miazhevich, G. (2007). Official media discourse and the self-representation of entrepreneurs in Belarus. *Europe-Asia Studies,* 59 (VIII): 1331-1348.

Nkamnebe, A. (2009). Towards market-oriented entrepreneurial university management for Nigerian universities. *International Journal of Management Education,* 7 (II): 9-19.

North, D. C. (1990). *Institutions, institutional change and economic performance.* Cambridge: Cambridge University Press.

O'Shea, R., Allen, T., Morse, K., O'Gorman, C. and Roche, F. (2007). Delineating the anatomy of an entrepreneurial university: the Massachusetts Institute of Technology experience. *R&D Management,* 37 (I): 1-16.

O'Shea, R., Chugh, H. and Allen, T. (2008). Determinants and consequences of university spinoff activity: a conceptual framework. *Journal of Technology Transfer,* 33 (VI): 653–666.

Packham, G., Jones, P., Miller, C., Pickernell, D. and Brychan, T. (2010). Attitudes towards entrepreneurship education: a comparative analysis. *Education+ Training,* 52 (VIII-IX): 568-586.

Rees, C. J. and Miazhevich, G. (2009). Socio-cultural change and business ethics in post-Soviet countries: The cases of Belarus and Estonia. *Journal of Business Ethics,* 86 (I): 51-63.

Sangren, A. (2004). Are Russian universities becoming entrepreneurial? In *Entrepreneurialism and the Transformation of Russian Universities* edited by Shattock M. 57-65. Paris: UNESCO/International Institute tor Educational Planning (IIEP).

Secundo, G., Dumay, J., Schiuma, G. and Passiante, G., 2016. Managing intellectual capital through a collective intelligence approach: An integrated framework for universities. *Journal of Intellectual Capital*, 17 (II): 298-319.

Schulte, P. (2004). The entrepreneurial university: A strategy for institutional development. *Higher Education in Europe*, 29 (II): 187-191.

Shattock, M. (2004). *Entrepreneurialism and the Transformation of Russian Universities*. (M. Shattock, Ed.) Paris: UNESCO/International Institute tor Educational Planning (IIEP).

Siegel, D. S. and Phan, P. H. (2005). Analyzing the effectiveness of university technology transfer: implications for entrepreneurship education. Advances in the study of entrepreneurship. *Innovation & Economic Growth*, 16: 1-38.

Sieger, P., Fueglistaller, U. and Zellweger, T. (2014). *Student Entrepreneurship Across the Globe: A Look at Intentions and Activities*. St. Gallen: Swiss Research Institute of Small Business and Entrepreneurship at the University of St. Gallen (KMU-HSG).

Solesvik, M. Z., Westhead, P., Matlay, H. and Parsyak, V. N. (2013). Entrepreneurial assets and mindsets: benefit from university entrepreneurship education investment. *Education + Training*, 55 (VIII-IX): 748-762.

Souitaris, V., Zerbinati, S. and Al-Laham, A. (2007). Do entrepreneurship programmes raise entrepreneurial intention of science and engineering students? The effect of learning, inspiration and resources. *Journal of Business Venturing*, 22 (IV): 566-591.

Subotzky, G. (1999). Alternatives to the entrepreneurial university: New modes of knowledge production in community service programs. *Higher Education,* 38 (IV), 401-440.

Tkachev, A. and Kolvereid, L. (1999). Self-employment intentions among Russian students. *Entrepreneurship & Regional Development,* 11 (III): 269-280.

Todorovic, Z. W. and Ma, J. (2010). Resolving the paradox of enterprising communities in Eastern Europe. *Journal of Enterprising Communities: People and Places in the Global Economy,* 4 (III): 234-251.

Toledano, N. and Urbano, D. (2008). Promoting entrepreneurial mindsets at universities: a case study in the South of Spain. *European Journal of International Management,* 2 (IV): 382-399.

Urbano, D. and Guerrero, M. (2013). Entrepreneurial universities: Socioeconomic impacts of academic entrepreneurship in a European region. *Economic Development Quarterly,* 27 (I): 40-55.

Uvarov, A. and Perevodchikov, E. (2012). The entrepreneurial university in Russia: from idea to reality. *Procedia-Social and Behavioral Sciences,* 52: 45-51.

Wright, M., Clarysse, B., Mustar, P. and Lockett, A. (2007). *Academic entrepreneurship in Europe.* Cheltenham: Edward Elgar Publishing.

Yar Hamidi, D., Wennberg, K., and Berglund, H. (2008). Creativity in entrepreneurship education. Journal of small business and enterprise development, 15(II): 304-320.

Yin, R. K. (2014). *Case study research: Design and methods* (5th ed.). Thousand Oaks: Sage Publications.

Zhang, Y., Duysters, G. and Cloodt, M. (2014). The role of entrepreneurship education as a predictor of university students' entrepreneurial intention. *International Entrepreneurship and Management Journal,* 10 (III): 623-641.

Zhou, C. and Peng, X. M. (2008). The entrepreneurial university in China: nonlinear paths. *Science and Public Policy,* 35 (IX): 637–646.

ANNEX 1. ROTATED COMPONENT MATRIX AND RELIABILITY INDICATORS

Items	Component			
	Attitude	PBC	Envir.	Norms
Being an entrepreneur implies more advantages than disadvantages to me.	0.812			
A career as entrepreneur is attractive for me.	0.892			
If I had the opportunity and resources, I would become an entrepreneur.	0.888			
Being an entrepreneur would entail great satisfactions for me.	0.904			
Among various options, I would rather become an entrepreneur.	0.856			
For me, being an entrepreneur would be very easy.		0.810		
If I wanted to, I could easily pursue a career as entrepreneur.		0.852		
As entrepreneur, I would have complete control over the situation.		0.777		
If I become an entrepreneur, the chances of success would be very high.		0.749		
How would react student's close family if a student became an entrepreneur?				0.733
How would react student's friends if a student became an entrepreneur?				0.866
How would react fellow students' friends if a student became an entrepreneur?				0.830
The atmosphere at my university inspires me to develop ideas for new businesses.			0.886	
There is a favorable climate for becoming an entrepreneur at my university.			0.888	
At my university, students are encouraged to engage in entrepreneurial activities.			0.819	
Cronbach's alpha	0.951	0.893	0.887	0.810
Extraction Method: Principal Component Analysis. Rotation Method: Varimax with Kaiser Normalization.				

ANNEX 2. ALUMNI SURVEY QUESTIONNAIRE

Year of graduation:
Year of Birth:
Gender:
Field of education: Business Administration; Logistics; Economics; Management; Other Social sciences; Art, Humanities, Linguistics; Natural sciences; IT
Form of education: full-time; part-time
Year of the first employment:
Kind of professional activity:
Doing business/Management and administration; Practical work according to profession acquired; R&D; Teaching; Professional activity is not related to specialization acquired; Baby-sitting; Study; Unemployed
How often do you apply knowledge obtained at university?: constantly; often; rarely
Type of organization you are employed at: private; public; non-commercial
Have you created or participated in business creation? Yes/No
Is it a family firm? Yes/No
Did you receive any support from the university during the creation of your company? Yes/No
Where is your firm located?
Which sector is your firm active in?
Information technology and communication; Trade (wholesale/retail); Consulting (law, tax, management, HR); Advertising/Marketing/Design; Education and training; Tourism and gastronomy; Health services; Other services (including finance, insurance, etc.); Architecture and engineering; Construction and manufacturing; Other
Number of employees at your firm:
How many employees do you expect to have in 5 years?
What are your market expectations? Regional market; National Market; International market
How many enterprises have created?
Have you initiated or participated in the creation of non-commercial organizations? Yes/No
Have you initiated organizational/process/product innovations in the firm you work for? Yes/No
What is proximally your personal income per month before taxes and without extra payments?
Is your salary/business income more than an average salary in the country? Yes/No

Please indicate the extent to which you agree to the following statements about the university environment. (1= lower level of agreement, 5=higher level of agreement):
The atmosphere at my university inspires me to develop ideas for new businesses
There was a favorable climate for becoming an entrepreneur at my university
At my university, students were encouraged to engage in entrepreneurial activities
My university influence in my propensity to becoming self-employment
I feel proud of being alumni of this university
Entrepreneurship course/program/education:
I did not attend a course on entrepreneurship
I attended at least one entrepreneurship course as elective
I attended at least one entrepreneurship course as compulsory part of my studies
I studied in a specific program on entrepreneurship
What did your university provide for business creation?
Financial support (yes/no); Contact points (yes/no); Mentoring/Coaching Programs (yes/no); Business plan contests (yes/no); Contact platform with investors (yes/no); Workshops/Networking with entrepreneurs.
Evaluate the level of your managerial skills acquired at a university:
(1 = low level, 5 = high level)
Evaluate the level of your skills of doing business acquired at a university:
(1= low level, 5=high level)
Evaluate the level of your academic (theoretical) education:
(1 = low level, 5=high level)
Evaluate the level of your practical education:
(1 = low level, 5 = high level)
Evaluate the level of your education for R&D activity:
(1 = low level, 5 = high level)
Evaluate the level of your computer skills and skills in using Internet acquired at a university: (1= low level, 5 = high level)
Evaluate the level of your skills in independent work acquired at a university:
(1= low level, 5 = high level)
Evaluate the level of your foreign language skills acquired at a university:
(1= low level, 5 = high level)
Evaluate the level of your business communication skills and skills of team work acquired at a university:
(1 = low level, 5 = high level)
To what extent are you satisfied with your education level obtained at a university:
(1 = low level, 5 = high level)

ANNEX 3. DESCRIPTIVE STATISTICS AND CORRELATION MATRIX ON THE SAMPLE OF BSU STUDENTS

	Mean	S.D.	1	2	3	4	5	6	7	8	9	10	11	12	13	14	15	16	17	18	19	20	21	22
1 The atmosphere at my university inspires me to develop ideas for new businesses.	4.14	1.58																						
2 There is a favorable climate for becoming an entrepreneur at my university.	4.29	1.59	0.827**																					
3 At my university, students are encouraged to engage in entrepreneurial activities.	4.19	1.80	0.668**	0.702**																				
4 Being an entrepreneur implies more advantages than disadvantages to me.	4.82	1.66	0.299**	0.330**	0.332**																			
5 A career as entrepreneur is attractive for me.	4.75	1.66	0.291**	0.322**	0.287**	0.819**																		
6 If I had the opportunity and resources, I would become an entrepreneur.	4.91	1.77	0.274**	0.260**	0.236**	0.724**	0.819**																	
7 Being an entrepreneur would entail great satisfactions for me.	4.97	1.65	0.301**	0.311**	0.293**	0.767**	0.834**	0.877**																
8 Among various options, I would rather become an entrepreneur.	4.79	1.73	0.307**	0.347**	0.306**	0.703**	0.816**	0.775**	0.823**															
9 Your close family	5.91	1.27	0.316**	0.300**	0.314**	0.377**	0.343**	0.374**	0.360**	0.340**														
10 Your friends	5.78	1.19	0.260**	0.286**	0.256**	0.298**	0.266**	0.322**	0.293**	0.277**	0.679**													
11 Your fellow students	5.27	1.40	0.239**	0.256**	0.197**	0.189**	0.186**	0.218**	0.230**	0.188**	0.471**	0.636**												
12 For me, being an entrepreneur would be very easy.	4.20	1.44	0.354**	0.408**	0.388**	0.455**	0.492**	0.407**	0.446**	0.416**	0.381**	0.287**	0.201**											
13 If I wanted to, I could easily pursue a career as entrepreneur.	4.26	1.47	0.316**	0.374**	0.363**	0.416**	0.420**	0.348**	0.372**	0.393**	0.348**	0.341**	0.211**	0.767**										
14 As entrepreneur, I would have complete control over the situation.	4.94	1.44	0.326**	0.340**	0.348**	0.437**	0.424**	0.416**	0.440**	0.411**	0.420**	0.395**	0.303**	0.640**	0.659**									
15 If I become an entrepreneur, the chances of success would be very high.	4.81	1.45	0.365**	0.391**	0.336**	0.459**	0.454**	0.427**	0.418**	0.445**	0.485**	0.406**	0.292**	0.628**	0.648**	0.714**								
16 Male	0.39	0.49	-0.134**	-0.104*	-0.083	-0.021	-0.051	-0.079	-0.063	-0.074	-0.125**	-0.056	-0.068	0.084	0.052	0.035	-0.047							
17 Self-empl. parents	0.35	0.48	0.099	0.121**	0.156**	0.109	0.146**	0.113*	0.127*	0.116*	0.017	0.014	0.021	0.216**	0.194**	0.120*	0.118*	0.139**						
18 Age Squared	362.15	102.22	-0.229**	-0.245**	-0.232**	-0.161**	-0.102	-0.044	-0.053	-0.067	-0.072	0.008	-0.182**	-0.154**	-0.103	-0.147**	0.000	-0.147**						
19 Employment	0.24	0.43	-0.145**	-0.132**	-0.039	0.080	0.116*	0.126*	0.069	0.034	0.026	-0.039	0.059	-0.002	0.050	-0.045	0.085	-0.076	0.273**					
20 Business field	0.63	0.48	0.248**	0.274**	0.323**	0.166**	0.194**	0.210**	0.205**	0.206**	0.333**	0.204**	0.190**	0.242**	0.199**	0.209**	0.289**	0.083	-0.252**	-0.054				
21 SBMT	0.56	0.50	0.213**	0.244**	0.279**	0.184**	0.225**	0.210**	0.204**	0.202**	0.334**	0.189**	0.203**	0.236**	0.189**	0.183**	0.211**	0.089	-0.259**	0.011	0.865**			
22 Entr. course	0.27	0.44	0.146**	0.144*	0.177**	0.167**	0.195**	0.132*	0.163**	0.149**	0.058	-0.004	0.025	0.240**	0.176**	0.154**	-0.034	-0.175**	0.006	-0.234**	0.114*	0.166**		
23 Entrepr. intention	0.71	0.46	0.181**	0.181**	0.143**	0.186**	0.256**	0.203**	0.246**	0.284**	0.155**	0.105	0.153**	0.267**	0.241**	0.253**	-0.070	-0.085	0.113*	-0.085	-0.019	0.133*	0.166**	0.185**

Pearson and Spearman correlation coefficients[50]

[50] Spearman correlation coefficients were computed for binary variables.

ANNEX 4. DESCRIPTIVE STATISTICS AND CORRELATION MATRIX ON THE SAMPLE OF BSU ALUMNI

		Mean	Std. Deviation	1	2	3	4	5	6	7	8	9	10	11	12
1	Personal (doing business skills)	2.37	1.193												
2	Behavioral (higher income)	0.56	0.497	0.041											
3	The atmosphere at my university inspires me to develop ideas for new businesses.	2.62	1.242	0.499**	0.108										
4	There is a favorable climate for becoming an entrepreneur at my university.	2.43	1.221	0.601**	0.046	0.737**									
5	At my university, students are encouraged to engage in entrepreneurial activities.	2.15	1.132	0.541**	0.011	0.644**	0.684**								
6	Male	0.32	0.466	0.005	0.125*	0.131*	0.101	-0.012							
7	Age squared	640.095	137.928	-0.202**	0.020	-0.158*	-0.084	-0.105	0.103						
8	Work experience	4.289	2.659	-0.149*	0.140*	-0.110	-0.048	-0.082	0.120	0.788**					
9	Years after graduation	3.37	2.483	-0.173**	0.055	-0.117	-0.035	-0.063	0.087	0.925**	0.771**				
10	Business field	0.46	0.499	0.505**	0.129*	0.347**	0.398**	0.402**	-0.036	-0.324**	-0.299**	-0.297**			
11	SBMT	0.384	0.487	0.493**	0.135*	0.364**	0.393**	0.385**	-0.048	-0.333**	-0.319**	-0.278**	0.855**		
12	Entr.course	0.456	0.499	0.476**	0.091	0.413**	0.413**	0.370**	-0.064	-0.193**	-0.163**	-0.149*	0.671**	0.658**	
13	Doing business	0.11	0.309	0.008	0.133*	0.097	0.120	0.041	0.270**	-0.015	0.041	-0.066	0.201**	0.133*	0.129*

Pearson and Spearman correlation coefficients[54]

---

[54] Spearman correlation coefficients were computed for binary variables

INDEX

A

accreditation, 4, 14, 15, 17, 20, 21, 25, 31, 35, 38, 40, 44, 61, 62, 66, 101, 102, 149
acquisition of knowledge, 26
administrative and technological need, x, 148, 153, 154, 155, 156, 157
administrators, x, 148, 151, 156, 161, 163
assessment, vii, viii, ix, 2, 7, 17, 20, 26, 29, 33, 35, 36, 37, 40, 43, 44, 46, 49, 52, 54, 57, 62, 64, 100, 102, 108, 113, 115, 116, 117, 122, 123, 124, 125, 126, 128, 129, 130, 132, 134, 135, 138, 141, 142, 149, 152, 170, 172
assessment models, 37
assessment procedures, 40, 44
assets, 70, 230, 233, 240
atmosphere, 214, 216, 228, 242, 244, 246
attitudes, xi, 30, 113, 122, 123, 125, 126, 132, 137, 139, 141, 158, 202, 207, 228, 229, 232

B

Bahrain, 24
Bangladesh, 24
Belarus, 201, 204, 210, 212, 216, 218, 219, 223, 228, 232, 233, 237, 239
Belorussia, 202
benchmarking, 4, 19, 37, 39, 57, 62, 139
Bologna Process, 60, 80, 127

C

CAF, 35, 39, 41, 43, 74, 101, 102
certification, 4, 20, 35, 40, 44, 49, 61, 62, 102, 139, 219
challenges, x, 108, 111, 113, 127, 128, 130, 132, 133, 137, 139, 141, 142, 151, 197, 198, 203, 223, 237
commercial, 206, 222, 228, 243
Commonwealth of Independent States, 204
communication, 118, 127, 130, 132, 133, 137, 158, 244
communication skills, 118, 130, 137, 244

competency-based education, 108, 111, 112, 113, 142, 143, 144
competition, 149, 152, 186, 192, 194, 195
competitive advantage, 153, 154
competitiveness, 5, 21, 144, 155, 156, 157, 165, 236
complexity, ix, 14, 33, 36, 108, 109, 111, 112, 114, 117, 119, 124, 126, 130, 136, 138, 209
conceptual model, 19, 44, 47, 114, 207, 209, 231
Council of the European Union, 143
curricula, 112, 116, 124, 224, 228
curriculum, vii, ix, 18, 20, 32, 101, 108, 114, 116, 117, 118, 120, 122, 123, 124, 128, 135, 138, 141, 219
curriculum development, 20, 114, 116, 117, 118, 120, 122, 123, 135, 138

D

DEA, 171, 172, 176, 177, 178, 179, 181, 182, 187, 188, 189, 190, 191, 193, 194, 195, 196, 197, 199

E

Eastern Europe, 203, 235, 237, 241
economic activity, 174
economic development, xi, 202, 232, 234, 238
economic growth, 236
economic performance, 5, 239
economic theory, 173, 174
economics, 25
ecosystem, 37, 229
educational assessment, 122
educational experience, 113, 128, 130, 136
educational institutions, 3, 5, 12, 38, 40, 43, 56, 60
educational policy, 16, 108, 113, 175

educational practices, 118
educational process, 124, 175, 207
educational programs, 219
educational quality, 100, 101
educational settings, 114
educators, 118
efficiency, v, vii, x, 11, 163, 169, 170, 171, 172, 174, 175, 176, 177, 178, 179, 180, 181, 182, 183, 184, 185, 187, 188, 190, 191, 192, 193, 194, 195, 196, 197, 198, 199, 223
e-learning, 124
entrepreneurial activities, vi, vii, xi, 201, 202, 203, 204, 205, 206, 207, 210, 214, 216, 220, 222, 228, 232, 237, 242, 244, 246
entrepreneurial universities, xi, 202, 203, 234, 236, 237, 241
entrepreneurs, 206, 212, 227, 228, 229, 237, 239, 244
entrepreneurship, xi, 112, 174, 202, 203, 204, 205, 206, 207, 212, 214, 215, 217, 222, 224, 226, 227, 228, 229, 230, 231, 232, 233, 235, 236, 237, 238, 239, 240, 241, 244
Europe, ix, 67, 74, 108, 113, 115, 118, 119, 123, 124, 144, 196, 237, 239, 240, 241
European Commission, 110, 116, 118, 119, 123, 144, 206, 235
European Union, 21, 143, 144, 235
evidence, 11, 18, 19, 23, 29, 31, 42, 46, 60, 99, 100, 101, 102, 104, 105, 106, 113, 133, 138, 190, 194, 226, 227, 234, 236

F

focus on client, x, 148, 153, 154, 156, 157
formal education, 142
formation, 111, 149, 203, 229, 239
funding, 16, 113, 186, 204, 220, 229, 232
fundraising, 221

G

general education, 120
general knowledge, 124
global economy, ix, 107
globalization, x, 108, 148, 151, 155
Google, 211, 213
governance, 15, 17, 20, 102, 205, 206, 222, 228, 231, 237

H

higher education, v, vii, ix, x, 1, 2, 3, 8, 11, 21, 24, 29, 31, 41, 43, 44, 48, 65, 66, 67, 68, 70, 71, 72, 73, 74, 75, 76, 77, 78, 79, 80, 81, 82, 83, 84, 85, 86, 87, 88, 89, 90, 91, 92, 93, 94, 95, 96, 98, 100, 101, 102, 104, 105, 106, 108, 109, 111, 112, 113, 115, 117, 118, 120, 122, 127, 129, 130, 131, 135, 138, 139, 141, 142, 143, 144, 145, 146, 148, 149, 151, 154, 155, 161, 162, 163, 164, 165, 166, 167, 169, 170, 171, 173, 174, 176, 177, 179, 180, 183, 185, 188, 192, 193, 194, 195, 197, 198, 199, 203, 218, 219, 220, 223, 228, 230, 231, 234, 235, 237, 238, 239, 240, 241
higher education institutions, v, vii, ix, x, 1, 2, 3, 48, 78, 81, 84, 87, 89, 91, 92, 93, 94, 98, 100, 101, 102, 104, 106, 108, 109, 111, 114, 115, 117, 118, 120, 122, 131, 135, 138, 148, 149, 161, 163, 164, 167, 169, 170, 173, 199, 232, 234, 239
human capital, 12, 13, 144, 186, 198, 239
human dignity, 128
human resources, 17, 103, 222
humanitarianism, 117

I

information systems, 2, 10, 16, 48, 66, 68, 70, 71, 73, 74, 75, 76, 78, 80, 83, 84, 85, 87, 88, 89, 90, 91, 92, 95, 96, 97, 106, 163
inputs, xi, 170, 171, 173, 174, 175, 176, 177, 178, 179, 180, 181, 183, 184, 186, 188, 193
Internal Quality Assurance System (IQAS), v, viii, 1, 2, 3, 4, 5, 6, 7, 8, 9, 10, 11, 13, 14, 15, 16, 17, 18, 19, 20, 21, 22, 23, 24, 25, 28, 29, 30, 31, 32, 33, 34, 35, 36, 37, 38, 40, 41, 42, 43, 44, 45, 46, 49, 50, 51, 52, 53, 55, 56, 57, 59, 60, 61, 62, 64, 65, 66, 70, 72, 75, 90, 92, 94, 96, 101, 102

K

Kenya, 24
knowledge acquisition, 117, 137
knowledge economy, 203

L

labor market, ix, 108, 109, 110, 112, 113, 114, 122, 139, 141, 170
labor market integration, 108
labour market, 16, 143
languages, 128, 133
leadership, 11, 14, 16, 21, 39, 124, 126, 132, 137, 150, 154, 158, 205, 206, 223
learner progress, 134
learners, 133, 135
learning, x, 6, 8, 17, 20, 40, 42, 43, 60, 100, 101, 102, 113, 114, 115, 116, 117, 118, 119, 120, 121, 122, 123, 124, 125, 126, 127, 128, 129, 130, 131, 132, 133, 134, 135, 136, 137, 138, 139, 140, 141, 142,

143, 144, 148, 151, 154, 161, 183, 208, 230, 240
learning environment, 154
learning outcomes, 113, 114, 115, 116, 117, 118, 119, 120, 121, 122, 123, 124, 126, 127, 128, 129, 130, 132, 134, 135, 136, 137, 138, 139, 140, 141, 142, 143, 144
learning process, 17, 101, 114, 131, 136, 140, 151
learning skills, 118
liberal education, 119, 136
lifelong learning, 111, 113, 123, 127, 128, 135, 137, 143
Likert scale, 156
linear programming, 179
literacy, 128, 130, 132, 137

M

maturity, v, vii, viii, 1, 2, 5, 6, 7, 16, 19, 24, 25, 26, 27, 28, 29, 30, 31, 32, 33, 34, 35, 36, 37, 38, 39, 40, 41, 42, 43, 44, 45, 46, 49, 50, 51, 52, 53, 54, 57, 59, 60, 61, 64, 65, 67, 68, 70, 71, 73, 75, 78, 79, 80, 81, 82, 83, 85, 86, 87, 88, 89, 90, 91, 93, 94, 95, 96, 97, 98, 99, 100, 102, 104, 105
Ministry of Education, 185, 219, 223, 232

N

natural sciences, 212, 224

O

OECD, x, 140, 145, 169, 195
outputs, xi, 17, 18, 32, 33, 34, 52, 55, 110, 143, 170, 171, 173, 174, 175, 176, 177, 178, 179, 180, 181, 183, 184, 185, 186, 188, 193

P

performance indicator, 49, 149, 170, 176, 195
post-Soviet countries, 204, 220, 223, 228, 239
process improvement, x, 18, 69, 70, 73, 81, 89, 148, 153, 154
productivity, x, 86, 90, 93, 109, 111, 169, 176, 186, 188, 192, 195, 196, 199
public universities, v, 169, 173, 176, 183, 184, 185, 188, 190, 193, 194, 198

Q

QAM, 88
qualifications, 112, 118, 119, 120, 123, 127, 130, 131, 135, 139, 140, 141, 143, 145, 219
quality assurance, vii, viii, 2, 3, 7, 8, 9, 10, 15, 16, 120, 127, 140, 145, 154, 165
quality control, 158
quality frameworks, 39, 45, 108
quality improvement, 3, 10, 30
Quality Management System (QMS), 5, 7, 8, 9, 11, 12, 13, 18, 28, 31, 32, 35, 38, 39, 41, 42, 43, 44, 45, 46, 60, 71, 74, 76, 77, 79, 84, 85, 87, 88, 89, 98, 99, 101

R

regression, xi, 17, 160, 173, 177, 178, 181, 182, 183, 185, 192, 202, 204, 218, 225, 227, 232, 236
regression analysis, xi, 17, 202, 204, 232
regression equation, 182
regression model, 218
Russia, 226, 233, 241

S

scores, 151, 171, 177, 179, 181, 182, 184, 188, 189, 190, 191, 192, 193, 218
secondary schools, 195
self-assessment, 4, 15, 17, 21, 38, 39, 40, 52, 57, 62, 132
self-efficacy, 208, 216, 234
self-employed, 214, 215, 217
self-employment, 244
self-improvement, 112
self-reflection, 134, 137
self-regulation, 132, 137
self-understanding, 126
skill shortages, 109, 143
skilled workers, 109
social responsibility, 45, 119, 126, 128, 132, 137
social sciences, 128, 129, 212
society, 5, 20, 21, 39, 56, 61, 101, 113, 127, 128, 134, 151, 175, 234
soft-skills, 108

T

teachers, 113, 115, 124, 125, 133, 138, 141, 142
teaching experience, 192
teaching quality, 25, 186
technical efficiency, 179, 188, 194
technological advancement, 151
technological change, x, 108
technologies, 134, 229
technology, ix, 27, 48, 49, 108, 109, 132, 133, 154, 174, 178, 179, 199, 205, 220, 222, 232, 234, 236, 240, 243
technology transfer, 206, 232, 234, 240
tertiary education, ix, 108

total quality management, v, vii, x, 8, 39, 44, 45, 68, 72, 76, 77, 81, 84, 86, 88, 90, 96, 147, 148, 149, 150, 155, 156, 157, 162, 163, 166, 167
training, 16, 34, 45, 102, 103, 110, 111, 112, 120, 130, 133, 134, 138, 149, 151, 158, 160, 165, 171, 220, 229, 235, 243

U

UNESCO, 3, 10, 18, 66, 72, 75, 79, 80, 82, 97, 235, 240
universities, x, xi, 3, 59, 63, 72, 113, 144, 148, 152, 161, 162, 170, 171, 173, 174, 175, 176, 177, 179, 183, 184, 185, 186, 188, 189, 190, 192, 193, 194, 196, 197, 198, 199, 202, 203, 204, 205, 206, 208, 209, 211, 212, 219, 220, 222, 224, 228, 229, 231, 233, 234, 235, 236, 237, 238, 239, 240, 241
university management, 20, 148, 158, 160, 235, 239

V

vocational education and training, 143

W

workers, x, 110, 111, 148, 152, 153, 154, 155, 156, 157, 158
workforce, 113, 152
working groups, 115
workload, 116, 118, 119, 120, 124, 125, 135
workplace, ix, 107, 108, 109, 111, 132
workplace-based competencies, 108

Related Nova Publications

HIGHER EDUCATION: GOALS AND CONSIDERATIONS

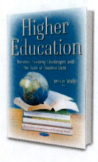

AUTHOR: Ronan Alvarado

SERIES: Education in a Competitive and Globalizing World

BOOK DESCRIPTION: The first chapter of this book is an introduction to the TRIO programs. The TRIO programs are the primary federal programs providing support services to the disadvantaged students to promote achievement in postsecondary education.

SOFTCOVER ISBN: 978-1-53614-157-3
RETAIL PRICE: $82

HIGHER EDUCATION: BENEFITS, FUNDING CHALLENGES AND THE STATE OF STUDENT DEBT

EDITOR: Spencer Wolfe

SERIES: Education in a Competitive and Globalizing World

BOOK DESCRIPTION: Higher education is one of the most important investments individuals can make for themselves and for our country. Many students access student loans to help finance their education, and last year federal student loans helped 9 million Americans to make that investment in their futures.

EBOOK ISBN: 978-1-53610-192-8
RETAIL PRICE: $95

To see complete list of Nova publications, please visit our website at www.novapublishers.com